Introduction to Qualitative Research Methods

Introduction to Qualitative Research Methods

THE SEARCH FOR MEANINGS

SECOND EDITION

STEVEN J. TAYLOR

ROBERT BOGDAN

A WILEY-INTERSCIENCE PUBLICATION

JOHN WILEY & SONS

New York • Chichester • Brisbane • Toronto • Singapore

Library of Congress Cataloging in Publication Data:

Taylor, Steven J., 1949–
    Introduction to qualitative research methods.

    "A Wiley-Interscience publication."
    Bibliography: p.
    Includes index.
    1. Sociology—Methodology.   2. Sociology—Research.
I. Bogdan, Robert.   II. Title.

HM24.T32   1984   301'.072   84-7522
ISBN 0-471-88947-4

Preface

In the preface to the first edition of this book we stated that the past decade had witnessed a growing interest in the subjective side of social life—how people view themselves and their world. This interest, we wrote, required methods that are descriptive and holistic: qualitative research methods.

Since the publication of the first edition in 1975, interest in studying social meanings and perspectives through qualitative methods has remained strong. Indeed, qualitative research approaches are accepted as never before. There are now journals devoted exclusively to reporting qualitative studies. There is an ever increasing number of books and articles written on field research, photography, and other qualitative methods. In education, social work, evaluation, and applied fields, qualitative methods are demanding serious attention. Qualitative research is coming of age.

This is a book on *how to conduct* qualitative research. There are some excellent books on specific qualitative approaches, especially participant observation, insightful personal accounts of researchers in the field, and treatises on the theoretical underpinnings of qualitative research. Yet these do not provide those unfamiliar with qualitative methods with an adequate introduction, an overview of the range of different approaches, and guidance on how to actually conduct a study. This book is intended to do these things.

The book is based on our own research experience, our theoretical perspective (which informs how we think about interacting with people in our society), our cultural knowledge of how to act in everyday life, and our sense of ethics. We have also drawn extensively on the first-hand accounts of other researchers and several of the recently published writings that challenge traditional conceptions of fieldwork.

This book contains an introduction and two major parts. The Introduction deals with qualitative methods in general and the theoretical tradition underlying qualitative research. Part 1 contains a "how to do it" approach to qualitative research. Chapters 2 and 3 deal with participant observation. In Chapter 4 we discuss in-depth interviewing. Chapter 5 considers a range of creative qualitative research approaches. Chapter 6 describes data analysis in qualitative research.

In Part 2 we move to the presentation of findings in qualitative research. After a short introduction, we present a number of articles based on the methods described in Part 1. Many of the examples used in Part 1 come from the studies reported in Part 2. All of these articles were written by us. We present them because they illustrate some of the ways in which to write up findings. We also chose them to catch the interest and imagination of those new to qualitative research.

A few words of thanks are due to those who helped with this book. We want to thank the many colleagues over the years who contributed directly or indirectly to this book, especially Burton Blatt, Douglas Biklen, Blanche Geer, Betsy Edinger, Stan Searl, Janet Bogdan, Irwin Deutscher, Bill McCord, Michael Baizerman, Seymour Sarason, and our friends at the Center on Human Policy. We also thank the many people who have worked with us in conducting qualitative research. Many of them have been called students, but they have been our teachers as well. Special thanks to Sue Smith-Cunnien for permission to include excerpts from her field notes in Chapter 3. We also want to thank Dianne Ferguson for tak- ing the time from her studies and many other activities to help in the preparation of the manuscript for this book and Helen Timmins for her general support. Finally, we thank Herb Reich of John Wiley & Sons for encouraging us to write this edition of this book.

STEVEN J. TAYLOR
ROBERT BOGDAN

Syracuse, New York
September 1984

Contents

Introduction to Qualitative Research Methods

1

Introduction

GO TO THE PEOPLE

The term *methodology* refers to the way in which we approach problems and seek answers. In the social sciences, the term applies to how one conducts research. Our assumptions, interests, and purposes shape which methodology we choose. When stripped to their essentials, debates over methodology are debates over assumptions and purposes, over theory and perspective.

Two major theoretical perspectives have dominated the social science scene (Bruyn, 1966; Deutscher, 1973). The first, *positivism*, traces its origins in the social sciences to the great theorists of the nineteenth and early twentieth centuries and especially to August Comte (1896) and Emile Durkheim (1938, 1951). The positivist seeks the *facts* or *causes* of social phenomena apart from the subjective states of individuals. Durkheim (1938:14) told the social scientist to consider social facts, or social phenomena, as "things" that exercise an external influence on people.

The second major theoretical perspective, which, following the lead of Deutscher (1973), we describe as *phenomenological,* has a long history in philosophy and sociology (Berger and Luckmann, 1967; Bruyn, 1966; Husserl, 1913; Psathas, 1973; Schutz, 1962, 1967).[1] The phenomenologist is committed to *understanding* social phenomena from the actor's own perspective. He or she examines how the world is experienced. The important reality is what people perceive it to be. Jack Douglas (1970b:ix) writes:

> The "forces" that move human beings, as human beings rather than simply as human bodies . . . are "meaningful stuff." They are internal ideas, feelings, and motives.

Since positivists and phenomenologists take on different kinds of problems and seek different kinds of answers, their research demands different methodologies. Adopting a natural science model of research, the positivist searches for causes through methods such as questionnaires, inventories, and demography that produce data amenable to statistical analysis. The phenomenologist seeks understanding through qualitative methods such as participant observation, in-depth interviewing, and others that yield descriptive data. In contrast to a natural science approach, the phenomenologist strives for what Max Weber (1968) called *verstehen,* understanding on a personal level the motives and beliefs behind people's actions.

This book is about qualitative methodology: how to collect descriptive data, people's own words and behavior. It is a book on how to study social life phenomenologically.

We are not saying that positivists cannot use qualitative methods to address their own research interests. Thus Durkheim (1915) used rich descriptive data collected by anthropologists as the basis for his treatise *The Elementary Forms of Religious Life.* We are saying that the search for social causes is neither what this book is about nor where our own research interests lie.

We return to the phenomenological perspective later in this chapter, for it is at the heart of this work. It is the perspective that guides our research.

A NOTE ON THE HISTORY OF QUALITATIVE METHODS

Descriptive observation, interviewing, and other qualitative methods are as old as recorded history (Wax, 1971). Wax points out that the origins of fieldwork can be traced to historians, travelers, and writers ranging from the Greek Herodotus to Marco Polo. It was not until the nineteenth and early twentieth centuries, however, that what we now call qualitative methods were consciously employed in social research.

Frederick LePlay's 1855 study of European families and communities stands as one of the first genuine pieces of participant observation research (Bruyn, 1966). Robert Nisbet (1966) writes that LePlay's research represents the first "scientific" sociological research:

> But *The European Working Classes* is a work squarely in the field of sociology, the first genuinely scientific sociological work in the century. . . . Durkheim's *Suicide* is commonly regarded as the first "scientific" work in sociology, but it takes nothing away from Durkheim's achievement to observe that it was in LePlay's studies of kinship and community types in Europe that a much earlier effort is to be found in European sociology to combine empirical observation with the drawing of crucial inference—and to do this acknowledgedly within the criteria of science.

In anthropology, field research came into its own around the turn of the century. Boas (1911) and Malinowski (1932) can be credited with establishing fieldwork as a legitimate anthropological endeavor. As Wax (1971:35-36) notes, Malinowski was the first professional anthropologist to provide a description of his research approach and a picture of what fieldwork was like. Perhaps due to the influence of Boaz and Malinowski, in academic circles field research or participant observation has continued to be associated with anthropology.

One can only speculate on the reasons why qualitative methods have been so readily accepted by anthropologists and so easily ignored by sociologists. Durkheim's *Suicide,* which equated statistical analysis with scientific sociology, has been extremely influential and has provided a model of research for several generations of sociologists. It would have been difficult for anthropologists to employ the research techniques such as survey questionnaires and demographics that Durkheim and his predecessors developed. One obviously cannot enter a tribal culture and ask to see the police blotter or administer a questionnaire. Further, whereas anthropologists have been unfamiliar with and hence deeply concerned with everyday life in the cultures they have studied, sociologists probably have taken it for granted that they already know enough about the daily lives of people in their own society to decide what to look at and which questions to ask.

Yet qualitative methods have a rich history in American sociology, even if they have not yet received widespread acceptance. The use of qualitative methods first became popular in the studies of the "Chicago School" in the period from approximately 1910 to 1940. During this period, researchers associated with the University of Chicago produced detailed participant observation studies of urban life (Anderson, *The Hobo*, 1923; Cressey, *The Taxi-Dance Hall*, 1932; Thrasher, *The Gang*, 1927; Wirth, *The Ghetto*, 1928; Zorbaugh, *The Gold Coast and the Slum*, 1929); rich life histories of juvenile delinquents and criminals (Shaw, *The Jack-Roller*, 1966; Shaw, *The Natural History of a Delinquent Career*, 1931; Shaw et al., *Brothers in Crime*, 1938; Sutherland, *The Professional Thief*, 1937), and a classic study of the life of immigrants and their families in Poland and America based on personal documents (Thomas and Znaniecki, *The Polish Peasant in Europe and America*, 1918–20). Up until the 1940s, people who called themselves students of society were familiar with participant observation, in-depth interviewing, and personal documents.

As important as these early studies were, interest in qualitative methodology waned toward the end of the 1940s and beginning of the 1950s with the growth in prominence of *grand theories* (e.g., Parsons, 1951) and quantitative methods. Even today it is possible for students to receive an advanced degree in sociology without ever hearing the phrase *personal documents*.

Since the 1960s, there has been a reemergence in the use of qualitative methods. So many powerful and insightful studies have been published based on these methods (e.g., Becker, 1963; Goffman, 1961) that they have been impossible to discount. What was once an oral tradition of qualitative research has been recorded in monographs (Lofland, 1971, 1976; Schatzman and Strauss, 1973; Van Maanen et al., 1982) and edited volumes (Emerson, 1983; Filstead, 1970; Glazer, 1972; McCall and Simmons, 1969; Shaffir et al., 1982). There also have been books published that examine the philosophical underpinnings of qualitative research (Bruyn, 1966), relate qualitative methods to theory development (Glaser and Strauss, 1967), and contain personal accounts of researchers' experiences in the field (Douglas, 1976; Johnson, 1975; Wax, 1971). There are even journals devoted to publishing qualitative studies (*Urban Life, Qualitative Sociology*).

The approaches of sociologists, anthropologists, psychologists, and others involved in qualitative research today are strikingly similar (Emerson, 1983). Indeed, it is difficult, if not impossible, at times to distinguish between cultural anthropology and qualitative sociology. Thus sociologists use terms such as *ethnography* and *culture,* terms with a distinct anthropological ring; anthropologists like Spradley (1979, 1980) adopt symbolic interactionism, a sociological perspective, as a theoretical framework. Liebow's (1967) "anthropological" study, *Tally's Corner,* is not unlike the "sociological" studies of Whyte (1955), *Street Corner Society,* and Suttles (1968), *The Social Order of the Slum.* Similarly, Coles (1964, 1971) and Cottle (1972, 1973), both psychologists, could be considered sociologists or anthropologists. Our description of qualitative research reflects the sociological tradition; most of the works we cite and examples we use come from sociology. However, the points we make in the following chapters apply generally to qualitative research, regardless of the discipline of the researcher.

QUALITATIVE METHODOLOGY

The phrase *qualitative methodology* refers in the broadest sense to *research that produces descriptive data: people's own written or spoken words and observable behavior.* As Ray Rist (1977) points out, qualitative methodology, like quantitative methodology, is more than a set of data gathering techniques. It is a way of approaching the empirical world:

1. *Qualitative research is inductive.* Researchers develop concepts, insights, and understanding from patterns in the data, rather than collecting data to assess preconceived models, hypotheses, or theories. In qualitative studies researchers follow a flexible research design. They begin their studies with only vaguely formulated research questions.

2. *In qualitative methodology the researcher looks at settings and people holistically; people, settings, or groups are not reduced to variables, but are viewed as a whole.* The qualitative researcher studies people in the context of their past and the situations in which they find themselves.

3. *Qualitative researchers are sensitive to their effects on the people they study.* Qualitative research has been described as naturalistic. That is, researchers interact with informants in a natural and unobtrusive manner. In participant observation they try to "blend into the woodwork," at least until they have grasped an understanding of a setting. In in-depth interviewing they model their interviews after a normal conversation, rather than a formal question and answer exchange. Although qualitative researchers cannot eliminate their effects on the people they study, they attempt to minimize or control those effects or at least understand them when they interpret their data (Emerson, 1983).

4. *Qualitative researchers try to understand people from their own frame of reference.* Central to the phenomenological perspective and hence qualitative research, is experiencing reality as others experience it. Qualitative researchers empathize and identify with the people they study in order to understand how they see things. Herbert Blumer (1969:86) explains it this way:

> To try to catch the interpretive process by remaining aloof as a so-called "objective" observer and refusing to take the role of the acting unit is to risk the worst kind of subjectivism—the objective observer is likely to fill in the process of interpretation with his own surmises in place of catching the process as it occurs in the experience of the acting unit which uses it.

5. *The qualitative researcher suspends, or sets aside, his or her own beliefs, perspectives, and predispositions.* As Bruyn (1966) notes, the qualitative researcher views things as though they were happening for the first time. Nothing is taken for granted. Everything is a subject matter of inquiry.

6. *For the qualitative researcher, all perspectives are valuable.* The researcher seeks not "truth" or "morality," but rather a detailed understanding of other people's perspectives. All people are viewed as equals. Thus the juvenile delinquent's perspective is just as important as the judge's or counselor's; the "paranoid's" just as important as the psychiatrist's.

In qualitative studies, those whom society ignores, the poor and the "deviant," often receive a forum for their views (Becker, 1967). Oscar Lewis (1965:xii), famous for his studies of the poor in Latin America, writes, "I have tried to give a voice to a people who are rarely heard."

7. *Qualitative methods are humanistic.* The methods by which we study people of necessity affect how we view them. When we reduce people's words and acts to statistical equations, we lose sight of the human side of social life. When we study people qualitatively, we get to know them personally and experience what they experience in their daily struggles in society. We learn about concepts such as beauty, pain, faith, suffering, frustration, and love whose essence is lost through other research approaches. We learn about ". . . the inner life of the person, his moral struggles, his successes and failures in securing his destiny in a world too often at variance with his hopes and ideals" (Burgess, as quoted by Shaw, 1966:4).

8. *Qualitative researchers emphasize validity in their research.* Qualitative methods allow us to stay close to the empirical world (Blumer, 1969). They are designed to ensure a close fit between the data and what people actually say and do. By observing people in their everyday lives, listening to them talk about what is on their minds, and looking at the documents they produce, the qualitative researcher obtains first-hand knowledge of social life unfiltered through concepts, operational definitions, and rating scales.

Whereas qualitative researchers emphasize validity, quantitative researchers emphasize reliability and replicability in research (Rist, 1977). As Deutscher (1973:41) writes, reliability has been overemphasized in social research:

> We concentrate on consistency without much concern about whether we are right or wrong. As a consequence we may have been learning a great deal about how to pursue an incorrect course with a maximum of precision.

This is not to say that qualitative researchers are unconcerned about the accuracy of their data. A qualitative study is not an impressionistic, off-the-cuff analysis based on a superficial look at a setting or people. It is a piece of systematic research conducted with demanding, though not necessarily standardized, procedures. In the chapters that follow we discuss some of the checks researchers can place on the accuracy of their data recording. However, it is not possible to achieve perfect reliability if we are to produce valid studies of the real world. LaPiere (quoted in Deutscher, 1973:21) writes:

The study of human behavior is time consuming, intellectually fatiguing, and depends for its success upon the ability of the investigator. . . . Quantitative measurements are quantitatively accurate; qualitative evaluations are always subject to the errors of human judgment. Yet it would seem far more worthwhile to make a shrewd guess regarding that which is essential than to accurately measure that which is likely to prove irrelevant.

9. *For the qualitative researcher, all settings and people are worthy of study.* No aspect of social life is too mundane or trivial to be studied. All settings and people are at once similar and unique. They are similar in the sense that some general social processes may be found in any setting or among any group of people. They are unique in that some aspect of social life can best be studied in each setting or through each informant because there it is best illuminated (Hughes, 1958:49). Some social processes that appear in bold relief under some circumstances appear only faintly under others.

10. *Qualitative research is a craft.* Qualitative methods have not been as refined and standardized as other research approaches. This is in part an historical artifact which is changing with the publication of books such as this one and first-hand accounts of field researchers, and in part a reflection of the nature of the methods themselves. Qualitative researchers are flexible in how they go about conducting their studies. The researcher is a craftsperson. The qualitative social scientist is encouraged to be his or her own methodologist (Mills, 1959). There are guidelines to be followed, but never rules. The methods serve the researcher; never is the researcher a slave to procedure and technique:

> If a choice were possible, I would naturally prefer simple, rapid, and infallible methods. If I could find such methods, I would avoid the time-consuming, difficult and suspect variants of "participant observation" with which I have become associated (Dalton, 1964:60).

THEORY AND METHODOLOGY

The phenomenological perspective is central to our conception of qualitative methodology. What qualitative methodologists study, how they study it, and how they interpret it: all of these depend upon their theoretical perspective.

The phenomenologist views human behavior, what people say and do, as a product of how people define their world. The task of the phenomenologist and, for us, the qualitative methodologist, is to capture this process of interpretation. As we have emphasized, the phenomenologist attempts to see things from other people's point of view.

The phenomenological perspective is tied to a broad range of theoretical frameworks and schools of thought in the social sciences.[2] We cannot discuss all of these here. Rather, we focus on two major theoretical approaches, symbolic interactionism and ethnomethodology, that have become dominant forces in the social sciences and fall within the phenomenological tradition.

Symbolic interactionism stems from the works of Charles Horton Cooley (1902), John Dewey (1930), George Herbert Mead (1934, 1938), Robert Park (1915), W. I. Thomas (1931), and others. Mead's (1934) formulation in *Mind, Self, and Society* was the clearest and most influential presentation of this perspective. Mead's followers, including Howard Becker (Becker et al., 1961; Becker et al., 1968), Herbert Blumer (1962, 1969), and Everett Hughes (1958), have applied his insightful analyses of the processes of interaction to everyday life.[3]

The symbolic interactionist places primary importance on the *social meanings* people attach to the world around them. Blumer (1969) states that symbolic interactionism rests on three basic premises. The first is that people act toward things, including other people, on the basis of the meanings these things have for them. Thus people do not simply respond to stimuli or act out cultural scripts. It is the meaning that determines action.

Blumer's second premise is that meanings are social products that arise during interaction: "The meaning of a thing for a person grows out of the ways in which other persons act toward the person with regard to the thing" (Blumer, 1969:4). People learn how to see the world from other people.

The third fundamental premise of symbolic interactionism, according to Blumer, is that social actors attach meanings to situations, others, things, and themselves through a *process of interpretation.* Blumer (1969:5) writes:

> This process has two distinct steps. First, the actor indicates to himself the things toward which he is acting; he has to point out to himself the things that have meaning. Second, by virtue of this process of communicating with himself, interpretation becomes a matter of handling meanings. The actor

selects, checks, suspends, regroups, and transforms the meanings in the light
of the situation in which he is placed and the direction of his action.

This process of interpretation acts as an intermediary between meanings
or predispositions to act in a certain way and the action itself. People
are constantly interpreting and defining things as they move through
different situations.

We can see why different people say and do different things. One
reason is that people have had different experiences and have learned
different social meanings. For example, people hold different positions
within an organization. Each has learned to see things in a certain way.
Take the example of a student who breaks a window in a school cafe-
teria. The principal might define the situation as a behavior problem;
the counselor sees it as a family problem; the janitor as a work problem;
the school nurse as a health problem; the student who broke the window
does not see it as a problem at all.

A second reason why people act differently is that they find themselves in different situations. If we want to understand why some adolescents become "delinquents" and others do not, we have to look at the
situations they confront.

Finally, the process of interpretation is a dynamic process. How a
person interprets something will depend on the meanings available and
how he or she sizes up a situation.

From a symbolic interactionist perspective, all organizations, cultures,
and groups consist of actors who are involved in a constant process of
interpreting the world around them. Although people may act within
the framework of an organization, culture, or group, it is their interpretations and definitions of the situation that determine action and not
norms, values, roles, or goals.

A great deal of controversy surrounds the influential writings of
Harold Garfinkel (1967) and his fellow ethnomethodologists (Mehan and
Wood, 1975; Turner, 1974; Zimmerman and Wieder, 1970). For some,
ethnomethodology falls squarely within the symbolic interactionist perspective (Denzin, 1970). For others, it represents a radical departure from
other sociological traditions (Zimmerman and Wieder, 1970). Mehan and
Wood (1975) characterize ethnomethodology as a separate enterprise from
sociology.[4] In this discussion we outline some common strains of thought
found in the works of ethnomethodologists.[5]

Ethnomethodology refers not to research methods but rather the subject matter of study: how (the methodology by which) people maintain a sense of an external reality (Mehan and Wood, 1975:5). For the ethnomethodologists, the meanings of actions are always ambiguous and problematic. Their task is to examine the ways people apply abstract cultural rules and commonsense understandings in concrete situations to make actions appear routine, explicable, and unambiguous. Meanings, then, are practical accomplishments on the part of members of society.

A study by D. Lawrence Wieder (1974) illustrates the ethnomethodological perspective. Wieder explores how "addicts" in a halfway house use a "convict code" (axioms such as "do not snitch" and "help other residents") to explain, justify, and account for their behavior. He shows how residents "tell the code," apply maxims to specific situations, when they are called upon to account for their actions:

> The code, then, is much more a *method* of moral persuasion and justification than it is a substantive account of an organized way of life. It is a way, or set of ways, of causing activities to be seen as morally, repetitively, and constrainedly organized (Wieder, 1974:158).

The ethnomethodologists thus bracket or suspend their own belief in reality to study the reality of everyday life. Garfinkel (1967) has studied the commonsense or taken-for-granted rules of interaction in everyday life through a variety of mischievous experiments he calls "breaching procedures" (see Chapter 5). Through an examination of common sense, the ethnomethodologists seek to understand how people "go about the task of *seeing, describing,* and *explaining* order in the world in which they live" (Zimmerman and Wieder, 1970:289).

In this chapter we have attempted to give a sense of some of the methodological and theoretical dimensions of qualitative research. The remainder of this book covers data collection, data analysis, and the presentation of findings in qualitative research. Part 1 deals with how to conduct qualitative research. We discuss participant observation, in-depth interviewing, and a host of creative qualitative approaches. In Part 2 we consider the presentation of findings in qualitative research and offer a series of articles based on qualitative data. After a concluding note in Chapter 13, we include a set of sample field notes in the Appendix.

NOTES

1. Like Deutscher (1973), we use the term phenomenology broadly to refer to a tradition within the social sciences concerned with understanding the social actor's frame of reference. Psathas (1973) and Bruyn (1966) provide a good overview of origins of this tradition. Some sociologists use the term more narrowly to refer to the European school of thought in philosophy represented by the writings of Alfred Schutz (1967). Heap and Roth (1973) argue that the original meaning of phenomenology has been lost.

2. There has been a proliferation of theoretical perspectives and schools of thought associated with phenomenology over the past 20 years or so. These include Goffman's (1959) dramaturgical model, the sociology of knowledge as defined by Berger and Luckmann (1967), labeling theory (Schur, 1971), existential sociology (Douglas and Johnson, 1977), formal sociology (Schwartz and Jacobs, 1979), and a sociology of the absurd (Lyman and Scott, 1970), in addition to symbolic interactionism and ethnomethodology. It is often difficult to understand how these perspectives differ from one another, if at all.

3. See Kuhn (1964) for a discussion of trends in symbolic interactionism.

4. This is typical of the ethnomethodologists who go to great lengths to distance themselves from other sociological perspectives, especially symbolic interactionism. It is for this reason that ethnomethodologists have been accused of acting like a clique or private club, complete with their own folk heros (Garfinkel, but never Mead or Blumer), language ("indexicality," "reflexivity," "et cetera principle"), and home base (California). It is difficult to evaluate the continuities between ethnomethodology and other perspectives within the phenomenological tradition. As sociologists who identify with symbolic interactionism, we find many useful ideas in the writings of ethnomethodologists. However, we suspect that most ethnomethodologists would be quick to disassociate themselves from the model of research described in this book.

5. This is not as easy as it sounds. First of all, many ethnomethodologists take the position that ethnomethodology can only be lived, and not described (see Mehan and Wood, 1975). Second, it is not always clear who is and is not an ethnomethodologist. Douglas sounds like one in books published in 1970 and 1971. However, he disassociates himself from this perspective in his later work (see Douglas, 1976:117–118).

Part 1

Among the People

HOW TO CONDUCT
QUALITATIVE RESEARCH

2

Participant Observation

In this and the following chapters we discuss participant observation, the mainstay of qualitative methodology. The phrase *participant observation* is used here to refer to *research that involves social interaction between the researcher and informants in the milieu of the latter, during which data are systematically and unobtrusively collected.* We begin our discussion of participant observation with the pre-fieldwork stage of research: locating and getting into the setting one wishes to study. The following chapter deals with participant observation in the field.

RESEARCH DESIGN

In contrast to most methods in which researchers' hypotheses and procedures are determined a priori, the research design in participant observation remains flexible both before and throughout the actual research. *Although participant observers have a methodology to follow and perhaps some general research interests, the specifics of their approach evolve as they proceed.*[1]

Until we enter the field, we do not know what questions to ask or how to ask them. In other words, the preconceived image we have of the people we intend to study may be naive, misleading, or downright false. Most participant observers attempt to enter the field without specific hypotheses or preconceptions. As Melville Dalton (1964) writes:

> (1) I never feel sure what is relevant for hypothesizing until I have some intimacy with the situation—I think of a hypothesis as a well-founded conjecture; (2) once uttered, a hypothesis becomes obligatory to a degree; (3) there is a danger that the hypothesis will be esteemed for itself and work as an abused symbol of science.

One of the authors was involved with a large-scale research project that highlights the dangers of beginning a study with a rigid research design. This study's research design revolved around the distinction between one- and two-parent families, a common distinction in social science research. Both the sampling and analytical procedures were designed around this distinction. When field researchers entered families' homes, however, they found that the differentiation between one- and two-parent families is a gross oversimplification of the living situation of families today. For example, in "two-parent families" they found couples where one spouse accepted no responsibility for the child and where one spouse, while trying to fulfill the parental role, spent weeks away from home at a time. In "one-parent" families they came across couples living together where the nonparent accepted equal responsibility for the child, divorced couples who had reunited, sometimes permanently and sometimes for only a night, couples living together where the nonparent ignored the child, and a host of other relationships. Further, the field researchers learned that living together, for married and unmarried couples alike, can be a fluid situation; living circumstances change regularly. Complicating the study even more, some families, especially those receiving public assistance, tried to conceal their living situation from the researchers. Despite these findings, the study was locked into the arbitrary distinction between one- and two-parent families and proceeded according to the assumption that this corresponded to the actual nature of family relationships.

Most researchers do, of course, have some general questions in mind when they enter the field. These typically fall into one of two broad categories: substantive and theoretical.[2]

The first includes questions related to specific issues in a particular type of setting. For instance, one might be interested in studying a mental hospital, school, bar, or juvenile gang. The second category, theoretical, is more closely tied to basic sociological issues such as socialization, deviance, and social control. For example, Goffman's stated purpose in studying a mental hospital was to develop a sociological version of the self by analyzing situations in which the self is assaulted.

These two categories are interrelated. A good qualitative study combines an in-depth understanding of the particular setting studied and general theoretical insights that transcend that particular type of setting.

After entering the field, qualitative researchers often find that their areas of interest do not fit their settings. Their questions may not be relevant to the perspectives and behaviors of informants. In a study of institutional wards for the "severely and profoundly retarded," one of the authors began the study with the intention of studying residents' perspectives on the institution only to find that many residents were nonverbal whereas others were reluctant to speak openly (Taylor, 1977). He then shifted attention to staff perspectives which proved to be a fruitful line of inquiry. The same occurred in a study of a "hard core unemployed" job training program (Bogdan, 1971). The researchers hoped to study "resocialization" in the program, but soon learned that other factors were far more important to understanding the phenomenon.

Once you begin your study, do not be surprised if the setting is not what you thought it to be (Geer, 1964). The researcher interested in theoretical questions is especially likely to find that a particular setting is ill-suited to his or her interests. If you are tied to a particular theoretical question, you must be prepared to leave the setting for another. Our advice is to not hold too tightly to any theoretical interest, but to explore phenomena as they emerge during observations. All settings are intrinsically interesting and raise important theoretical questions.

Just as participant observers begin a study with general research questions and interests, they usually do not predefine the nature and number of "cases"—settings or informants—to be studied. In traditional quantitative studies, researchers select cases on the basis of statistical probability. Random sampling, stratified sampling, and other probability techniques are designed to ensure the representativeness of cases studied of a larger population in which the researcher is interested.

Qualitative researchers typically define their sample on an ongoing basis as the study progresses. Glaser and Strauss (1967) use the phrase *theoretical sampling* to refer to a procedure whereby researchers consciously select additional cases to be studied according to the potential for developing new insights or expanding and refining those already gained. Through this procedure, researchers examine whether and to what extent findings in one setting apply to others. According to Glaser and Strauss, the researcher should maximize variation in additional cases selected in order to broaden the applicability of theoretical insights.

In participant observation, the best advice is to get your feet wet: enter the field, understand a single setting, and only then decide upon other settings to study. Any study suggests almost limitless additional lines of inquiry. Until you are actually engaged in the study, you do not know which of these lines will be most fruitful.

In the state institution study, the researcher spent the first year conducting participant observation on a single ward. By the end of this year, he had acquired an in-depth understanding of the perspectives and routines of the attendants on this ward. In the words of Glaser and Strauss (1967), he had reached the "theoretical saturation" point. Additional observations did not yield additional insights. Once deciding to continue his study, the researcher was faced with selecting other settings to observe. He could pursue either substantive or theoretical (formal) interests. The major possibilities included the following:

Substantive Focus

Other aspects of attendants' lives

Other aspects of attendants' work (e.g., attendant training programs)

Other wards at the same institution

Other wards at other institutions

Other staff at the institution (e.g., administrators, professionals)

Theoretical Focus

Other types of total institutions (e.g., mental hospitals, prisons)

Other types of organizations that deal with the mentally retarded

Other types of "people processing" organizations (e.g., schools, social service agencies)

Other types of organizations (e.g., factories)

The researcher pursued his substantive interest in institutions for the mentally retarded by studying attendants and administrators at additional institutions. Other researchers might have adopted a different substantive focus, developed a theoretical focus, or concluded the study as an ethnography of a single ward.

SELECTING SETTINGS

The ideal research setting is one in which the observer obtains easy access, establishes immediate rapport with informants, and gathers data directly related to the research interests. Such settings seldom exist. Getting into a setting is usually hard work. It requires diligence and patience. The researcher must negotiate access, gradually win trust, and slowly collect data that only sometimes fit his or her interests. It is not uncommon for researchers to "spin their wheels" for weeks, even months, trying to break into a setting.

You cannot always determine beforehand whether you will be able to get into a setting and pursue your interests. If you encounter difficulties, keep trying! There are no guidelines for determining when you should give up on a setting. However, if you cannot give your best effort to obtain access to a setting, it is unlikely that you will be able to deal with the problems that inevitably arise in the course of fieldwork.

We recommend that researchers stay away from settings in which they have a direct personal or professional stake.[3] There is a tendency for novice observers to want to study friends and familiar surroundings. When one is directly involved in a setting, one is likely to see things from only one point of view. In everyday life people take their ways of seeing things for granted. They equate their views with an objective reality. As a researcher, you must learn to see their version of reality as only one out of many possible ways of viewing the world. One might also tend to limit what is written in research reports in the fear that friends will be offended.

Those who observe in their own professional domains face similar problems. It is difficult for people trained in an area of professional expertise to hold their own perspectives and feelings in abeyance. They will tend to share common sense assumptions with informants. For example, we know one observer of a "behavior modification" program who characterized clients' behavior as "appropriate" and "inappropriate."

Jack Douglas (1976) argues that researchers should stay away from areas in which they have deeply felt commitments. Although this is sound general advice, research is never "value free" (Becker, 1966–1967; Gouldner, 1970; Mills, 1959). Researchers almost always develop some sympathies with the people they study. Further, as the institutional researcher learned, there are some settings which so offend the human sensitivities of the researcher that it is impossible to remain detached and dispassionate.

ACCESS TO ORGANIZATIONS

Participant observers usually gain access to organizations by requesting permission from those in charge. We refer to those persons as *gatekeepers* (Becker, 1970). Getting into a setting involves a process of managing your identity; projecting an image of yourself that will maximize your chances of gaining access (Kotarba, 1980). You want to convince gatekeepers that you are a nonthreatening person who will not harm their organization in any way.

Students are especially likely to put gatekeepers at ease. Most people expect students to have class assignments or program requirements. The naive, eager students can often attract sympathy and help. Gatekeepers will probably assume that students want to learn concrete facts and tasks from "experts."

In many organizations a straightforward approach will work. People are usually surprised at how accessible most organizations are. One of the authors conducted a study of door-to-door salespersons in two companies (Bogdan, 1972). Although these companies trained prospective salespersons in the techniques of calculated misrepresentation, the heads of the branch offices opened their doors to the researcher within minutes of his request to observe. In fact, one of the branch heads gave permission over the phone after the researcher responded to a "come-on" in the newspaper to lure trainees into the program.

Not all organizations are studied so easily. The upper echelons of corporations (Dalton, 1964), hospitals (Haas and Shaffir, 1980), and large government agencies are notoriously difficult to infiltrate. The researcher can expect to get the "run-around" or to be turned down outright. The same researcher who studied the door-to-door salespersons tried first to observe a U.S. Air Force fireman's training program. Officials at each of a number of levels wanted to interview him personally. After each interview, they told him that they would have to get written permission from someone else before granting him access. By the time he finally received tentative permission to conduct the study, he had given up hope and turned to the study of salespersons.

When a straightforward approach does not work, you can use other tactics to gain access to a setting. Many researchers have gotten into organizations by having someone else vouch for them. As Hoffmann (1980) notes, most researchers have friends, relatives, and acquaintances who have contacts within organizations. These people can be enlisted to help win over reluctant gatekeepers. Similarly, a mentor or colleague can write a supportive letter on official letterhead to prospective gatekeepers (Johnson, 1975).

If all else fails, you can try to get into an organization "through the back door." For example, we have observed institutions by tagging along with family members and staff from other agencies. In one instance one of us obtained official permission to visit and then negotiated regular access with lower level staff. Although being a volunteer at a setting can interfere with research, some observers have gained their initial entree to a setting by assuming this role and proving themselves as trustworthy individuals.

One of the ironies of observing organizations is that once researchers have obtained access from gatekeepers, they typically must disassociate from them (Van Maanen, 1982; 108–109). Many organizations are characterized by tension, if not conflict, between the upper and lower levels of the hierarchy. If researchers are interested in studying people at the lower levels, they must go out of the way to avoid the appearance of collaborating or siding with gatekeepers or officials. They must also be alert to the possibility that gatekeepers may request reports on what they observe. When negotiating access, most observers are only prepared to provide gatekeepers with a very general report, a report so general that no one can be identified.

As should be apparent, there can be a significant lapse of time between the initial attempt to gain access and the beginning of observations. In some cases you will be unable to obtain access to an organization and have to start all over again somewhere else. Keep this in mind when you design your study. It is not unusual for inexperienced researchers, especially students working on theses and dissertations, to leave insufficient time to gain entree and complete a study.

ACCESS TO PUBLIC AND QUASI-PUBLIC SETTINGS

Many studies are conducted in public (parks, government buildings, airports, train and bus stations, beaches, street corners, public restrooms, etc.) and semipublic (bars, restaurants, pool halls, theaters, stores, etc.) settings. In these settings researchers do not ordinarily have to negotiate access with gatekeepers. Anyone can go to these places. Of course, in quasi-public settings—private establishments—the researcher may have to obtain permission from the owner to continue observations.

Although obtaining access to these settings does not present a problem, the participant observer, as a participant as opposed to passive observer, does have to develop strategies to interact with informants. *If you hang out long enough in the right position, sooner or later something will happen.* Prus (1980) recommends that observers situate themselves in "high action spots" in public places. In other words, go to where the people are and try to engage someone in casual conversation.

Liebow (1967) describes how he met Tally, the key informant in his study of black street corner men, while discussing a puppy in the street in front of a carry-out restaurant. Liebow spent four hours with Tally that day, drinking coffee and lounging around in the carry-out. After meeting Tally, Liebow's study blossomed. Before long, Tally was introducing him to others and vouching for him as his friend.

However, if you are going to hang out in a spot for a long time, you had better find an acceptable role to play. Although it is acceptable for strangers to engage each other in casual conversation, people suspect the motivations of someone who acts too interested in others or asks too many questions. The participant observer is easily confused with the mugger, voyeur, flirt, or, in certain circles, undercover agent (Karp, 1980). William Foote Whyte (1955) recounts his first efforts at locating an informant in his study of "Cornerville." Acting on the advice of a colleague who suggested that he go to a bar, buy a woman a drink, and encourage her to tell him her life history, Whyte found himself in an awkward situation. Whyte (1955:289) writes:

> I looked around me again and now noticed a threesome: one man and two women. It occurred to me that here was a maldistribution of females which I might be able to rectify. I approached the group and opened with something like this: "Pardon me. Would you mind if I joined you?" There was a moment of silence while the man stared at me. He then offered to throw me down the stairs. I assured him that this would not be necessary and demonstrated as much by walking right out of there without any assistance.

Some researchers who have conducted successful studies of public and quasi-public settings have adopted an acceptable participant role. In a study of hustlers and criminals, Polsky spent hours playing pool. According to Polsky, if you want to study criminals, go to where they spend their leisure time and win the trust of a few of them. Laud Humphreys (1975), whose study generated criticism on ethical grounds, but who has demonstrated enormous sensitivity to the people he studied, played the role of "voyeur-lookout" and "waiter" in a study of impersonal sex in public restrooms.

Although it is not necessary for observers in these settings to introduce themselves as researchers and explain their purposes to people with whom they will have only fleeting contact, they should explain themselves to people with whom they will have a sustained relationship. *Identify yourself before people begin to doubt your intentions, especially if they are involved in illegal or marginal activities.* Thus Liebow explained his intentions to informants after his first or second contact with them, whereas Polsky advises researchers to identify themselves to criminals shortly after meeting them.

ACCESS TO PRIVATE SETTINGS

The task of the participant observer in gaining access to private settings (homes) and situations (some activities take place in a range of settings) is similar to the interviewer's in locating informants. Settings and individuals must be tracked down; consent for the study must be negotiated with each individual.

The basic approach in obtaining access to private settings is the "snow-balling" technique: start with a small number of people, win their trust, and ask them to introduce you to others. Polsky (1969:124) writes:

> In my experience the most feasible technique for building one's sample is "snowballing"; get an introduction to one criminal who will vouch for you with others, who in turn will vouch for you with still others. (It is of course best to start at the top if possible, that is, with an introduction to the most prestigious person in the group you want to study.)

There are several places to start. First of all, check with friends, relatives, and personal contacts. People are usually surprised at the number of different persons their personal contacts know. In an experiment conducted with a class of students, Polsky reports that a third of the students found that friends and relatives could arrange a personal introduction to a career criminal.

Second, involve yourself with the community of people you wish to study. For his study of an inner city ethnic neighborhood in Boston, Herbert Gans (1962) moved into the neighborhood and became a member of the community. He made friends with neighbors, used local stores and facilities, and attended public meetings. Through these activities, he eventually received invitations to homes, parties, and informal gatherings in the neighborhood.

Third, go to agencies and social organizations that serve the people in whom you are interested. For example, depending on your interests, you might go to local churches, neighborhood centers, self-help groups, day care centers, schools, or fraternal associations. Bercovici (1981) conducted a participant observation study of boarding homes and other settings for the mentally retarded by accompanying a team of occupational therapists who visited the facilities. Whyte's (1955) study got off the ground when he was introduced to Doc, who turned out to be his key informant and sponsor, by a social worker at a neighborhood settlement house. In contrast to the time when Whyte's study was begun, the late 1930s, researchers today can expect organizations to set up hurdles in their path in the form of confidentiality and privacy.

A final tactic researchers have used to locate private settings and informants is advertising (Kotarba, 1980). Researchers have placed ads in local papers, made appearances on local talk shows, and prepared hand-outs describing their studies for distribution among local groups.

WHAT DO YOU TELL GATEKEEPERS AND INFORMANTS?

Explaining one's research procedures and interests to gatekeepers and informants is one of the most sensitive issues faced in field research. *Our own approach is to be truthful, but vague and imprecise.*[4] We take this position not only on ethical grounds, but pragmatic ones as well. If you deliberately misrepresent your intentions, you have to live with the fear and anxiety of getting caught. There is also the real possibility of having your cover blown and either being booted out of the setting or shattering your relationship with informants. Perhaps the greatest disadvantage of covert research is the limitations it places on the researcher. The overt researcher can transcend the narrow roles people in a setting play and engage in actual research activities. Further, many people will be more open and willing to share their perspectives with a researcher than with a co-worker or fellow participant.

It is unwise to give details concerning your research and the precision with which notes will be taken. If they knew how closely they were going to be watched, most people would feel self-conscious in your presence. In the unlikely case that you are pressed on the matter, you can tell people that you jot down some notes afterwards or keep a diary.

One way we have found useful in explaining our research interests is to let people know that we are not necessarily interested in that particular organization or the specific people there. In all studies, the researcher's interests are broader than a particular setting and concern the general type of organization. If you are seeking access to a school, for example, you should suggest that you are interested in understanding what *a* school is like, rather than the nature of that specific school. You might want to explain why that particular organization would make an ideal research setting, especially if people take pride in what they do.

It is a common experience among field researchers in large organizations for informants to assume that they are there to learn about people at another level. In the institutional study, attendants naturally assumed that the observer was there to observe the behavior patterns of the "severely and profoundly retarded" and to learn about the retarded from attendants. Whether or not researchers should cultivate false impressions, as Douglas (1976) suggests, there is no need to correct such misunderstandings.

Some gatekeepers will demand an elaborate explanation and defense of the research. Participant observers can get bogged down in extended discussions of research methodology trying to get into an organization. The standard objections to participant observation include: "We have to protect the privacy and confidentiality of our clients"; "We're too busy to answer a bunch of questions"; "You'll interfere with what we're trying to do"; "You won't find much interesting here anyway"; and "Your study doesn't sound scientific."

Anticipate the objections and have your responses ready. We are usually prepared to make certain guarantees to gatekeepers. This is sometimes called the *bargain*. Observers should emphasize the fact that their research will not disrupt the setting. Gatekeepers often assume that research involves questionnaires, structured interviews, clipboards, and other obtrusive methods. In contrast to these approaches, participant observation involves nondisruptive and unobtrusive activities. In fact, it is as important to most researchers to minimize disruption as it is to gatekeepers.

You should also guarantee the confidentiality and privacy of the people you study. We go out of our way to let informants know that any notes we take will not contain the names or identifying information about individuals or the organization and that we are as bound to confidentiality as the people in the organization.

How exactly you respond to questions about your research design will depend on how you size up the people in the organization. Critical questions about the research design usually reflect concerns about the findings (Haas and Shaffir, 1980). For instance, gatekeepers at institutions sometimes use client confidentiality to hide substandard conditions.

In the institutional study, the observer spent hours defending the integrity of his research to officials at one institution who happened to be trained in psychology. It was not until he stumbled upon the phrase "unobtrusive measures" that the officials finally granted him permission to observe. Johnson (1975) reports that his fumbling performance explaining his research to a group of social workers was a key factor in gaining access to a social service agency. The social workers concluded that they had nothing to fear from someone who had such difficulty explaining his aims.

Douglas (1976) advocates "playing the boob" or the "hare-brained academic ploy" when people seem afraid of the research. That is, the researcher tries to convince gatekeepers that the study is so academic and abstract that it could not possibly threaten anyone. Douglas (1976:170) gives an example:

> It is especially effective to tell them in some detail how, "We're doing a phenomenological–ethnomethodological reduction of your natural attitude in order to display and document the invariant interpretative procedures which are constitutive of the transcendental-ego and hence of intersubjective cognition."

Assuming this kind of ploy works, you will have to live for a while with this identity. We know one observer who identified himself to informants as an "ethnographer." He later heard one person whisper to another, "Don't make any racial jokes in front of that guy. He's an ethnographer."

It is not uncommon today for gatekeepers to ask participant observers to prepare a written proposal or to submit their research design to a "protection of human subjects committee." The same general guidelines apply to written documents: be honest, but vague. A bland and rambling discussion of qualitative research methods, grounded theory, and the like will usually suffice.

COLLECTING DATA

Detailed field notes should be kept during the process of gaining entry to a setting. As in later research, notes should be recorded after both face-to-face encounters and telephone conversations. The data collected during this time may prove extremely valuable at a later date. During the getting-in stage of the institutional study, the researcher spent time with the director of the facility. In addition to setting the ground-rules, the director offered her perspective on the institution: "Nobody's perfect"; "We are overcrowded"; "We could use more money from the state." After concluding his study of attendants, the researcher studied the perspectives of officials. These statements by the director helped him understand how institutional officials project a favorable image of themselves to the outside world.

The process of gaining access to a setting also lends insight into how people relate to one another and how they process others. One good way to learn about the structure and hierarchy of an organization is to be handed around through it. Finally, the notes collected at this time will help the observer later understand how he or she is viewed by people in the organization.

COVERT RESEARCH

Throughout this chapter we have emphasized overt research; that is, studies in which researchers communicate their research interests to prospective gatekeepers and informants. Yet many successful and important participant observation studies have been conducted using a covert approach (Festinger et al., 1956; Humphreys, 1975; Rosenhan, 1973; Roy, 1952a). Quite apart from pragmatic considerations, *there are serious ethical issues raised by covert research.*

Ethical decisions necessarily involve one's personal morality. One must choose among a number of moral alternatives and responsibilities. Some social scientists, such as Kai Erikson (1967:254), argue that undercover research and deception jeopardize the goodwill of potential research subjects and the general public on whom researchers depend: "It probably goes without saying that research of this sort is liable to damage the reputation of sociology in the larger society and close off promising areas of research for future investigators." In a similar vein, Warwick (1975) warns that a "public be damned" attitude among field workers has already created a societal backlash against social research.

Other researchers believe that the scientific knowledge gained through research justifies otherwise distasteful practices.[5] Glaser (1972:133) reports that Arthur Vidich justified deceptive assurances about the protection of identities as the price inherent in contributing to knowledge. Denzin (1978) takes the position that each researcher should decide on what is ethical behavior. Denzin (1978:331) argues for ". . . the absolute freedom to pursue one's activities as one sees fit." Jack Douglas (1976) characterizes society as a dog-eat-dog world. Since lies, evasions, and deceptions are part of everyday social life, according to Douglas, researchers must lie to, evade, and deceive their informants if they are to get the "truth."

Still other social scientists subscribe to situation ethics (Humphreys,

1975). In other words, the practical social benefits of research may justify deceptive practices. For Rainwater and Pittman (1967), social science research enhances the accountability of public officials.

Finally, there are those who condemn the deception of people on face value and advocate a "right not to be researched" (Sagarin, 1973). Thus some social scientists argue that researchers never have a right to harm people and the only ones who can judge whether research might cause harm, even if only in the form of exposure of group secrets, are informants themselves (Spradley, 1980).

In matters of ethics, then, researchers must counterbalance their multiple responsibilities to their profession, the pursuit of knowledge, the society, their informants, and, ultimately, themselves.

Our own view is that there are situations in which covert research is both necessary and ethically justified. It depends on what you are studying and what you intend to do with the results. Since powerful groups in our society are the least likely to grant access to researchers, social science research tends to concentrate on the powerless. We have far more studies of workers than corporate managers, poor people than politicians, and deviants than judges. Researchers expose the faults of the powerless while the powerful remain unscathed. To study powerful groups covertly, therefore, may well be warranted. However, we find it difficult to justify outright deception of anyone merely for the sake of completing one's degree requirements or adding a publication in an obscure journal to one's vita.

It is also true, as Roth (1962) points out, that the distinction between overt and covert research is an oversimplification. That is, all research is to some extent secret in the sense that researchers never tell their informants everything. What of researchers who observe in public places? Must they inform a crowd of people that they are being observed? Should researchers be compelled to give informants a blow-by-blow account of their emerging hypotheses and hunches?

There are no hard-and-fast rules in the realm of ethics. *Research in the field must involve the researcher in a great deal of soul-searching.*[6] Whatever ethical decisions researchers make, they should not be cavalier or casual about deceiving people.

This chapter dealt with the pre-fieldwork stage of participant observation research. More specifically, we focused on matters related to the decisions observers must make before they enter the field and the initial contacts they must make to conduct their research. The following chapter shifts to the issues and dilemmas the observer faces in the field: "Now that you're in, where do you go from here?"

NOTES

1.   Of course, proposal writing for outside funding requires the researcher to specify the research design. When we write proposals for qualitative studies, we provide a review of the qualitative literature on the subject matter and a detailed description of qualitative methods, similar to that in this book.

2.   Glaser and Strauss (1967) make the distinction between "substantive" and "formal" theory. This is similar to the distinction we are making here.

3.   This issue is much more complicated than we present it here. There have been some outstanding studies written by people who were participants of the settings they observed. Becker's (1963) study of jazz musicians and Roth's (1963) study of a TB hospital are excellent examples. Riemer (1977) provides a good review of research conducted by participants of settings. For the reasons stated here, we still maintain that it is preferable not to be too intimately tied to what you study, especially if you do not have experience conducting participant observation. The closer you are to anything, the harder it is to develop the critical perspective necessary to conduct solid research.

4.   However, see our discussion of covert observation in this chapter.

5.   Apparently, few social scientists would carry this belief to its logical extension. Lofland (1969:301), who justifies his own covert research among an Alcoholics Anonymous group, writes, "The 'research' activities of Nazi Germany taught us (or should have) very well that there are definite moral limits on what can be done in the name of science." Also see Lofland (1961).

6.   In recent years "protection of human subjects" committees have sprung up at universities across the country, largely in response to federal research guidelines (Department of Health, Education and Welfare, 1974, 1978). These committees often seem designed to protect universities and funding agents from controversy, rather than to safeguard the interests of potential "subjects." In any case, the fact that a research proposal has passed the scrutiny of a "protection of human subjects" committee does not let the researcher off the hook in making ethical decisions on the spot. It is also true, as Klockars (1977) and Wax (1983) point out, that federal "informed consent" procedures seem inappropriate in qualitative studies since the researcher cannot always, if ever, specify beforehand which people or settings will be studied, what questions will be asked, and what risks will be entailed by informants. Klockars (1977:217) quotes a marvelous statement from Margaret Mead made in reference to federal research guidelines: "Anthropological research does not have subjects. We work with informants in an atmosphere of mutual trust and respect."

3

Participant Observation

IN THE FIELD

In this chapter we consider the fieldwork phase of participant observation. Fieldwork involves three major activities. The first relates to inoffensive social interaction: putting informants at ease and gaining their acceptance. The second aspect deals with ways to elicit data: field strategies and tactics. The final aspect involves recording data in the form of written field notes. We discuss these and other issues that arise in the field in this chapter.

ENTERING THE FIELD

Participant observers enter the field with the hope of establishing open relationships with informants. They conduct themselves in such a way that they become an unobtrusive part of the scene, people whom participants take for granted. Ideally, informants forget that the observer is there to do research. Many of the techniques used in participant observation correspond to everyday rules about inoffensive social interaction; skills in this area are a necessity.

Observers remain relatively passive throughout the course of the fieldwork, but especially during the first days in the field (Geer, 1964).[1] Participant observers "feel out the situation," "come on slow," "play it by ear" (Johnson, 1975), and "learn the ropes" (Geer, 1964). The first days in the field are a period in which observers try to put people at ease, dispelling notions of obtrusive research approaches, establish their identities as "OK" persons, and learn how to act appropriately in the setting. What clothes should I wear? Can I smoke? Who looks too busy to talk to me? Where can I sit without being in the way? Can I walk around? What can I do to avoid sticking out like a sore thumb? Can I talk to the clients? Who looks approachable?

During the initial period, collecting data is secondary to getting to know the setting and people. Questions are designed to help break the ice. Since some people may ask you what you want to know, it's a good idea to jot down some general questions before you enter the field. Questions such as "Could you give me an overview of this place?" and "How did you get into this sort of thing?" are usually good openers.

Different people will probably exhibit different degrees of receptivity to you. Although the gatekeeper may have consented to your study, others may resent your presence. Sue Smith-Cunnien, in the first day of a participant observation study, overheard one person ask another: "What's she going to do—stand around and watch us all the time?" As Johnson (1975) notes, it is not uncommon for observers to find themselves in the middle of a power struggle over their presence. It's important to explain who you are to *all* people in the setting. In a study of teachers' use of the media, for example, the researchers interviewed each teacher individually to explain the study and obtain permission to observe in each classroom, even though this had been granted by administrators.

You should also try to let people know in subtle ways that what they say to you will not be reported to others. (Of course, you don't introduce yourself by saying that you're a researcher and ethically bound not to violate their confidentiality.) On the second observation in the institutional study, one of the attendants asked the researcher, "Did you tell (the director) about the boys here on this ward?" The researcher responded with something like: "No, I didn't even tell him where I was. I don't tell people on the outside about the institution so why should I tell him about all of you." In Smith-Cunnien's study, she seized on the opportunity to explain the confidentiality of her research during the following exchange:

OBSERVER: "Would you want to be Editor-in-Chief next year?"

INFORMANT: "Who are you going to tell all of this to anyway?"

OBSERVER: "I'm sorry, I should have told you from the start that everything you tell me is confidential. I won't be repeating any of this around here."

During the first days in the field, researchers invariably feel uncomfortable. Many of us shun unnecessary interaction with strangers. No one feels comfortable in a new setting with no definable role to play. Smith-Cunnien reflects on her first day observing:

I felt fairly uncomfortable in this setting. Most of this was my own shyness, I think, although some of it definitely stemmed from the fact that a stranger sitting there is conspicuous and I was doing nothing but looking around— didn't write any field notes. Part of the uncomfortableness came from the fact that at some moments there was literally very little to watch—all the action was going on in the offices and I could just overhear things. Next time I observe, I will try to be a little more aggressive without being too aggressive—I will have to try to observe more specific settings and try to find out who more people are.

All observers are faced with embarrassing situations in the field. Al-though it is true, as Shaffir, Stebbins, and Turowetz (1980) write, that fieldwork is characterized by feelings of self-doubt, uncertainty, and frustration, take comfort in the fact that *you will feel more comfortable in the setting as the study progresses.*

When first entering the field, observers are often overwhelmed by the amount of information they receive. For this reason, you should try to limit the amount of time spent in the setting during each observation. An hour is usually enough time. As you become more familiar with a setting and adept at observation skills, you can increase the length of time in the setting.

Field research can be especially exciting early in a study. Some observers are inclined to stay in a setting so long that they leave the field drained and filled with so much information that they never record it. Observations are useful only to the extent that they can be remembered and recorded. *Don't stay in the field if you will forget much of the data or not have the time to write your field notes.*

NEGOTIATING YOUR ROLE

The conditions of field research—what, when, and whom you observe— must be negotiated continually. *You must strike a balance between conducting your research as you see fit and going along with informants for the sake of rapport.*

The first problem you are likely to face is being forced into a role incompatible with conducting research. People often do not understand participant observation, even when it has been explained to them carefully. In many settings gatekeepers and informants will place observers into roles commonly performed by outsiders. The personnel in schools, mental hospitals, and other institutions often try to force observers into a volunteer role, especially in the case of women and students. Observers may be expected to sign the volunteer book, work with certain clients, and report to the volunteer supervisor. We know one observer who was pushed into a tutoring relationship with a boy in a detention home, despite the fact that he had explained his interests to the institution's director. Similarly, Easterday, Papademas, Schorr, and Valentine (1977) report that women researchers in male-dominated settings often get put in the role of "gofer," among others.

There are sometimes advantages in being placed in a familiar role in a setting: access is more easily obtained; the observer has something to do; people are not as self-conscious in the researcher's presence; some data are more accessible. We are familiar with one observer who, in a study of a charitable organization, was given a volunteer assignment to record information on donors. As a study progresses, however, the researcher will lose control of the study and have limitations imposed on collecting data if he or she is confined to a narrow organizational role.

A second problem encountered by field researchers is being told what and when to observe. All people attempt to present themselves in the best possible light to outsiders (Goffman, 1959). Informants will share those aspects of their lives and work in which they are seen in a favorable light and hide, or at least downplay, those in which they are not. Many organizations appoint tour guides to give tours to outsiders. Although these tours are valuable in certain respects, they tend to give a selective view of the setting. At total institutions, for example, tour guides will often show visitors the best wards and model programs and discourage visitors from seeing other parts of the institution (Goffman, 1961; Taylor and Bogdan, 1980).

In many organizations, people also try to structure the times at which observers can visit. Total institutions are notorious for denying visits on weekends, since this is when the least programming occurs and most staff members have days off. Typically, organizational officials and staff will try to limit observers to special events, such as a holiday party or open house.

Women sometimes face special problems in having informants limit their research (Easterday et al., 1977; Warren and Rasmussen, 1977). For example, Easterday et al. note that older males often act paternalistically with younger women; in a study of a morgue, a medical examiner attempted to "protect" a young woman researcher from seeing the "bad cases."

You should try to resist attempts of informants to control your research. Ideally, researchers should select their own places and times to observe. As observers establish some level of rapport, they usually find they can gain access to more places and people.

ESTABLISHING RAPPORT

Establishing rapport with informants is the goal of every field researcher. It is an exciting and fulfilling feeling when one begins to establish rapport with those one is studying. Rapport is not an easily defined concept. It means many things:

Communicating a feeling of empathy for informants and having them accept it as sincere.

Penetrating people's "defenses against the outsider" (Argyris, 1952).

Having people "open up" about their feelings about the setting and others.

Being seen as an "OK" person.

Breaking through the "fronts" (Goffman, 1959) people impose in everyday life.

Sharing in informants' symbolic world, their language, and perspectives (Denzin, 1978).

Rapport comes slowly in most field research. Even then, it may be tentative and fragile. It is doubtful whether anyone completely trusts anyone else at all times and under all circumstances. As John Johnson (1975) tells us, rapport and trust may wax and wane in the course of fieldwork. With some informants, one may never develop true rapport. Johnson (1975:141–142) writes:

Near the end of the welfare investigations I finally concluded that it is not a realistic possibility to develop relations of trust as such. This was especially true in a setting that included a radical leftist, a militant women's liberationist, older people, younger people, mods and squares, Republicans, Democrats, third-party members, Navy chiefs and commanders, Reserve Army majors, pacifists, conscientious objectors, and so on. . . . During the final months of the field research I gradually developed a notion of "sufficient trust" to replace the earlier presuppositions gained from a reading of the traditional literature. Sufficient trust involves a personal, common-sense judgment about what is accomplishable with a given person.

Although there are no hard-and-fast rules for establishing rapport with informants, a number of general guidelines can be offered.

Paying Homage to Their Routines

Observers can only establish rapport with informants if they accommodate themselves to informants' routines and ways of doing things. All people like to do things in certain ways and at certain times. Observers must stay out of their hair. Polsky (1969:129) offers advice on how to observe criminals that applies to observing anyone: "If he wants to sit in front of his TV set and drink beer and watch a ball game for a couple of hours, so do you; if he wants to walk the streets or go barhopping, so do you; if he wants to go to the racetrack, so do you; if he indicates (for whatever reason) that it's time for you to get lost, you get lost." We know one observer who, in a study of a hospital, came late to two staff meetings and then asked the physicians, who felt pressed for time themselves, to reschedule the meetings to suit his schedule. These kinds of people give participant observers a bad name.

Establishing What You Have in Common with People

Probably the easiest way to build relationships with people is to establish what you have in common with them. The casual exchange of information is often the vehicle through which observers can break the ice. In the study of the unemployed training program, the observer got to know many of his informants through conversations about fishing, children, sickness, past jobs, and food. It is natural for people to want to know about the observer's interests and pastimes.

Helping People Out

One of the best ways to begin to gain people's trust is to do favors for them. Johnson (1975) reports that during his fieldwork, he served as a driver, reader, luggage porter, baby-sitter, moneylender, ticket-taker at a local conference, notetaker, phone answerer when business was heavy, book reader, book lender, adviser on the purchase of used automobiles, bodyguard for a female worker, letter writer, messenger, and other things. We know one researcher studying an understaffed ward for 40 young children at an institution for the mentally retarded who was having a terrible time relating to the staff. The attendants were abrupt with him and did their best to ignore him totally. The situation became increasingly uncomfortable until the observer offered to help the two attendants feed the children one day. As he began to feed the first child, the attendants opened up and started to share their concerns and complaints. For the first time, they invited him to join them for a break in the staff lounge.

Being Humble

It is important for people to know that the researcher is the type of person to whom they can express themselves without fear of disclosure or negative evaluation. Many observers, ourselves included, try "to appear as a humble person who would be a regular guy and do no one any dirt" (Johnson, 1975:95).

Observers frequently become the people with the most knowledge and understanding of what everyone in the setting thinks. Keep this knowledge to yourself. Researchers should be careful not to reveal certain things that informants have said even if they were not related in private. To display too much knowledge makes the observer threatening and potentially dangerous.

Informants may also be reluctant to express their feelings if the observer acts too knowledgeable. Let people speak freely. You will find that many people hold beliefs that are inaccurate if not patently absurd. There's no need to correct these beliefs. You will only make people self-conscious in your presence.

Acting Interested

It should go without saying that you should act interested in what people have to say. Yet, it is sometimes easy to act bored in the field, especially if one finds oneself in a situation with someone who monopolizes the conversation about seemingly irrelevant or trivial matters. There are ways to channel a conversation and to subtly avoid people. We cover some of these later in this chapter and in our discussion of interviewing.

PARTICIPATION

When active involvement in people's activities is essential to acceptance, then by all means participate, but know where to draw the line. In some settings, you have to participate in marginal activities. Van Maanen (1982:114), who witnessed many instances of police brutality, writes, "Only practical tests will demonstrate one's trustworthiness."

The attendants in the institutional study often cruelly teased and abused their charges: beat them, threw buckets of water on them, forced residents to engage in fellatio, encouraged some to hit others, forced them to swallow burning cigarettes, and tied them to beds spread-eagled (the attendants' folk wisdom included ways to do these things without leaving marks). Although the attendants subtly encouraged the observer to participate in these abuses, they never exerted strong pressures on him to join. However, they did watch him closely for signs of disapproval. For his part, he tried to ignore these acts as best he could.[2]

Fine (1980) reports that he was tested by children in his study of little league baseball. For example, kids would engage in rowdiness and roughhousing in his presence as a way of sizing him up. Given the difficulties of overcoming generational differences, it was important for him to distance himself from an adult role of supervising in order to gain the kids' trust.

The participant observer walks a thin line between active participant—"participant-as-observer"—and passive observer—"observer-as-participant" (Gold, 1958; Junker, 1960). There are clearly times in which it is best not to be accepted as a genuine member of the setting or group.

Where involvement places one in a competitive situation with informants, it is best to withdraw. It is sometimes difficult to set aside your own ego. Like other people, observers have a self-concept to defend and want to be thought of as witty, bright, and sexually attractive. In a study of a newsroom, Rasmussen found that although the "cute young datable guy" approach worked in winning over some female reporters, this alienated the male reporters (Warren and Rasmussen, 1977).

You should also avoid acting and talking in ways that don't fit your own personality. For example, although you should dress in such a way as to blend into the setting (if people dress casually, dress casually; if they dress formally, do the same; if people dress in different ways, try to find a neutral form of dress), you should not wear anything in which you feel unnatural or uncomfortable. Similarly, it is wise not to use people's vocabulary and speech patterns until you have mastered them and they come naturally. Whyte (1955:304) learned this lesson when he was walking down the street with a street corner group and, entering the spirit of the small talk, let loose with a string of obscenities. Whyte reports what happened: "Doc shook his head and said: 'Bill, you're not supposed to talk like that. That doesn't sound like you.' "

"Rapping" was a common pastime among trainees in the job training program. Here, rapping, also called "playing the dirty dozen" and "joking," refers to a competitive verbal exchange the object of which is to put down another person by the clever use of phrases with double meanings (Hannerz, 1969; Horton, 1967). The observer found himself to be the object of trainees' jokes and, after a few days of observation, was encouraged by them to engage in verbal exchanges about his potency as a lover and his capacity as a drinker. Although he gradually began to participate in these exchanges, he soon realized that he lacked the ability to perform well on this level. At first, he saw this inability to rap as a barrier. As the study progressed, however, he found this inability to be an asset. Since he couldn't rap well, he was not forced into these exchanges, which had become progressively repetitive, and could concentrate on collecting data.

There are also situations in which you want to go out of your way to point out the differences between yourself and informants. Polsky (1969) discusses the tightrope field researchers walk trying to blend into the social scenery without pretending to be something they are not. In studying heroin users, Polsky made a point of wearing short-sleeved shirts and an expensive watch, both of which let any newcomer know that he was not a junkie.

Any participation that interferes with the researcher's ability to collect data should be avoided. In their rush to be accepted by informants, some observers get sucked into active participation. We know an observer who, on his first day at a school, overheard teachers express a desire to have a sensitivity training workshop. Since he had led a number of such workshops previously, he immediately offered to help them. He ended up abandoning his research.

Field researchers also have to guard against being exploited by informants. There's a difference between establishing rapport, on the one hand, and being treated as a stooge. Polsky suggests that researchers have to know where to draw the line with informants. Polsky (1969:128) offers this example: "I have heard of one social worker with violent gangs who was so insecure, so unable to 'draw the line' for fear of being put down, that he got flattered into holding and hiding guns that had been used in murders."

No discussion of rapport would be complete without a mention of *over-rapport* (Miller, 1952). Although there are instances of field researchers "going native," abandoning their role and joining the groups they are studying, the more common problem is over-identification with informants. As Miller notes, it is easy to be coopted by friendships in the field to the point of giving up embarrassing lines of inquiry or, worse, abandoning the critical perspective fieldwork requires. The problem of over-rapport underscores the importance of collaborate relationships such as team research in the field.

KEY INFORMANTS

Ideally, participant observers develop close and open relationships with all informants. However, as mentioned previously, rapport and trust come slowly in field research. With some informants, the researcher will never develop rapport.

Field researchers usually try to cultivate close relationships with one or two respected and knowledgeable people in the early stages of the research. These people are called *key informants*. In the folklore of participant observation, key informants are almost heroic figures. They are the researcher's best friend in the field. Whyte's (1955) Doc and Liebow's (1967) Tally are notable examples.

Key informants are the researcher's sponsor in the setting and primary sources of information (Fine, 1980). During the first days in the field especially, observers try to find people who will "take them under their wing": show them around, introduce them to others, vouch for them, tell them how to act, and let them know how they are seen by others. Whyte (1955:292) recounts Doc's words to him in their first meeting:

> ". . . You tell me what you want to see, and we'll arrange it. When you want some information, I'll ask for it, and you listen. When you want to find out their philosophy of life, I'll start an argument and get it for you. If there's something else you want to get, I'll stage an act for you. . . . You won't have any trouble. You come in as my friend. . . . There's just one thing to watch out for. Don't spring (treat) people. Don't be too free with your money."

Participant observers also look to key informants to provide them with a deep understanding of the setting. Since field research is limited in time and scope, key informants can give the history of the setting and fill in the researcher on what happens when he or she is not there. Zelditch (1962) calls the informant the "observer's observer." In some studies participant observers have used key informants to check out emerging themes, hunches, and working hypotheses. Whyte reports that Doc became, in a real sense, a collaborator in the research by reacting to Whyte's interpretations and offering those of his own.

Although researchers are always on the lookout for good informants and sponsors, it is generally wise to hold back from developing close relationships until one has developed a good feel for the setting. In the initial phase of the research, there is a tendency to latch onto anyone who seems open and friendly in a strange situation. Yet the most outgoing and friendly people in a setting may be marginal members themselves. It is often difficult to know who is or is not respected in a setting initially. If researchers attach themselves to an unpopular person, they are likely to find that others regard them as an arm or ally of that person.

It is also important to avoid concentrating exclusively on one or a handful of people. Do not assume that all informants share the same perspective. They seldom do.

In the institutional study, Bill, the "ward charge" or supervising attendant, tended to monopolize the observer's time. He took the observer on long coffee breaks in the staff room during which he freely expressed his perspectives on the institution, residents, his supervisors, and life in general. As the study progressed, Bill began to repeat himself, telling the same stories and expressing the same views on every observation session. It was not until the observer scheduled his visits on Bill's days off that he began to talk at length with other attendants and learn about their perspectives. The observer in the job training program study encountered similar problems with a staff member who was particularly friendly. Although it helped to have a sponsor and informant in the setting, the staff member kept him from interacting with other staff and the trainees. The observer withdrew from the relationship and only reestablished it after he had gotten to know others.

Close relationships are essential in field research. The right key informant can make or break a study. However, you have to be prepared to stand back from relationships formed early in a study if and when circumstances demand it.

DIFFICULT FIELD RELATIONS

Fieldwork is characterized by all of the elements of human drama found in social life: conflict, hostility, rivalry, seduction, racial tension, and jealousy. Observers often find themselves in the middle of difficult and sensitive situations in the field.

Age, gender, race, and other features of personal identity can have a powerful influence on how informants react to the observer (Warren and Rasmussen, 1977). Liebow (1967) conducted his study of black street corner men as a white researcher. Although he developed strong and friendly relationships with his informants, Liebow (1967:248) does not pretend to have overcome the barriers to insider status imposed by race: "In my opinion, this brute fact of color, as they understood it in their experience and I understood in mine, irrevocably and absolutely relegated me to the status of outsider."

In some situations women enjoy certain advantages in conducting field research (Easterday et al., 1977; Warren and Rasmussen, 1977). Obviously, women stand a better chance than men in being accepted as an insider in female-dominated settings. Warren and Rasmussen (1977) also point out that male and female researchers alike can use sexual attraction to gain information.

However, women researchers are often confronted with problems in the field that men usually do not face. In the family study with which one of the authors was involved, women interviewers occasionally found themselves to be the objects of husbands' sexual advances and, consequently, wives' jealousy. Easterday et al. (1977) describe being hustled as a common problem of young female researchers in male-dominated settings. They recount the following exchange during an interview:

> I was in the midst of industriously questioning the attendant about his job at the morgue and he came back with, "Are you married?"
>
> OBSERVER: "No. How long have you worked here?"
>
> ATTENDANT: "Three years. Do you have a steady boyfriend?"
>
> OBSERVER: "No. Do you find this work difficult?"
>
> ATTENDANT: "No. Do you date?"
>
> OBSERVER: "Yes. Why isn't this work difficult for you?"
>
> ATTENDANT: "You get used to it. What do you do in your spare time?"
>
> And so our interview went on for over an hour, each of us working at our separate purposes. I doubt whether either of us got any "usable data." (Easterday et al., 1977:339)

As Easterday et al. note, in these situations every encounter can become a balancing act between cordiality and distance.

Hostile informants can be just as troublesome as overly attentive ones. In many settings—almost surely in large organizations—observers come across people who seem to resent their very presence. Van Maanen (1982: 111–112) offers the following quote as an example of unambiguous rejection in his study of the police:

"Sociologists? Shit. You're supposed to know what's going on out there. Christ, you come around here asking questions like we're the fucking problem. Why don't you go study the goddamn niggers and find out what's wrong with them. They're the fucking problem, not us. I haven't met a sociologist yet who'd make a pimple on a street cop's ass."

Johnson (1975) uses the term "freeze-out" to refer to an informant who expresses an unwillingness to aid the research. In his study of a social service agency, he encountered 2 freeze-outs out of 13 case workers. What he eventually discovered was that both of the freeze-outs padded their case loads, meaning that they kept files on people to whom no services were provided.

Although some people may never accept you, don't assume that hostile informants will remain hostile forever. People often soften over time. In the institutional study, one attendant, Sam, avoided the observer for over six months. Although other attendants seemed to accept the observer, Sam remained very guarded in his presence. The observer visited the ward one evening when only Sam and one other attendant were on duty. Sam, who was in charge, was sitting in the staff office. The observer stopped by the office and asked Sam if it was all right for him to hang around for a while. Suddenly, Sam went off on a long monologue on why it was necessary to maintain strict discipline on the ward. He explained why he thought attendants had to hit and scream at the residents. It seems that Sam had not trusted the observer up until that point. He was afraid that the observer was some kind of a spy. After that visit, Sam, although never overly friendly, was cordial to the observer and appeared at ease around him.

You should try to provide hostile informants with opportunities to change their minds. Continue to be friendly without pushing them into interaction. Even if you can't win their acceptance, you might avoid making them your enemies and allowing them to turn others against you. Observers can find themselves torn by conflict and organizational power struggles (Roy, 1965). People on both sides of a controversy may vie for their allegiance. Support for one side may be expected as the *quid pro quo,* or exchange, for information. Johnson (1975) found himself being manipulated for information by a supervisor who was trying to build a case against one social worker.

Probably the best way to deal with conflict is to lend a sympathetic ear to both sides. The trick is to make both sides believe that you're secretly agreeing with them without actually taking a position or giving either side ammunition. Observers often walk a tightrope and have to be able to sense when they are off-balance.

FIELD TACTICS

Establishing and maintaining rapport with informants is an ongoing activity throughout field research. As fieldwork moves beyond the first days in the field, however, observers devote increasing attention to finding ways to broaden their knowledge of settings and informants. Here are some tactics.

Acting Naive

Many observers find that presenting themselves as naive but interested outsiders is an effective way of eliciting data (Lofland, 1971; Sanders, 1980). Sanders (1980:164) notes that presenting oneself as an "acceptable incompetent" enables one to ask questions about "what everyone knows." Outsiders are expected to possess a degree of naiveté about a setting. For example, an observer at a school would not be expected to know about educational curricula and standardized testing. In the institutional study, the observer developed a strategy to get access to ward records by asking naive questions about residents' IQs and ward events that he knew attendants could not answer without consulting the files.

Being at the Right Place at the Right Time

Perhaps the most effective field tactic to use is placing yourself in situations likely to yield the data in which you are interested. You can tag along, wrangle invitations to go places or see things, show up unexpectedly, or "play both sides against the middle" (Johnson, 1975). The latter is a variation of the tactic children use to get permission to do things from their parents: imply to both parents that it's OK with the other, without specifically saying so, thereby leaving yourself an out if you get caught. At the institution, the researcher developed a number of ways to gain information in an unobtrusive manner and stumbled upon a number of others:

1. He frequently visited the ward late at night, after residents had been sent to bed and when the attendants had the time to engage in long conversations, and at shift changes, when accounts of the day's events and most recent institutional rumors were given to one set of attendants by another.

2. On the first day of his study, the observer hung around with attendants at the conclusion of their shift as they were talking about going out for a drink. By placing himself in this awkward position, he wrangled an invitation to go to a local bar frequented by attendants.

3. The observer broke down Sam's resistance by happening to visit the ward on an evening when only Sam and another attendant were working and finding him alone in the staff office.

Most observers catch themselves eavesdropping on conversations and lifting extra copies of memos and other documents. The subtle eavesdropper sometimes gains important data that would not otherwise have been obtained. Of course, the discovered eavesdropper faces embarrassment (Johnson, 1975).

Don't Let Informants Know Exactly What You Are Studying

It's usually wise not to let informants know what you want to learn about or see (if you know yourself). In the first place, as Hoffmann (1980) notes, it is sometimes useful to camouflage the real research questions to reduce self-consciousness and the perceived threat. Hoffmann (1980:51) reports:

> Many of my respondents became reticent when they perceived themselves to be the object of study—that is, when I told them that I was interested in how the old elite system worked. I found, however, that they were prepared to offer their views more freely on "external" topics, such as reorganization policy or problems of the new membership. With respondents who appeared

defensive about the old system . . . or who countered direct questions with front work, I presented myself as being interested in the consequences of reorganization or organizational problems rather than in the board as a social group or in board work as an elite social institution.

In the second place, when informants know too much about the research, they are likely to either hide those things from the observer or stage events for his or her benefit. The design of the family study described earlier called for a series of interviews with the parents and home observations, including observations of the bedtime routines of children. The fieldworkers observed dramatic differences in how some parents acted during the interviews and the prescheduled observations. In most families children were better dressed and had more toys around on the days of the observations. During evening interviews, the fieldworkers found that in many families there is no bedtime routine per se. Children fall asleep in front of a television some time after early evening. When the fieldworkers returned to conduct the preannounced bedtime observations, some parents actually staged bedtime routines for them to observe (telling the child to get ready for bed at an early hour, tucking the child in, etc.). By informing parents what they wanted to see, the fieldworkers unwittingly encouraged some parents to fabricate events, because they wanted either to look like "good parents" or to be cooperative and give the researchers what they wanted.

You Can Use Aggressive Field Tactics Once You Have Developed an Understanding of the Setting

Early in a study, you conduct yourself in such a way as to minimize *reactive effects* (Webb et al., 1966); your goal is for people to act as naturally as possible in your presence (knowing that you have some effect by virtue of being there). For instance, participant observers don't walk around with clipboards or questionnaires, take notes, or ask a lot of structured questions. As Jack Douglas (1976) argues, the more controlled the research, the farther it departs from natural interaction, the greater the likelihood that one will end up studying the effects of research procedures.

At a later stage of research, you can employ obtrusive or aggressive tactics, knowing enough about the setting to gauge how these tactics affect what people say and do. Some observers conduct structured interviews toward the end of their research. Altheide (1980) reports that as he was about to exit the field, he became much more aggressive in his questioning, probing sensitive political issues.

ASKING QUESTIONS

Although participant observers enter the field with broad questions on their minds, they allow themes to emerge before pursuing specific lines of inquiry. Initially, *field researchers ask questions in such a way as to enable people to talk about what is on their minds and what is of concern to them without forcing them to respond to the observers' interests, concerns, or preconceptions.*

Early in a study, observers ask nondirective and nonjudgmental questions. Use the phrases with which you usually initiate conversations: "How's it going?" "How do you like it here?" "Can you tell me a little about this place?" These kinds of questions allow people to respond in their own ways and with their own perspectives. Another good way of getting people to talk initially is to wait for something to happen and then ask about it. As discussed earlier, newcomers are expected to be naive and to ask questions about things they haven't seen before.

Knowing what not to ask can be just as important as knowing what to ask. Sanders (1980) points out that when one is studying people who are engaged in legally questionable activities, inappropriate questions can reasonably be interpreted as an indication that the researcher is an informer. Van Maanen (1982) argues that any form of sustained questioning implies evaluation. In the institutional study, the observer directly questioned only one attendant about abuse (and this was after a few beers), even though this was a major focus of the research. The subject was too sensitive and explosive to explore in a straightforward way.

We know of one group of observers who, on a tour of a mental hospital, questioned a supervisor about a ward's "time-out," or isolation rooms: "Are they allowed to go to the bathroom?" "Do they still get meals when they're in there?" The supervisor was infuriated by the questions and shot back: "What do you think we are here—sadists?"

It is also important to know *how* to ask questions. Questions should be phrased in sympathetic terms that support informants' definitions of themselves. One researcher referred to the "funeral business" during her first visit to a funeral home. The funeral director was taken aback. This seemingly innocuous phrase contradicted his view of his work as a profession and not merely a business.

It was not uncommon for institutional attendants to strait jacket or tie residents. The observer was always careful to ask questions that would not intimidate the attendants or challenge their perspectives: "Does he always give you problems?" "How long do you have to keep him in there?" There is no doubt that if he had asked questions requiring the attendants to justify their actions—"How often do you let them out?" "What's the institution's policy on restraint?"—they would have frozen him out.

Once informants start talking, you can encourage them to say more about topics in which you are interested. Encouraging words, cues, and gestures that indicate your interest are usually sufficient to keep someone on track: "That's interesting." "Is that right?" "I always wondered about that." Small signs of sympathy demonstrate support and encourage people to continue: "I know what you mean." "That's rough."

You should ask for clarification of informants' remarks. *Don't assume that you understand what people mean.* Use phrases like "What do you mean by that?," "I don't follow you exactly," and "Explain that again." You can also restate what informants say and ask them to confirm your understanding.

As observers acquire knowledge and understanding of a setting, questioning becomes more focused and directive (Denzin, 1978; Spradley, 1980). Once themes and perspectives have emerged, researchers begin to round out their knowledge of the setting and check out information previously gathered.

In participant observation, data analysis is an ongoing activity. Observers move back and forth between the field and data already collected. What they try to observe and ask about in the field depends on what they think they have learned. It's a good idea to keep a running record of themes to explore and questions to ask (as described later, we use "Observer's Comments" to do this).

After they have developed some working hypotheses, observers round out their knowledge by asking informants to elaborate on subjects they mentioned previously and following up on things mentioned by some informants with others. In the institutional study the observer had a hunch that attendants' work careers (previous jobs) and personal networks (family members and friends who worked at the institution) played a role in shaping their perspectives on work after talking to several attendants about previous jobs and relatives. Over the next couple of months, he made a point of casually asking other attendants what they did before they worked at the institution and whether they had friends and relatives there.

Jack Douglas (1976:147) stresses the importance of *checking out* informants' accounts and stories: "Checking out consists essentially of comparing what one is told by others against what can be experienced or observed more directly, and therefore more reliably, or against more trustworthy accounts." Accounts that the researcher suspects early in the study can be checked out after he or she has a sense of who can and cannot be believed and to what extent.

Most observers also employ more aggressive questioning tactics once they have developed a feel for a setting and informants. Especially toward the end of a study, observers pose "devil's advocate" questions (Strauss et al., 1964), confront informants with falsehoods, probe "taboo" subjects (Altheide, 1980), and ask informants to react to their interpretations and conclusions (Strauss et al., 1964).

The observer who has spent some time in a setting can use knowledge already gained to obtain more information. The idea is to act as if you already know about something to get people to talk about it in depth. Douglas (1976) calls this the "phased-assertion" tactic. Hoffmann (1980: 53) describes how she used inside information when people seemed reluctant to talk too freely:

> First, respondents learned that I was "in the know," that I had penetrated through the public veneer to the underlying social reality. Front work was discouraged because they know that I could distinguish it from backstage information and because it might look as if they were covering something up. Second, the use of insider details possibly acted to reassure reticent informants. I often had the impression that respondents felt relieved by the knowledge that they were not the only persons to make such disclosures, that initial responsibility lay with someone else, and that this person must have had reason to trust me in the first place.

Hoffmann also notes that by dropping inside information the researcher discourages informants from going over familiar points and encourages them to make responses relevant to his or her interests.

LEARNING THE LANGUAGE

An important aspect of participant observation is learning how people use language (Becker and Geer, 1957; Spradley, 1980). *Field researchers must start with the premise that words and symbols used in their own worlds may have different meanings in the worlds of their informants.* They must also be attuned to and explore the meanings of words with which they are not familiar.

Observers almost always come across new words and symbols. Any group, especially one cut off from the broader society, develops its own special vocabulary. For example, Wallace (1968) provides a glossary of terms used on "skid row": *beanery,* a cheap restaurant; *dead one,* a retired hobo; *dingbat,* the lowest type of tramp; *jack,* money; *slave market,* street corner employment office. Similarly, Giallombardo (1966) offers the argot, special language, of a women's prison: *bug house,* institution for the "mentally insane" or "defective"; *butcher,* a prison doctor; *flagging,* an older inmate attempting to involve a younger one in sex.

The vocabulary used in a setting usually provides important clues to how people define situations and classify their world and thus suggests lines of inquiry and questioning. In the job training program the staff and trainees used special terms to refer to each other which indicated the distrust in the setting. Some of the staff used the phrase "professional trainee" to refer to people who had been involved in other training programs. Some trainees, on the other hand, referred to staff members as "poverty pimps," a phrase that suggested that they were living off of the plight of others.

Certain assumptions may be built into a vocabulary. In institutions for the so-called "mentally retarded," for example, mundane activities are referred to as "therapy" and "programming"; "motivation training" and "recreation therapy" refer to going for walks, coloring, and similar activities (Taylor and Bogdan, 1980).

Some observers are unable to cut through professional jargon and vocabularies. They uncritically accept the assumptions behind professional categories. Terms like "schizoid," "paranoid," and "psychotic" have little concrete meaning and are based on psychiatric ideologies, rather than "scientific knowledge" (Szasz, 1970). Likewise, the vocabulary used in many educational settings reflects class and racial bias (Cicourel and Kitsuse, 1963). Lower-class children who cannot read or are disruptive are labeled "educable retarded," "culturally deprived," and "emotionally disturbed," whereas middle-class children with the same behavior are likely to be called "learning disabled" or "minimally brain-damaged."

People use a special vocabulary to build lines of action in some settings. Calling a person "profoundly retarded" or "severely handicapped" can be used to keep that person institutionalized. Calling a child "emotionally disturbed" may allow the child to be kicked out of school.

You must learn to examine vocabularies as a function of the assumptions and purposes of the users, rather than an objective characterization of the people or objects of reference. This applies to even clear-cut words. A person described as "nonambulatory" might be thought of as someone who cannot walk at all. Yet in understaffed nursing homes and institutions the term might be used to refer to people who could walk if they had minimal assistance.

The meaning and significance of people's verbal and nonverbal symbols can only be determined in the context of what they actually do and after an extended period of time. There is a danger of imputing meanings that people did not intend. Polsky (1969:123–124) warns against assuming that a person's vocabulary reflects deep-seated feelings:

> I have seen it seriously argued, for example, that heroin addicts must unconsciously feel guilty about their habit because they refer to heroin by such terms as "shit," "junk," and "garbage." Actually, the use of any such term by a heroin addict indicates, in itself, nothing whatever about his guilt feelings or the lack thereof, but merely that he is using a term for heroin traditional in his group.

Although the words people use lend insight into the meanings they attach to things, it is naive to presume that the intricacies of a social setting can be revealed by vocabulary alone.

FIELD NOTES

As an analytical research method, *participant observation depends upon the recording of complete, accurate, and detailed field notes.* You should record field notes after each observation as well as after more casual contacts with informants such as chance encounters and phone conversations. As noted earlier, field notes should be recorded during the pre-fieldwork stage of the research.

Since field notes provide the raw data of participant observation, you should strive to write up the most complete and comprehensive field notes possible. This requires a tremendous amount of self-discipline, if not compulsiveness. It is not uncommon for observers to spend four to six hours recording field notes for every hour of observation. Those who want to use qualitative methods because they seem easier than statistics are in for a rude awakening. Anyone who has done a participant observation study knows that recording field notes can be drudgery.

Many beginning observers try to cut corners by writing sketchy summaries, omitting details, or postponing recording the notes. "Nothing much happened" is a common rationalization. Yet the observer's frame of mind should be such that everything that occurs in the field is a potentially important source of data. You don't know what is important until you have been in the setting for a while. Even "small talk" can lend insight into people's perspectives when viewed in context at a later time. A common experience in participant observation is to go back to your initial notes when you begin to analyze your data to look for something you vaguely remember being said or done only to find that you never wrote it down. Of course, as you get to know the setting and people and focus your research interests, you can be more selective in what you record. We've found that we can spend half as much time recording notes in the latter stages of fieldwork than in the early ones.

Try to find a mentor or colleague to read your field notes. This is probably the best way to get the motivation to record field notes session after session over a period of time. By virtue of their distance from the dynamics of a setting, readers can also point out emerging themes that escape the observer.

The field notes should include descriptions of people, events, and conversations as well as the observer's actions, feelings, and hunches or working hypotheses. The sequence and duration of events and conversations are noted as precisely as possible. The fabric of the setting is described in detail. In short, the field notes represent an attempt to record on paper everything that can possibly be recalled about the observation. A good rule to remember is that *if it is not written down, it never happened.*

HINTS IN RECALLING WORDS AND ACTIONS

Participant observers must *strive for* a level of concentration sufficient to remember most of what they see, hear, feel, smell, and think while in the field (they can also "cheat" by using mechanical recording devices and pay the price in rapport as we discuss later). Although precise recall may seem like a difficult, if not impossible, task, most observers are amazed at the accuracy with which they can recall details through training, experience, and concentration. Some observers use the analogy of a switch to describe the ability they have developed to remember things; they can "turn on" the concentration needed to observe and recall. This analogy is a good one if only for the reason that it sets the tone for the goal of observation skills.

People vary in the amount that they can remember and in the techniques that enable them to recall things. We've found the following techniques useful in recalling details in a broad range of settings.

1. *Pay attention.* The reason most people don't recall things in everyday life is that they never notice them to begin with. As Spradley (1980) remarks, participant observers must overcome years of selective inattention. Watch, listen, concentrate. In characteristic fashion, Yogi Berra is said to have remarked, "You can see a lot by just looking."

2. *Shift focus from a "wide angle" to a "narrow angle" lens.* In busy places observers are usually overwhelmed by the sheer number of activities and conversations occurring at the same time. It is literally impossible to concentrate on, let alone remember, everything that is happening. One especially effective recall technique that can be perfected with practice is to focus on a specific person, interaction, or activity, while mentally blocking out all the others.

In the institutional study, over 70 residents and anywhere from 1 to 10 attendants could be in one large dayroom at a single time. The number of activities occurring simultaneously seemed infinite: several residents rocking on benches, one removing his clothes, another urinating on the floor, two residents cleaning up feces and urine with a rag and bucket, a handful of residents sitting in front of the television, three lying on the floor, several pacing back and forth, two residents hugging each other, a couple of residents in strait jackets, one attendant scolding a resident, two other attendants reading a newspaper, another attendant preparing to dispense tranquilizers and seizure control drugs, and so on, and so on.

When first entering the room, the observer tried to take a "wide angle" picture of the room for a few minutes, noting the various activities occurring. After that, however, he would shift focus to a single activity or corner of the room, ignoring everything else. By concentrating on specific activities one at a time he could later reconstruct much of what was happening at the time.

3. *Look for "key words" in people's remarks.* Although your notes should be as accurate as possible, it is not necessary to remember every word that people say. However, you can concentrate on and commit to memory key words or phrases in every conversation that will enable you to recall the *meanings* of their remarks. It is with meanings that you are concerned.

You will find that certain words and phrases stand out in your mind. In a study of a hospital neonatal unit (Bogdan et al., 1982) doctors and nurses used special, easy to remember terms to refer to infants: for example, "feeders and growers," "nonviable," and "chronics." Other, more familiar words or phrases, such as "very sick baby" and "good baby," although less striking, were easily recalled once the researchers were attuned to how medical staff defined the infants.

4. *Concentrate on the first and last remarks in each conversation.* Conversations usually follow an orderly sequence. A certain question elicits a certain response; one remark provokes another; one topic leads into a related one. If you can remember how a conversation started, you can often follow it through to the end in your own mind. Even when conversations do not follow a logical or orderly sequence, remarks that "come out of nowhere" should not be difficult to recall. You should find that the *substance* of long monologues, which usually confuse the novice observer, is retrievable.

5. *Play back remarks and scenes in your mind.* After you see or hear something, repeat it to yourself mentally. Try to visualize the scene or remark. It is also a good idea to take a break from talking or observing every once in a while during a session to play back in your mind what has already happened.

6. *Leave the setting as soon as you have observed as much as you can remember.* Although this point has been made already, it bears repeating. In a new setting you probably should not spend more than an hour observing unless something important is happening. As you get to know a setting and learn to remember things, you can spend more time in the field.

7. *Record your field notes as soon as possible after observing.* The longer you wait between observing and recording the data, the more you will forget. Try to schedule your observations when you will have the time and energy to write up your notes.

8. *Draw a diagram of the setting and trace your movements through it.* In a sense, walk through your experience. Doing this is a valuable aid to help recall events and people. A seating chart similarly can be helpful. The diagram or chart will help you in recalling who did what and remembering less conspicuous people.

9. *Once you have drawn a diagram and traced your own movements, outline specific events and conversations that occurred at each point in time before you record your field notes.* The outline will help you recall additional details and approximate the sequence in which events occurred. The outline does not have to be elaborate; it only needs to contain key words, scenes, and events that stand out in your mind, the first and last remarks in conversations, and other reminders. The time you take to construct an outline will be well worth it in terms of the accuracy and clarity it adds to your notes.

10. *If there is a time lag between observing and recording the field notes, tape record a summary or outline of the observation.* One of the sites we've studied was located an hour's drive away. The observer taped a detailed summary of the observation on the way home. He let conversations and events flow freely from his mind during this time. Later, after arriving home, he transcribed the summary, organizing events according to the sequence in which they occurred. From this summary he wrote up a detailed account of the day's events. Between observations in his study of impersonal sex in public restrooms, Humphreys (1975) occasionally went to his car to tape record what he had just observed.

11. *Pick up pieces of lost data after you have recorded your field notes.* Observers often recall things days or even weeks after an observation. Sometimes events and conversations are remembered after the next observation. These pieces of data should be incorporated into the field notes.

TAPING AND TAKING NOTES IN THE FIELD

Although most participant observers rely on their memories to record data, some researchers take notes in the field or use mechanical recording devices for data collection. Indeed, there is a growing number of qualitative studies in which researchers use tape recorders, videotape machines, and time-lapse photography (Dabbs, 1982; Whyte, 1980).

Participant observers seem divided on the pros and cons of recording notes and using mechanical recording devices in the field. Some researchers take the position that obtrusive recording devices draw unnecessary attention to the observer and disrupt the natural flow of events and conversations in the setting. Douglas (1976:53) writes, ". . . there is every reason to believe that obtrusive recording devices have fundamental effects in determining what actors think and feel about the researcher (mainly, it makes them terribly suspicious and on guard) and what they do in his presence." Other researchers, especially those identified with linguistic ethnomethodology and formal sociology, question whether the observer can accurately remember and subsequently record the important details of what happens in the setting (Schwartz and Jacobs, 1979).

Our view is that *researchers should refrain from taping and taking notes in the field at least until they have developed a feel for the setting and can understand the effects of recording on informants.* In our experience mechanical recording devices have untoward effects on people. One of the authors used a tape recorder during the first interview with the mother of a young child in her home. In the "warm up" prior to the interview, the researcher casually mentioned that he previously lived in her neighborhood and asked her how she liked living there. She proceeded to complain about how many blacks had recently moved into the neighborhood and how they had "taken over" the parks and playgrounds. Then came the interview which included questions on likes and dislikes about the neighborhood. As the interviewer questioned the mother with the tape recorder playing, she gave bland responses to questions about what she liked about the neighborhood and what changes had occurred since she had been living there. Never was race mentioned. After the interview had been completed and the tape recorder turned off, the interviewer again struck up a conversation about the neighborhood and again the mother complained about the number of blacks who had moved there. The conclusion: no one, or at least few people, want to be a racist "for the record." In other words, it is naive to assume that people will immediately reveal their private behavior and thoughts while they are being filmed or taped.

There are situations and settings in which observers can get by using mechanical recording devices without dramatically altering the research.

Whyte's (1980) excellent photographic study of small urban places demonstrates that a camera can be an effective research tool in public places. Similarly, there have been many insightful documentaries by Frederick Wiseman and others filmed by a camera operator who seemed to move in with a group of people and capture an incredible amount of their private lives, although one is left wondering to what extent the people put on performances for the cameras. In our interviewing we have found that over a period of time people seem to forget about a tape recorder and speak relatively freely while it is recording.

It is also true that there are some social patterns that cannot be studied and analyzed without audio or video recording devices. Thus observers are not likely to recall, or even notice, all of the minute details of interactional patterns and conversations sufficient for ethnomethodological analysis and certain other lines of inquiry. In a study of children's interaction patterns and peer socialization, Lothar Krappmann and Hans Oswald of the Max Planck Institute at the Free University of Berlin have utilized two observers taking detailed notes and a videotape machine at the same time in school classrooms.

In most symbolic interactionist studies researchers do not need to rely on mechanical recording devices to collect important data. Through training and experience, the researcher can develop *sufficient recall* to remember events and conversations necessary to understand people's meanings, perspectives, and definitions. In fact, the accuracy the experienced observer interested in this level of analysis gains with the use of a tape recorder is probably illusory.

There are few instances when it is advisable to take notes in the field. More so than recording, note-taking reminds people that they are under constant surveillance and tips them off to areas in which the researcher is interested. As noted earlier, in many situations the observer wants to deflect informants' attention from the research concerns. One of the few times at which notes can be taken unobtrusively is when other people are also taking notes, as in a classroom or formal meeting. Even in these situations, the researcher should be discreet.

Some observers go to a private place such as a bathroom to jot down key words and phrases that will help them later recall events during long observation sessions. You can buy a small reporter's notebook that will fit easily and inconspicuously into a pocket. If this helps you remember things and can be done secretly, so much the better.

THE FORM OF THE NOTES

Everybody develops his or her own way of writing up the field notes. Although the form varies from observer to observer, the field notes should be written in such a way as to allow you to retrieve data easily and to code (and cut up) themes or topics. Here are some guidelines we try to follow.

1. *Start each set of notes with a title page.* The title page should include the date, time, and place of observation, and the day and time when the notes were recorded. Some observers title each set of notes with a phrase that will remind them what they contain generally when they go to their notes to check on something.

2. *Include the diagram of the setting at the beginning of the notes.* Trace your movements and indicate the page of your notes on which each movement is described. This will serve as an easy reference when you want to check specific events. For those who are fortunate enough to have someone read their notes, a diagram provides a useful point of reference for the reader.

3. *Leave margins wide enough for your and others' comments.* Wide margins also enable you to add forgotten items at a later time and to code your notes in the analysis stage of your research.

4. *Form new paragraphs often.* As noted in the chapter on data analysis, the best way to analyze your data is literally to cut up your notes according to themes or topics. The task of coding and cutting up your notes will be easier if you have formed new paragraphs for every event, thought, or topic.

5. *Use quotation marks to record remarks as often as possible.* It is not necessary to have a flawless reproduction of what was said. What is important is capturing the meaning and approximate wording of remarks. If you can't recall the wording, paraphrase: "John said something like—I've got to go home. Bill agreed and John walked out." Strauss et al. (1964) suggest that the researcher use quotation marks for exact recall, apostrophes to signify less precision in wording, and no marks to indicate reasonable recall.

6. *Use pseudonyms for the names of people and places.* More than a few participant observers have fretted over what would happen if their data fell into the wrong hands (Humphreys, 1975; Johnson, 1975; Van

Maanen, 1982, 1983). You never know what you might see or hear that would jeopardize the people you're studying if someone else found out. You also don't know whether readers of your notes might have relationships with the people described in your notes. Nothing is lost by using pseudonyms for people and places.

7. *Make at least three copies of your notes.* Keep one set handy, place one in safekeeping, and use a third set for any readers of your notes. Once you begin analyzing your data, you will also need at least one extra set and probably more to code and cut up the notes.

OBSERVER'S COMMENTS

The field notes should include not only descriptions of what occurs in a setting, but also a record of the observer's feelings, interpretations, hunches, preconceptions, and future areas of inquiry. These subjective comments should be clearly distinguished from descriptive data through the use of parentheses and the designation "O.C." for "Observer's Comment."

It may be difficult for those trained in "objective" research to accept the observer's own feelings and interpretations as an important source of understanding. Yet as a participant in the setting and a member of the general society and culture, the researcher is likely to share many feelings and perspectives with those within a setting. Indeed, participant observers must learn to empathize with informants, to experience vicariously their experiences, and to share their sufferings and joys. To distance oneself from subjective feelings is to refuse to take the role of the other person and to see things from his or her point of view (Blumer, 1969).

What you feel *may* be what informants feel or may have felt in the past. You should use your own feelings, beliefs, preconceptions, and assumptions to develop *potential* insights into others' perspectives. By recording these subjective definitions in "Observer's Comments," you identify areas for future investigation and analysis. The following comments are excerpted from field notes in the state institution study:

(O.C. I feel quite bored and depressed on the ward tonight. I wonder if this has anything to do with the fact that there are only two attendants working now. With only two attendants on, there are fewer diversions and less bantering. Perhaps this is why the attendants always complain about there not being enough of them. After all, there is never more work here than enough to occupy two attendants' time so it's not the fact that they can't get their work done that bothers them.)

(O.C. Although I don't show it, I tense up when the residents approach me when they are covered with food or excrement. Maybe this is what the attendants feel and why they often treat the residents as lepers.)

In the following excerpt from the job training study, the observer reflects upon one of his first contacts with a trainee after having spent the initial stages of the research with staff:

I approached the two trainees who were working on assembling the radio. The male trainee looked up. I said, "Hi." He said, "Hi" and went back to doing what he had been doing. I said, "Have you built that (the radio) right from scratch?" (O.C. After I said this I thought that that was a dumb thing to say or perhaps a very revealing thing to say. Thinking back over the phrase, it came across as perhaps condescending. Asking if he had built it right from scratch might imply that I thought he didn't have the ability. He didn't react in that way but maybe that's the way people think of the "hard core" unemployed out at the center. Doing well is treated with surprise rather than as standard procedure. Perhaps rather than expecting that they are going to produce and treating them as if they are going to produce, you treat doing well as a special event.)

The observer thus gained a possible insight into how staff members define trainees by reflecting on his own remark.

The participant observer also records emerging ideas and interpretations in the "Observer's Comments." These comments provide a running record of the observer's attempts to understand the setting and become extremely valuable during the analysis phase of the research. The comment below is taken from the field notes in the institutional research:

(O.C. Many residents on this ward collect and hoard seemingly insignificant things. This is similar to what Goffman writes about in institutions of this kind. I'll have to start looking into this.)

DESCRIPTIONS OF SETTINGS AND ACTIVITIES

The research setting and people's activities should be described in the field notes. When writing field notes, you should force yourself to describe the setting and activities in sufficient detail to paint a mental picture of the place and what occurred there. Some researchers write their field notes in such a way as to present narratively what a camera would capture in film.

You should be careful to use descriptive and not evaluative words when you write your field notes. For example, you would not describe a room simply as "depressing"; rather, you would write something like the following: "The room was relatively dark, with dust and cobwebs in the corners and on the window sills and chipped paint on the walls." Similarly, you would not say that people were receiving "occupational therapy"; you would record the activities in descriptive terms: "The three women were sitting at the table. One was caning a chair, while the other two were crayoning in coloring books. The staff member in charge referred to these activities as 'occupational therapy.' "

Your own feelings, evaluations, or interpretations should be included in the "Observer's Comments." By doing this, you can identify possible areas for investigation or analysis without assuming that everyone sees things exactly the same way that you do. The following excerpt comes from the notes in the institutional study:

> A strong smell of feces and urine mixed with antiseptic permeated the air as I entered the smaller dormitory. (O.C. I find the smell to be repulsive, so much so that I immediately want to leave. Yet the attendants do not seem to mind the smell. Some claim to have gotten used to it. Others never mention it. I wonder if this reflects the difference between myself and them or the fact that I am a newcomer to the ward compared to them.)

You will find that a detailed description of the setting and people's positions within it will give you important insights into the nature of participants' activities, interaction patterns, perspectives, and ways of presenting themselves to others. At many total institutions, the front regions—areas visible to outsiders—are arranged to present an appearance of benign, idyllic retreats where residents receive appropriate care and treatment (Goffman, 1961; Taylor, 1977; Taylor and Bogdan, 1980). Thus the grounds of most institutions are filled with tall trees, meticulously cared for gardens, and stately buildings. The administration building is likely to be an old Victorian or colonial structure, with carefully polished woodwork and floors on the inside. Institutions sometimes have special rooms set aside for family visits. As Goffman (1961) notes, the furnishings and decor of these rooms more closely approximate outside standards than residents' actual living quarters.

In dramatic contrast to these front regions, institutional back regions, where residents actually live, are designed to facilitate the staff's control over residents and efficient maintenance of ward order and cleanliness (Taylor, 1977). The following are common features on institutional wards:

Locked doors and areas within the ward.

Televisions and stereos located high on the walls out of residents' reach.

Heavy, destruction-proof furniture.

Wire mesh on windows.

Light switches and temperature controls inaccessible to residents.

Bathrooms lacking toilet paper, soap, towels, and mirrors.

Clothing and personal objects stored in locked rooms.

Staff offices and "nursing stations" positioned in such a way as to maximize staff surveillance of residents.

Sparse furnishings and decorations (wall paintings, curtains).

Not all aspects of a setting will be significant. However, you should note and question the meaning of everything you observe.

Although you need to fully describe a setting only once in your field notes, you should be attuned to changes that occur. These changes may reflect changes in how people see themselves or others. For example, a change in the seating pattern in a teachers' lunchroom may reflect a change in social relationships in the school.

DESCRIPTIONS OF PEOPLE

Like settings and activities, *people should be carefully described in the notes.* People convey important things about themselves and make assumptions about others on the basis of clothing, hair styles, jewelry, accessories, demeanor, and general appearance. Goffman (1959, 1963, 1971) uses the phrase "impression management" to describe how people actively try to influence how others think about them through their looks and actions.

You should note those features of people that lend insight into how they view themselves or how they want to be viewed by others. What kinds of clothing do they wear? Casual or formal dress? Do men have long hair and beards or short haircuts? What is the condition of their teeth and what might this tell you about them? How do people walk?[3] What kind of glasses are they wearing? Are people wearing jewelry? Do women have handbags and do men carry briefcases? These and other features should be described in the field notes.

People, as settings, should be described in specific and nonevaluative terms. Words like "shy," "flashy," "aggressive," and "fancy" are interpretative, not descriptive words. Your own impressions and assumptions about people based on their appearance should be relegated to "Observer's Comments." The following excerpt comes from field notes in the door-to-door salesmen study:

> The door leading from the corridor opened and a man paused for a moment and tiptoes in. (O.C. He looked surprised when he opened the door, like he didn't expect to see all the people. His tiptoeing seemed to be an attempt not to cause any excess noise. His carriage was one of "I'm imposing.") He was approximately 5'7" and had a deep brown suntan. (O.C. It looked like he was tan from working outside.) His skin was leathery. His hair was black and combed back. It had a few streaks of gray and he was slightly bald in front. He was maybe 45 years old. He was thin. His clothes were cleaned and well-pressed and fit him well. A set of keys was hanging from his belt on a key ring in back. He had on dark brown flannel straight-leg trousers with a light tan stretch belt with the buckle worn on his hip. He had on a dark brown plaid sport shirt with a button down. He was wearing well-polished loafers and had on black horn-rimmed glasses.

In many settings, especially organizations, dress and appearance differentiate people according to their position and status. Sometimes the signs of status are obvious; for example, some people wear work clothes or uniforms, whereas others wear dresses or coats and ties; hats and name plates also may indicate a person's status. In other settings signs that indicate status are subtle and will strike the observer only after a period of time in the field. One researcher noticed that women employees in an organization carried their handbags with them wherever they went. It took the researcher a while to realize that the women held subordinate positions in the organization and were not provided with lockers. At many total institutions, staff members have heavy key rings hanging from their belts. It is not uncommon to observe residents copying the staff by hanging keys on strings from their belts.

RECORD DIALOGUE ACCESSORIES

People's gestures, nonverbal communications, tone of voice, and speed of speaking help to interpret the meaning of their words. Everyone can recall instances in which someone said "no" in such a way as to imply "yes." These dialogue accessories are important to understanding interaction and should be included in the field notes. The following excerpts are examples of the kinds of gestures that should be recorded in your notes:

Joe loosened his tie and said, ". . ."

As Pete spoke, the sound of his voice got louder and louder and he began pointing his finger at Paul. Paul stepped back and his face turned red.

Bill raised his eyes to the ceiling as Mike walked past. (O.C. I interpret this as a ridiculing gesture.)

You should also try to capture accents and speech patterns when these might be significant; that is, when they tell something important about the person or how others are likely to view him or her.

RECORD YOUR OWN REMARKS AND ACTIONS

Participant observers should record their own behavior in the field. People's words and actions can only be understood if they are examined in the context in which they are said or done. You, as a participant observer, are part of that context. For instance, you will find that comments made in response to a question must be interpreted differently than volunteered remarks or that certain remarks are meaningless when viewed apart from the questions that elicited them. Further, recording and analyzing your own actions will help you revise your field tactics or develop new ones.

RECORD WHAT YOU DON'T UNDERSTAND

Participant observers often hear phrases and conversations that they do not fully understand. Since these comments are difficult to recall precisely, there is a tendency to omit them from the notes. However, *even the most incomprehensible remarks may become understandable when viewed in light of later conversations or events.* In the institutional study, attendants made frequent reference to "bung hole," which sometimes sounded like "bungle." Although he didn't understand the word, the observer included these references in the field notes. It was only later that he learned that "bung holing" was an institutional term for anal intercourse.

There are also remarks the observer overhears that seem inappropriate or out of context. Such data should be recorded as is. Don't try to reconstruct what you heard to make it read better.

BOUNDARIES OF A STUDY

As noted in the last chapter, the research design is flexible in participant observation and other qualitative research. That is, qualitative researchers usually start modestly; they enter the field, understand a single setting, and then decide upon other settings to study.

Sooner or later, you will have to set some boundaries for your research in terms of the number and types of settings studied. The selection of additional settings or informants will hinge on what you have learned and your own research interests. Thus in the institutional study the researcher could have pursued a large number of different lines of investigation, ranging from attendant training programs to other types of organizations. Since he had developed a strong substantive interest in total institutions and the social meaning of mental retardation, he proceeded to study attendants and officials at other institutions in addition to interviewing people labeled retarded themselves.

It is difficult to set limits on a study. There are always more people and places to study. However, many excellent studies have been conducted that were based on a single setting, whether a classroom, hospital ward, or street corner. What is important is that no matter how many settings you study, you develop an understanding of something that was not understood before.

Many observers prefer to take a break from fieldwork after they have spent some time in a setting. Doing this will allow you time to clear your mind, review and analyze your data, set priorities, develop field strategies and tactics, and decide whether to move on to other areas or settings. A respite from the intensive observation the research requires will also give you a second breath and the endurance needed to continue the study.

LEAVING THE FIELD

Participant observers almost never reach a point when they feel that their studies are complete. There is always one more person to interview, one more loose end to tie up, or one more area to pursue. Yet most field researchers arrive at a stage when the long hours spent in the field yield diminishing returns. Glaser and Strauss (1967) use the phrase *theoretical saturation* to refer to the point in field research at which the data become repetitive and no major new insights are gained. This is the time to leave the field.

Field studies last anywhere from a few months to well over a year. In fact, the study of the door-to-door salesmen lasted only three weeks. However, the researcher observed daily and focused on a narrow aspect of the sales training program. In the institutional study, the observer made weekly or biweekly visits to a single ward for over a year. During the last two months, the observer learned relatively few new things about attendants and institutional life, although he was able to round out his understanding of the setting and confirm many hunches and working hypotheses. After completing his research at this institution, the observer spent the next couple of years focusing on other institutions and, indeed, continues to study institutions today.

In most instances researchers should spend at least several months in a setting regardless of the frequency of their visits. It is common for field researchers to develop a deeper understanding of a setting and to reject or revise working hypotheses after the first several months. One often stumbles across some insight that ties everything together only after a prolonged period of time in the field. Sometimes it takes quite a while for informants to let down their guard around the observer.

Leaving the field can be a difficult time personally for participant observers (Shaffir et al., 1980; Snow, 1980). It means breaking attachments and sometimes even offending those one has studied, leaving them feeling betrayed and used. Perhaps for this reason, many observers end up

staying in the field longer than they need to for the purposes of the research (Wax, 1971).

A common way of leaving the field is "easing out" (Junker, 1960) or
"drifting off" (Glaser and Strauss, 1968); that is, gradually cutting down
on the frequency of visits and letting people know that the research is
coming to an end. It is a good idea not to cut off contacts with informants too abruptly, although this is easy to do. Miller and Humphreys
(1980) point out that there are sound reasons for concluding the research
on good terms with informants and leaving the door open to future
contacts. Thus they have been able to study people over a long period
of time, since the mid1960s in Humphreys' case, learning about changes
in people's lives and their definitions of themselves. On a more human
level, Miller and Humphreys have been able to assess the impact of the
research on informants by sending them copies of publications and maintaining phone and mail contact with them.

TRIANGULATION

In the literature on participant observation, the term *triangulation*
means the combination of methods or sources of data in a single study
(Denzin, 1978; Patton, 1980). Although field notes based on first-hand
experience in a setting provide the key data in participant observation,
other methods and approaches can and should be used in conjunction
with fieldwork. Triangulation is often thought of as a way of guarding
against researcher bias and checking out accounts from different informants. By drawing on other types and sources of data, observers also
gain a deeper and clearer understanding of the setting and people being
studied.

Practically all participant observers conduct interviews and analyze
written documents during or at the conclusion of their field research.
Especially toward the end of the research, after the observer has established relationships with people and gained "insider knowledge," open-
ended interviews with informants can be relatively focused and specific.
Altheide (1980) reports that as he was about to leave the field, he conducted aggressive interviews, probing areas that were too sensitive to
explore earlier in the research. Of course, you can also interview new
people toward the end of the study to obtain background information
relevant to the research or to check out different people's perspectives.

Written documents such as official reports, memos, correspondence, contracts, salary schedules, files, evaluation forms, and diaries provide an important source of data. As emphasized in later chapters, these documents should be examined not as "objective" data, but to lend insight into organizational processes and the perspectives of the people who write and use them and to alert the researcher to fruitful lines of inquiry. Since written documents are sometimes regarded as confidential, it is usually wise to wait until you have been in the field for a while before asking to see them.

Researchers can also analyze historical and public documents to gain a broader perspective on a setting. Newspapers, organizational archives, and local historical societies may be valuable repositories of information. The observer in the training program for the hard core unemployed analyzed these data in great depth in his research. He not only reviewed materials relevant to the formation of that particular program, but also researched materials on the local and national history of poverty programs. Through an historical perspective, researchers can view a setting in the context of its past and in relation to other settings.

Another form of triangulation is *team research*: two or more field workers studying the same or similar settings (see Becker et al., 1961, 1968; Bogdan et al., 1974; Geer et al., 1966; Strauss et al., 1964). In most team research the basic techniques of participant observation remain the same with the exception that field tactics and areas of inquiry are developed in collaboration with others.

Jack Douglas (1976) makes a convincing case in favor of team research as an alternative to the traditional "Lone Ranger" approach in fieldwork. As Douglas notes, the research team can develop an in-depth understanding typical of participant observation, while grasping the broader picture by studying different settings or different people within the same setting. Team research also permits a high degree of flexibility in research strategies and tactics. Since researchers differ in social skills and ability to relate to different people, they can play different roles in the field and study different perspectives. For example, in team research one observer can be aggressive while another is passive within a setting; men and women researchers will be viewed and reacted to differently and hence can pursue different areas of study.

As in many cooperative endeavors, it is a good idea to establish clear ground rules regarding each person's responsibilities and to be sure people can work together prior to entering into team research. Haas and

Shaffir (1980:250) report how personal pressures and professional competition led to the destruction of a three-member research team: "Differences of opinion about research roles, methods of collecting and analyzing data, and the publication and authorship of findings created strains among the researchers and threatened the veneer of collegiality."

Team research also raises the danger of a "hired hand" relationship between a research director, usually a tenured professor, and research assistants, usually graduate students, in which field workers are reduced to the status of "data collectors" who have no say in research design and analysis and, therefore, no stake in the research (Roth, 1966). Hired hands invariably cheat, fudge data, and otherwise subvert the research. The only way to avoid a hired hand mentality, as Roth so persuasively argues, is for each researcher to be actively involved in the process of formulating the research questions, deciding on field strategies, and making sense out of the data.

ETHICS IN THE FIELD

In the last chapter we discussed the ethical issues raised by covert research. The choice between overt as opposed to covert research is only one of many of the difficult ethical dilemmas in field research. As a research method that involves you in people's day-to-day lives, participant observation reveals both the best and the worst of others and very often places you in unresolvable morally and ethically problematic situations.

Getting into a setting usually involves some sort of bargain: explicit or implicit assurances that you won't violate informants' privacy or confidentiality, expose them to harm, or interfere in their activities. Once you are in the field, you try to establish rapport with informants, a certain level of trust and openness, and to be accepted as a nonjudgmental and nonthreatening person. So what do you do when informants engage in acts you consider distasteful, illegal, or immoral?

Published field studies are filled with reports of researchers having witnessed a broad range of illegal and, more important, immoral acts. Thus Van Maanen (1982, 1983) observed police brutality first-hand. Johnson (1975) observed numerous illegal acts committed by caseworkers in his study of social service agencies. Laud Humphreys (1975), whose excellent research has become synonymous with ethical controversy in many commentators' eyes, was accused of being an "accomplice" to over 200 acts of fellatio.[4]

In the institutional study, Taylor regularly observed acts of beating, brutality, and abuse of residents by attendants. Complicating the situation, how attendants define and account for abuse was a major focus of the study.

The literature on research ethics generally supports a noninterventionist position in fieldwork. Most researchers owe their loyalty to the pursuit of research goals or to their informants. Any involvement that would interfere with their research or their commitments to informants is to be avoided. We know one observer who, while studying a juvenile gang, witnessed the brutal beating of a young girl by a gang member. He admitted that he had difficulty sleeping that night, but argued, "What could I do? I was just an observer. It wasn't my place to intervene."

After observing illegal behavior, Humphreys, Johnson, and Van Maanen all state that they would go to jail before they would violate the confidentiality of informants (although a reading of qualitative studies of prison life might make them think twice). Van Maanen went so far as to refuse on the nonexistent legal grounds of research confidentiality to turn over subpoenaed materials in a court case involving an incident of police brutality he witnessed.[5]

Yet one is not absolved of moral and ethical responsibility for one's actions or inactions merely because one is conducting research. To act or fail to act *is* to make an ethical and political choice. It is to say that research goals and attachments to informants outweigh other considerations.

The field researcher is also faced with the possibility that his or her presence may encourage people to engage in immoral or illegal activities. Van Maanen strongly suspected that police officers were showing off for his benefit when they beat one suspect. In the institutional study, attendants frequently teased residents or forced them to do certain things such as swallowing burning cigarettes to amuse themselves and the observer. Even when observers do not provoke certain behavior, a strong case can be made that to do nothing, to stand by passively, is to condone behavior and hence perpetuate it.

Participant observers are not unlike reporters who wittingly or unwittingly create news events through their presence. A recent incident involving two camera operators created an uproar in television circles.

The camera operators passively filmed a man as he covered himself with flammable liquid and set himself on fire, even though they could have stopped him easily. In fact, it was apparent that the man staged the incident for the cameras. In a television interview shortly afterwards one of the camera operators awkwardly attempted to account for his and his colleague's role in the incident: "It's my job to report what happened." Of course, this is the same rationale used by fieldworkers to justify nonintervention. The pursuit of the "good story," like the pursuit of the "good study," excuses otherwise amoral or immoral actions.

So we return to the question: What do you do when you observe people engaging in immoral acts? What do you do when your informants, the people on whom you depend for information and with whom you have worked hard to establish rapport, harm other people? There is neither a simple nor correct answer to this question. The institutional study illustrates this quite well.

In this study, the observer could have intervened directly when attendants mistreated the residents or reported them to their supervisors. That he chose not to did not reflect any commitment to uphold the research bargain or to protect the interests of informants. As in most fieldwork, the research bargain was struck with institutional gatekeepers, the administrators. Although he suggested to attendants that he could be trusted with information, he did not make any formal guarantees to that effect. Further, although the research literature presents informants' interests as unitary, people in the setting, and perhaps in most settings, had competing interests. Thus the administrators, attendants, and residents each had different interests. Whereas one might take the position that a researcher would not have the right to harm attendants by violating their confidentiality, one could also argue that residents' interests would be harmed by this cloak of secrecy. Rather, the decision not to do anything in the setting at the time reflected the researcher's own uncertainty about how to deal with the situation and his estimation of the effect of intervention. It would not have done much good.

As the observer spent time in the setting, he learned that attendants used a number of evasion strategies to conceal their activities from supervisors and outsiders. For example, they placed a resident—a so-called "watchdog"—by the door to warn them of the arrival of visitors and were careful not to leave marks when they hit or tied residents. If the observer had attempted to intervene in their actions or even expressed outward disapproval, they simply would have treated him as an outsider, closing off opportunities for truly understanding the setting.

An event that occurred toward the conclusion of the research also illustrated the futility of reporting abusive attendants to administrators or others. As a result of a parent's complaint, the state police placed an undercover agent at the institution to pose as an attendant and uncover abuse. The scam resulted in the arrests of 24 attendants on abuse charges. All of the 24 attendants were suspended amid proclamations by the director of the institution that, "There are a few rotten apples in every barrel." Yet not one of these was an attendant in the study, each of whom routinely abused residents. Eventually, the 24 attendants were cleared of abuse charges on the basis of "insufficient evidence" and reinstated in their jobs. Any attempt by the observer to blow the whistle on attendants might have met the same fate.

None of this should be taken as a justification for turning one's back on the suffering of fellow human beings. To the contrary, we believe that researchers have a strong moral obligation to act based on what they observe, even though the choices in the specific situation may be severely limited. Over the course of the institutional study, the researcher came to see abuse and dehumanization as being rooted in the nature of total institutions (Goffman, 1961; Taylor, 1977). Attendant abuse was rampant at the institution. However, the attendants were not sadistic or brutal individuals otherwise. They were not as much "bad people" as "good people," or at least as good as most of us, in a "bad place." In a real sense they were dehumanized by the institution also. Further, although one might condemn the attendants for blatant physical abuse, professionals at the institution sanctioned and prescribed control measures, such as drugging residents into oblivion and placing them in strait jackets, that were equally abusive and dehumanizing. Attendants are often scapegoats for an abusive system. Little would be served by scapegoating them further.

What you learn through your research *and* what you do with your findings may at least partially absolve you from the moral responsibility for standing by as people are harmed. It is doubtful whether publishing one's findings in professional journals alone can justify participating in immoral actions. However, you can use your findings to try to change the circumstances that lead to abuse.

There is a long tradition of qualitative researchers engaging in social action as a result of their studies. Becker was an early leader in the National Organization for the Reform of Marijuana Laws; Goffman was a founder of the Committee to End Involuntary Institutionalization; Humphreys has been active in the gay rights movement. Less than two years after completing his initial study, Taylor led a half-dozen television and newspaper reporters through the institution in a widely publicized exposé. Subsequently, he has been involved in exposés in many other states and has testified as an expert witness in deinstitutionalization cases based on his knowledge of institutional conditions and abuse.

Not all researchers will find themselves in the difficult moral and ethical situations we describe in this section. We suspect, though, that these situations are more common than reported by researchers. Before you get too involved in a study, too close to informants, and too sympathetic to their perspectives, it is wise to know where you will draw the line.

As Van Maanen (1983) notes, there are no easy stances to be taken by the observer in field situations. Clearly, there are situations in which researchers can and should intervene on behalf of other people. However, people who cannot tolerate some moral ambiguity probably should not do fieldwork or at least have the good sense to know when to get out of certain situations.

As researchers, we recognize the fact that to withdraw from all morally problematic situations would prevent us from understanding and, indeed, changing many things in the world in which we live. In Van Maanen's (1983:279) words, "The hope, of course, is that in the end the truth, when it is depicted fully, will help us all out."

The last two chapters dealt with learning about the world first-hand. The next chapter turns to a discussion of learning about the world through second-hand accounts: in-depth interviewing.

NOTES

1. An increasing number of field researchers emphasize the importance of understanding one's effects on a setting, rather than trying to eliminate them altogether (see Emerson, 1981). Some researchers also advocate active involvement in the field as a means of revealing social processes that would otherwise remain hidden (Bodemann, 1978). Although these points make sense, we still feel that it is essential to "come on slow" in the field until one has developed an understanding of the setting and the people within it.

2. See the section on "Ethics in the Field" in this chapter for a discussion of the ethical issues raised by this research.

3. Ryave and Schenkein (1974) have conducted an ethnomethodological study of how people "do walking." As they demonstrate, walking is a practical accomplishment in which people produce and recognize appearances to navigate in public places.

4. Humphreys' research has generally been criticized on the grounds of violating people's privacy and confidentiality. Although the charge of being an "accomplice" to acts of fellatio seems frivolous today, this demonstrates how researchers place themselves in jeopardy by observing acts others consider illegal or immoral.

5. As Van Maanen (1983:276–277) points out, there is no legal protection guaranteed to social scientists on the grounds of research confidentiality (also see Nejelski and Lerman, 1971). Researchers are not legally bound to report criminal acts, but they are legally obligated to testify and turn over data in court proceedings.

4

In-Depth Interviewing

The preceding chapters described the methodology of participant observation: field research in natural settings. This chapter deals with in-depth qualitative interviewing, a related, but in many ways different, research approach. After a discussion of the types of interviewing and the strengths and limitations of this method, we discuss specific strategies and tactics for qualitative interviewing.[1]

TYPES OF INTERVIEWING

As Benney and Hughes (1970) point out, the interview is the "favored digging tool" of sociologists. Social scientists rely largely on verbal accounts to learn about social life.

When most people hear the term "interviewing," they think of structured research tools such as attitude surveys, opinion polls, and questionnaires. These interviews are typically "administered" to a large group of "respondents" or "subjects" (Benney and Hughes, 1956). People may be asked to rate their feelings along a scale, select the most appropriate answer from among a preselected set of questions, or even respond to open-ended questions in their own words. Although these research approaches differ in many respects, they all adopt a standardized format: the researcher has the questions and the research subject has the answers. In fact, in most structured interviewing each person is asked identically worded questions to assure comparable findings. The interviewer serves as a cheerful data collector; the role involves getting people to relax enough to answer the predefined series of questions completely.

In stark contrast to structured interviewing qualitative interviewing is flexible and dynamic. Qualitative interviewing has been referred to as nondirective, unstructured, nonstandardized, and open-ended interviewing. We use the phrase "in-depth interviewing" to refer to this qualitative research method. *By in-depth qualitative interviewing we mean repeated face-to-face encounters between the researcher and informants directed toward understanding informants' perspectives on their lives, experiences, or situations as expressed in their own words.* The in-depth interview is modeled after a conversation between equals, rather than a formal question-and-answer exchange. Far from being a robotlike data collector, *the interviewer, not an interview schedule or protocol, is the research tool.* The role entails not merely obtaining answers, but learning what questions to ask and how to ask them.

As a qualitative research approach, in-depth interviewing has much in common with participant observation. Like observers, interviewers "come on slow" initially. They try to establish rapport with informants, ask nondirective questions early in the research, and learn what is important to informants before focusing the research interests.

The primary difference between participant observation and in-depth interviewing lies in the settings and situations in which the research takes place. Whereas participant observers conduct their studies in "natural" field situations, interviewers conduct theirs in situations specifically arranged for the purposes of the research. The participant observer gains first-hand experience of the social world. The interviewer relies exclusively on second-hand accounts from others.[2] The problems this creates for the interviewer are discussed in the next section.

Three closely related types of in-depth interviewing can be distinguished. The first is the *life history* or sociological autobiography.[3] In the life history, the researcher attempts to capture the salient experiences in a person's life and that person's definitions of those experiences. The life history presents people's views on their lives in their own words, much the same as in a common autobiography. E. W. Burgess (in Shaw, 1966:4) explains the importance of life histories:

> In the life history is revealed as in no other way the inner life of the person, his moral struggles, his successes and failures in securing his destiny in a world too often at variance with his hopes and ideals.

What distinguishes the life history from popular autobiographies is that the researcher actively solicits the person's experiences and views and constructs the life history as a final product. Howard Becker (1966: vi) describes the role of the researcher in sociological life histories:

> The sociologist who gathers a life history takes steps to ensure that it covers everything we want to know, that no important fact or event is slighted, that what purports to be factual squares with available evidence and that the subject's interpretations are honestly given. The sociologist keeps the subject oriented to the questions sociology is interested in, asks him about events that require amplification, tries to make the story told jibe with matters of official record and with material furnished by others familiar with the person, event, or place being described. He keeps the game honest for us.

The life history has a long tradition in the social sciences and figures prominently in the work of the Chicago School in the 1920s, '30s, and '40s (Shaw, 1931, 1966; Shaw et al., 1938; Sutherland, 1937; also see Angell, 1945 and Frazier, 1978). Much of the discussion in this chapter is based on the life histories of a "transsexual" (Bogdan, 1974) and two "mentally retarded" persons (Bogdan and Taylor, 1982).

The second type of in-depth interviewing is directed toward learning about events and activities that cannot be observed directly. In this type of interviewing the people being interviewed are informants in the truest sense of the word. They act as the researcher's observer, his or her eyes and ears in the field. As informants, their role is not simply to reveal their own views, but to describe what happened and how others viewed it. Examples of this kind of interviewing include Erikson's (1976) study of a town's reaction to a natural disaster in West Virginia and Domhoff's (1975) study of power elites. Erikson's research could not otherwise have been conducted unless he happened to stumble across a natural disaster, an unlikely occurrence, whereas Domhoff probably would not have been able to gain access to intimate places frequented by the powerful.

The final type of qualitative interviewing is intended to yield a broad picture of a range of settings, situations, or people. Interviewing is used to study a relatively large number of people in a relatively short period of time compared to what would be required in participant observation research. For instance, one could probably conduct several in-depth interviews with 20 teachers in the same amount of time it would take to conduct a participant observation study of a single classroom. Rubin's (1976) study of working-class families based on 100 detailed interviews with husbands and wives is a good example of this type of interviewing.

Although researchers select in-depth interviewing for different purposes, the basic interviewing techniques are similar for these three types of interviewing. In each case interviewers establish rapport with informants through repeated contacts over time and develop a detailed understanding of their experiences and perspectives. This chapter describes approaches and strategies for in-depth interviewing, as defined here. However, many of the points in the following pages can be applied to any interviewing approach.

CHOOSING TO INTERVIEW

Every research approach has its strong points and drawbacks. We tend to agree with Becker and Geer (1957) that participant observation provides a yardstick against which to measure data collected through any other method. That is, no other method can provide the detailed understanding that comes from directly observing people and listening to what they have to say at the scene.

Yet participant observation is not practical or even possible in all cases. The observer can hardly go back in time to study past events or force entry to all settings and private situations. Erikson's (1976) and Domhoff's (1975) studies illustrate this point. Further, participant observation requires a commitment of time and effort that is not always warranted by the additional understanding gained as opposed to other methods. Our life histories of people labeled mentally retarded provide a ready example. Although one might take the position that the best way to construct life histories is to follow people around for a lifetime, it would be foolish to suggest this as an alternative to in-depth interviewing.

Thus no method is equally suited for all purposes. The choice of research method should be determined by the research interests, the circumstances of the setting or people to be studied, and practical constraints faced by the researcher. In-depth interviewing seems especially well suited in the following situations.

The research interests are relatively clear and well-defined. Although research interests are necessarily broad and open-ended in qualitative research, researchers vary according to the clarity and specificity of what they are interested in studying. For instance, one researcher may be generally interested in schools and teachers, whereas another may be interested in how teachers got into the profession. One's prior direct experiences and reading of other qualitative studies can help narrow one's research interests. This is why in-depth interviewing goes hand-in-hand with participant observation.

Settings or people are not otherwise accessible. As noted previously, in-depth interviewing is called for when one wishes to study past events or cannot gain access to a particular type of setting or people.

The researcher has time constraints. Participant observers sometimes "spin their wheels" for weeks, even months, at the beginning of the research. It takes time to locate settings, negotiate access, arrange visits, and get to know informants. Although interviewers can face similar problems, studies based on interviewing usually can be completed in a shorter period of time than participant observation. Whereas the participant observer's time can be taken up waiting for someone to say or do something, the interviewer usually collects data throughout the period spent with informants. The pressure to produce results in grant-funded studies or to write dissertations can severely limit the length of time the researcher can devote to a study. Interviewing makes the most efficient use of the researcher's limited time. Needless to say, this is not a justification for superficial or shoddy research.

The research depends on a broad range of settings or people. In qualitative research, an "N of One" can be just as illuminating as a large sample (and very often more so). However, there are instances in which the researcher may want to sacrifice the depth of understanding that comes with focusing intensively on a single setting or person for the breadth and generalizability that comes with studying a range of places and people. For example, analytic induction is a method of constructing theories from qualitative data that requires a sizable number of cases (Robinson, 1951; Turner, 1953). Through analytic induction Lindesmith (1968) developed a theory of opiate addiction based on interviews with a large number of opiate users.

The researcher wants to illuminate subjective human experience. We are referring here to life histories based on in-depth interviews. More than through any other social science approach, the life history enables us to know people intimately, to see the world through their eyes, and to enter into their experiences vicariously (Shaw, 1931). Life histories stand as a rich source of understanding in and of themselves. As Becker (1966) notes, life histories provide a touchstone with which to evaluate theories of social life. In our own research with the mentally retarded the life histories challenge myths and misconceptions of mental retardation.

It is also important to point out the drawbacks of interviewing that stem from the fact that interview data consist solely of verbal statements or talk. First of all, as a form of conversation, interviews are subject to the same fabrications, deceptions, exaggerations, and distortions that characterize talk between any persons. Although people's verbal accounts may lend insight into how they think about the world and how they act, there can be a great discrepancy between what they say and what they actually do (Deutscher, 1973). Benney and Hughes (1970:137) describe this problem quite well:

> Every conversation has its own balance of revelation and concealment of
> thoughts and intentions: Only under very unusual circumstances is talk so
> completely expository that every word can be taken at face value.

Similarly, Becker and Geer (1957) note that people see the world through
distorting lenses and that the interviewer must not uncritically accept
the factual validity of informants' descriptions of events.

Second, people say and do different things in different situations.
Since the interview is a kind of situation, one must not assume that what
a person says in the interview is what that person believes or says in other
situations. Irwin Deutscher (1973) has written and edited a superb book
that deals head-on with the difference between people's words and deeds.
Deutscher is especially critical of attitude and public opinion research in
which it is assumed that people carry around attitudes in their heads
that determine what they will do in any given situation.

Deutscher reprints and spends a good deal of time discussing a study
by Richard LaPiere (1934–1935). In the early 1930s LaPiere accompanied
a Chinese couple to hotels, auto camps, tourist homes, and restaurants
across the United States. Out of 251 establishments, only 1 refused to
accommodate them. Six months later, LaPiere sent a questionnaire to
each of the establishments asking them if they would accept members of
the Chinese race as guests. Of 128 establishments that replied, only 1 indicated that it would accept Chinese people! As Deutscher painstakingly
explains, the artificiality of the questionnaire and tightly controlled
interview produces "unreal" responses.

Third, since interviewers, as interviewers, do not directly observe people in their everyday lives, they are deprived of the context necessary to
understand many of the perspectives in which they are interested. In
their comparison of participant observation and interviewing Becker
and Geer (1957) list a number of shortcomings of interviews that relate
to this general point: interviewers are likely to misunderstand informants' language since they do not have opportunities to study it in common usage; informants are unwilling or unable to articulate many
important things and only by observing them in their daily lives can
researchers learn about these things; interviewers have to make assumptions about things that could have been observed and some of the assumptions will be incorrect.

Despite these limitations, few, if any, researchers would argue for
abandoning interviewing as a basic approach for studying social life.

Becker and Geer (1957:32) state that interviewers can benefit from an awareness of these limitations and "perhaps improve their batting average by taking account of them."

It is precisely because of these drawbacks that we emphasize the importance of *in-depth* interviewing, getting to know people well enough to understand what they mean and creating an atmosphere in which they are likely to talk freely. Our own view is that through interviewing the skillful researcher can usually learn how informants view themselves and their world, sometimes obtain an accurate account of past events and current activities, and almost never predict exactly how an informant will act in a new situation.

SELECTING INFORMANTS

Like participant observation, qualitative interviewing calls for a flexible research design. Neither the number nor type of informants is specified beforehand. The researcher starts out with a general idea of what people to interview and how to find them, but is willing to change course after the initial interviews.

It is difficult to determine how many people to interview in a qualitative study. Some researchers try to interview as many people familiar with a topic or event as possible. In a study of a New York City teachers' union, Cole (1976) conducted in-depth interviews with 25 union leaders, which represented almost all of the leaders in New York.

The strategy of theoretical sampling can be used as a guide for selecting people to interview (Glaser and Strauss, 1967). In theoretical sampling the actual number of "cases" studied is relatively unimportant. What is important is the potential of each "case" to aid the researcher in developing theoretical insights into the area of social life being studied. After completing interviews with several informants, you would consciously vary the type of people interviewed until you had uncovered the full range of perspectives held by the people in whom you are interested. You would have an idea that you had reached this point when interviews with additional people yielded no genuinely new insights.

Informants can be found in a number of ways. As discussed in the chapter on pre-fieldwork in participant observation, the easiest way to build a pool of informants is "snowballing": getting to know some informants and having them introduce you to others. Initially, you can locate potential informants through the same sources the participant observer uses to gain access to private settings: checking with friends, relatives, and personal contacts; involving yourself with the community of people you want to study; approaching organizations and agencies; advertising. In the research with families of young children with which one of the authors was involved, the study used a range of techniques to locate the families, including checking birth records, contacting day care centers, neighborhood centers, preschools, churches, and social clubs, passing out hand-outs at local stores, and, in some neighborhoods, conducting a door-to-door survey (the researchers had ID cards that indicated their affiliation with a university research project).

Life histories are written based on in-depth interviews with one or a small handful of people. Although all people have one good story to tell—their own—some people have better stories and make better research partners for the purpose of constructing a life history. Obviously, it is essential that a person have the time to devote to the interviewing. Another important consideration is people's willingness and ability to talk about their experiences and articulate their feelings. People simply do not have equal ability to provide detailed accounts of what they have been through and what they feel about it. It also usually seems as though strangers make better informants than friends, relatives, clients, and others with whom one has a prior relationship (Spradley, 1979).

In constructing life histories the researcher looks for a particular type of person who has had certain experiences. For example, life histories have been written on the experiences of juvenile delinquents (Shaw, 1931, 1966; Shaw et al., 1938), a professional fence (Klockars, 1974), a transsexual (Bogdan, 1974), and a professional thief (Sutherland, 1937). Although you might be interested in studying a certain type of person, keep in mind that people's past experiences may not have had an impact on their lives and current perspectives. What is important to you may not be important to a potential informant. Practically all youth engage in activities that someone could define as juvenile delinquency. Yet for most youth participation in these activities has little to do with how they view themselves. Spradley (1979) suggests that one of the requirements for good informants is "thorough enculturation"; that is, knowing a culture (or subculture, group, or organization) so well that they no longer think about it.

There are no easy steps to take to find a good informant for a life history. In this kind of research informants are seldom "found"; rather, they emerge in the course of one's everyday activities. You just happen to stumble across someone who has an important story to tell and wants to tell it. Of course, the more involved you are in circles outside of university settings, the more likely you are to establish the contacts and reputation necessary to find a good informant.

We met Ed Murphy and Pattie Burt (the subjects of *Inside Out*) through our involvement with local groups concerned with people labeled mentally retarded. Ed was recommended to us as a guest speaker for a course one of us was teaching. Ed was articulate in his presentation of his experience living at an institution and being labeled mentally retarded. In fact, the word "retarded" lost meaning as he spoke. We kept in touch with him after his talk at the course, running into him at a local association. About two years after we first met him, we approached him with the idea of working on his life history. One of us met Pattie when she was living at a local institution. When she told him that she wanted desperately to leave the institution, he helped her get out. For a brief period of time, she lived with the other author and his family. We saw Pattie frequently over the next 15 months when she was living in a series of different homes. We began interviewing her shortly after she moved to her own apartment in a nearby town.

The life history of Jane Fry, *Being Different*, came about in a similar manner. One of us met her when she spoke to a class taught by a colleague. Her presentation of life as a transsexual was striking in the insight it provided and the vividness of her description of her experiences. Some time after that the author ran into her again at a local crisis intervention center at which she was volunteering. Through that meeting and several other encounters, he got to know her well enough to ask her about writing her life history.

APPROACHING INFORMANTS

In most in-depth interviewing, you will not know how many interviews to conduct with informants until you actually begin speaking with them. Some people will warm up only gradually; others will have a lot to say and you will want to spend quite a few sessions with them. Interviewing projects usually take anywhere from several sessions to over 25 sessions, and 50 to 100 hours of interviewing, for life histories.

Since you cannot always tell beforehand exactly how many interviews you will want to conduct, it is advisable to come on slow with informants initially. Tell them that you would like to set up an interview or two with them, but don't ask for a commitment to spend a lot of time being interviewed. After you have conducted a couple of interviews, you can discuss your plans more directly. We met with Ed Murphy and Jane Fry several times before we raised the possibility of writing their life histories. Interestingly enough, both had thought about writing their autobiographies previously (most people have probably thought about this at some point in their lives). Jane had even attempted to write her life history several years earlier, only to have abandoned the project after writing a few pages. Ed and Jane were both enthusiastic about the project by the end of our first serious discussions with them.

It is usually not too difficult to line up people for initial interviews, as long as they can fit you into their schedules. Most people are willing to talk about themselves. In fact, people are often flattered at the prospect of being interviewed for a research project. In the family study many parents felt honored that they were selected to participate in a university study of child-rearing. Of course, it is very flattering to be asked to tell your life story. When approaching potential informants, we tell them that it seems like they have had some interesting experiences or have something important to say and that we would like to sit down with them and talk about it some time. If they seem receptive to the idea, we schedule the first meeting.

If, after a couple of sessions, you decide that you will want to interview an individual for a number of sessions over time, you should try to clarify any issues that might be on his or her mind and any possible misunderstandings. Life histories, in particular, are a collaborative endeavor. The tone you want to establish is that of a partnership rather than a researcher–subject relationship (Klockars, 1977). The following issues are those that are most easily misunderstood and hence the most important to raise.

1. *Your motives and intentions.* Many people will wonder what you hope to get out of the project. They may even fear that the final product will be used to their disadvantage. If you are a social scientist, your motivation will probably have something to do with contributing knowledge to your field and professional advancement. You can discuss this with informants. Although people may not grasp your precise research

interests, most will be able to understand educational and academic goals.

You probably will not be clear on whether and where the results of your study will be published. However, you should explain that you will try to have the study published in a book or journal or, in the case of students, as a dissertation or thesis. In very few instances are studies of this kind published commercially. This should be explained also. Finally, although you would not be willing to spend your time on the project unless you thought that something would come of it, you should alert informants to potential difficulties in having the study published.

2. *Anonymity.* It is almost always wise to use pseudonyms for people and places in written studies. There are few legitimate research interests served by publishing people's names. The risks are substantial: embarrassment of the informant or others; legal problems; self-aggrandizement; concealment of important details and information. Although people might want to have their names published for a variety of reasons, you should resist doing so and explain this to informants. In Jane Fry's life history, she wanted very much to see her name in print and the researcher initially agreed to this. However, as the interviewing progressed, it soon became apparent that this would create numerous problems and both agreed to the use of pseudonyms.

3. *Final say.* One way to gain informants' trust is to tell them that they will have the opportunity to read and comment on drafts of any books or articles prior to publication. Some researchers even guarantee veto power to informants over what is published. Although we are reluctant to give informants final say over the content of written materials, it strengthens the researcher's relationships with informants and the quality of the study to have informants review draft manuscripts.

4. *Money.* Money can corrupt the relationship between the interviewer and informant, turning it into an employer–employee relationship rather than a research partnership. It also raises the specter of encouraging the informant to fabricate "a good story" to get some money. Yet many large-scale research projects pay informants for interviews.[4] The family study paid parents nominal fees for participating in interviews. This clearly served as an inducement for some parents to stay involved in the study when they wanted to drop out. However, if people have to be paid to be interviewed, it is debatable whether they will talk candidly about anything of real importance in their lives.

Splitting book royalties with informants is a different matter than paying them for interviews. This creates a spirit of partnership in the research endeavor. Since informants usually do not have their names appear in print or receive professional credit, they probably deserve a share of the proceeds from a book, although most academic books do not earn sizable royalties.

The author of Jane Fry's life history worked out her royalties with a lawyer. Like many subjects of life histories, she was poor at the time and received public assistance. To make sure that the royalty payments did not affect her benefits, the lawyer helped set up a special trust fund for her.

5. *Logistics.* Finally, you will have to settle on a rough schedule and place to meet. The frequency and length of the interviews will depend on your respective schedules. You will usually need about two hours for an interview. Anything less is too short to explore many topics, whereas much more will probably burn out both of you. In order to preserve the flow of interviews you should try to meet every week or so. It is too difficult to pick up where you left off when you are not interviewing regularly. The length of the overall project will depend on how freely the person speaks and what you hope to cover. Life histories take at least a few months to complete. Klockars' (1974) life history of a professional fence took 15 months of weekly or biweekly meetings (Klockars, 1977).

You should try to find a private place where you can talk without interruption and where the informant will feel relaxed. Many people feel most comfortable in their own homes and offices. However, in many people's homes it is difficult to talk privately. In the family study some parents tried to listen in surreptitiously on their spouse's interviews, an obvious inhibiting factor. In our research with Ed Murphy and Jane Fry we conducted the interviews in our private offices, located in a converted house, after working hours. We interviewed Pattie Burt at her own apartment. Nothing prevents the researcher from setting up interviews in a public restaurant or bar as long as privacy is assured.

STARTING THE INTERVIEWS

The hallmark of in-depth qualitative interviewing is learning about what is important in the minds of informants: *their* meanings, perspectives, and definitions; how *they* view, categorize, and experience the world.

Presumably, researchers have some general questions to ask prior to starting the interviews. Yet they have to be careful not to push their agenda too early in the interviewing. By asking directive questions initially, the researcher creates a mind-set in informants about what is important to talk about that can make it difficult, if not impossible, to get at how they really see things.

It is during the early interviews that the researcher sets the tone of the relationship with the informant. In these initial interviews, the interviewer should come across as someone who is not quite sure what questions to ask and is willing to learn from the informants. Robert Coles (1971:39) eloquently describes this frame of reference when he writes:

> My job . . . is to bring alive to the extent I possibly can a number of lives . . . entrusted to a person like me, an outsider, a stranger, a listener, an observer, a doctor, a curious . . . fellow who one mountaineer described as "always coming back and not seeming to know exactly what he wants to hear or know."

The qualitative interviewer has to find ways of getting people to start to talk about their perspectives and experiences without structuring the conversation and defining what they should say. Unlike the participant observer, the interviewer cannot stand back and wait for people to do something before asking questions. There are many ways to guide initial interviews in this kind of research: descriptive questioning, solicited narratives, the log-interview approach, and personal documents.

Descriptive Questioning

Probably the best way to start off interviewing informants is to ask them to describe, list, or outline key events, experiences, places, or people in their lives. In practically any interviewing you can come up with a list of descriptive questions that will enable people to talk about what they see as important without structuring their responses. In our life histories with mentally retarded people we started the interviewing by asking the informants to give us chronologies of the major events in their lives. Pattie Burt listed such events as her birth, placement in various foster homes, institutionalization, and renting her own apartments. Ed Murphy listed the deaths of his father, mother, and sister, in addition to the places where he lived.

In our interviewing with Ed Murphy, we frequently started sessions by having him list events and experiences (sometimes this took an entire session). Since his institutionalization had a profound effect on his life, we pursued this experience in great depth. For instance, we asked him to outline such things as the wards where he lived at the institution, a typical day on different wards, his friends at the institution, and his work assignments.

As informants mention specific experiences, you can probe for greater detail. It is also a good idea to take note of topics to return to at a later time.

Solicited Narratives

Many of the classic life histories in the social sciences have been based on a combination of in-depth interviews and narratives written by informants themselves. Shaw (1931, 1966), Shaw, McKay, and McDonald (1938), and Sutherland (1937) made extensive use of this approach in their life histories of delinquents and criminals.

Shaw and his colleagues used various techniques to construct life histories of delinquents in the 1930s. Shaw (1966) reports that although they relied heavily on personal interviews, they preferred written documents as a basis for these life histories. In *The Jack-Roller,* Shaw (1966) first interviewed Stanley, the subject of the life history, to prepare a detailed chronology of his delinquent acts and experiences. He then returned this to Stanley to use as a guide for writing his own story. Shaw (1966:23) writes that Stanley was instructed "to give a detailed description of each event, the situation in which it occurred, and his personal reactions to the experience." In other life histories, such as *Brothers in Crime* (1938), Shaw and his collaborators gave their informants no more instruction than to give a detailed description of their experiences during childhood and adolescence.

Sutherland was somewhat more directive in soliciting the life history, *The Professional Thief* (1937). Although he does not describe his approach in detail, he indicates that the bulk of the life history was written by the thief on questions and topics suggested by the researcher. Sutherland then met with the thief for approximately 7 hours a week for 12 weeks to discuss what the thief had written. The final life history includes the thief's original narrative, the interview material, minor passages written by Sutherland for editorial reasons, and footnotes based on a broad range of sources, including interviews with other thieves and detectives.

In *Being Different,* the researcher asked Jane Fry to write a detailed chronology of her life prior to starting the interviews. He used this chronology as a basis for his interviewing with her. Toward the end of the interviewing, he and Jane went over the chronology point by point to pick up any forgotten items.

Not all people are able or willing to write about their experiences. However, even sketchy outlines and chronologies can be used to guide open-ended, in-depth interviews.

The Log-Interview Approach

In the log-interview approach, informants keep a running record of their activities for a specified period of time which is used to provide a basis for in-depth interviews. Zimmerman and Wieder (1977), who refer to this as the "diary-interview method," have described specific procedures associated with this approach.

In a study of "counterculture life styles" Zimmerman and Wieder asked informants to maintain an annotated chronological log of their activities. They instructed informants to record activities in as much detail as they could, to make entries at least daily, and to address a standard set of questions regarding each activity: Who/What/When/Where/How? Since Zimmerman and Wieder were interested in sexual activities and drug use, they instructed informants to describe these activities specifically.

Zimmerman and Wieder had two researchers review each diary and prepare a set of questions and probes to ask informants based on the narrative. They report that for every 5 to 10 pages of diary entries, the researchers generated 100 questions that involved 5 hours of interviewing.

Like solicited narratives, the log-interview approach is ill-suited for informants who are not adept at recording their activities in writing. As Zimmerman and Wieder point out, daily telephone interviews and tape recording can be used as substitutes for having informants maintain written logs.

Personal Documents

Personal documents—people's own diaries, letters, pictures, records, calendars, and memorabilia—can be used to guide interviews without imposing a structure on informants. Most people store old documents and records and are willing to show at least some of these to others. If you have at least a general idea of what experiences you want to cover in the interviews, you can ask informants to see documents relating to these experiences before starting the interviews. Later in the interviewing, these materials can spark memories and help people recall old feelings.

Jane Fry kept old letters and other documents and had actually written autobiographical narratives at critical points in her life. She shared these freely with the researcher. These documents not only provided a framework for interviewing, but were eventually incorporated into her life history.

In some interviewing research the interviewer has a good sense of what is on informants' minds prior to starting the interviews. For example, some researchers turn to interviewing after conducting participant observation; some also use their own experiences to guide their research. Becker's study of jazz musicians stemmed from his own experience in a band. In our research, we had spent a considerable amount of time with some of our informants before we started to interview them formally. We had heard Ed Murphy talk about his life in institutions before the idea of writing his life history ever occurred to us. When researchers have a body of direct experience to build on, they can be somewhat more directive and aggressive in their initial questioning.

THE INTERVIEW GUIDE

In large-scale interviewing projects some researchers use an *interview guide* to make sure key topics are explored with a number of informants. The interview guide is not a structured schedule or protocol. Rather, it is a list of general areas to cover with each informant. In the interview situation the researcher decides how to phrase questions and when to ask them. The interview guide serves solely to remind the interviewer to ask about certain things.

The use of an interview guide presupposes a certain degree of knowledge about the people one intends to study (at least in in-depth interviewing). Thus an interview guide is useful when the researcher has already learned something about informants through fieldwork or preliminary interviews or other direct experience. The interview guide can also be expanded or revised as the researcher conducts additional interviews.

An interview guide is especially useful in team research and evaluation or other funded research (Patton, 1980). In team research, the guide provides a way of ensuring that all the interviewers are exploring the same general areas with informants. One of the authors used an interview guide in a research project that involved short-term, intensive field visits to a number of sites by a half-dozen researchers (see Taylor, 1982). In funded research and qualitative evaluation the interview guide can be used to give sponsors a sense of what the researcher will actually cover with informants.

THE INTERVIEW SITUATION

The interviewer must create an atmosphere in which people feel comfortable to talk freely about themselves. In what kinds of situations are people most likely to express their views? In structured interviewing the interviewer is instructed to act as a disinterested figure; the interview situation is designed to resemble laboratory conditions. Yet, as Deutscher (1973:150) notes, people seldom express their true feelings and views under these circumstances: "Real expressions of attitude or overt behavior rarely occur under conditions of sterility which are deliberately structured for the interview situation."

In qualitative interviewing the researcher attempts to construct a situation that resembles those in which people naturally talk to each other about important things. The interview is relaxed and conversational, since this is how people normally interact. The interviewer relates to informants on a personal level. Indeed, the relationship that develops over time between the interviewer and informant is the key to collecting data.

Certainly, there are differences between the interview situation and those in which people normally interact: interviewers sometimes have to hold back from expressing their views; the conversation is understood to be private and confidential; the flow of information is largely, though not exclusively, one-sided; interviewers communicate a genuine interest in people's views and experiences and are willing to listen to them talk for hours on end. However, it is only by designing the interview along the lines of natural interaction that the interviewer can tap into what is important to people. In fact, the interviewer has many parallels in everyday life: "the good listener," "the shoulder to cry on," "the confi-dante."

Like participant observation, in-depth interviewing requires an ability to relate to others on their own terms. There is no simple formula for successful interviewing, but the following points set the tone for the atmosphere the interviewer should try to create.

Being Nonjudgmental

As informants begin to share more experiences and feelings with the interviewer, they let down their public fronts and reveal parts of them-selves they ordinarily keep hidden. It is common for people to preface or conclude revelations with disclaimers and comments such as: "You must think I'm crazy for doing that," and, "I can't justify what I did, but . . . ."

An important part of interviewing is being nonjudgmental. Benney and Hughes (1970:140) write: ". . . the interview is an understanding between two parties that, in return for allowing the interviewer to direct their communication, the informant is assured that he will not meet with denial, contradiction, competition, or other harassment." In other words, if you want people to open up about their feelings and views, you have to refrain from making negative judgments about them or "putting them down."

Of course, the best way to avoid the appearance of judging people is to try to accept them for who and what they are, and keep from judging them in your own mind. When you simply cannot do this, you can state your position, but gently and without condemning the person as a whole.

During the interview, you should go out of your way to reassure people that they are "all right" in your eyes after they have revealed something personal, embarrassing, or discrediting. Communicate your understanding and empathy: "I know what you mean," "That happened to me once," "I've thought of doing that myself," and "I have a friend who did the same thing."

Letting People Talk

In-depth interviewing sometimes requires a great deal of patience. In-formants can talk at length about things in which you have no interest. Especially during initial interviews, you should try to force yourself not to interrupt an informant even though you are not interested in a topic.

You can usually get a person back on track through subtle gestures, such as stopping nodding your head and taking notes (Patton, 1980), and gently changing the subject during breaks in the conversation: "I'd like to go back to something you said the other day." Over time, informants usually learn to "read" your gestures and know enough about your interests to talk about some things and not others.

When people start talking about something important, let the conversation flow. Sympathetic gestures and relevant questions can keep them on a subject.

Paying Attention

It is easy to let your mind drift during extended interviews. This is especially true when you tape record sessions and don't have to concentrate on remembering every word.

Paying attention means communicating a sincere interest in what informants are saying and knowing when and how to probe and ask the right questions. As Thomas Cottle (1973b:351) so clearly expresses it, paying attention also means being open to seeing things in a new and different way:

> If there is a rule about this form of research it might be reduced to something as simple as pay attention. Pay attention to what the person does and says and feels; pay attention to what is evoked by these conversations and perceptions, particularly when one's mind wanders so very far away; and finally, pay attention to the responses of those who might, through one's work, hear these people. Paying attention implies an openness, not any special or metaphysical kind of openness, but merely a watch on oneself, a self-consciousness, a belief that everything one takes in from the outside and experiences within one's own interior is worthy of consideration and essential for understanding and honoring those whom one encounters.

Being Sensitive

Interviewers always have to be attuned to how their words and gestures affect informants. They sometimes have to "play dumb," but not be insulting. They must be sympathetic, but not patronizing. They have to know when to probe, but stay away from open wounds. They have to be friendly, but not ingratiating. Being sensitive is an attitude one must bring to interviewing and, for that matter, participant observation. Robert Coles (1971b:29) strikes at the heart of the matter when he writes:

> Somehow we all must learn to know one another . . . Certainly I ought to say that I myself have been gently and on occasion firmly or sternly reminded how absurd some of my questions have been, how misleading or smug were the assumptions they convey. The fact is that again and again I have seen a poor, a lowly, an illiterate migrant worker wince a little at something I have said or done, smile a little nervously, glare and pout, wonder a little in his eyes about me and my purposes, and through his grimace let me know the disapproval he surely has felt; and yes, the criticism he also feels, the sober, thought-out criticism, perhaps not easily put into words . . .

PROBING

One of the keys to successful interviewing is knowing when and how to probe. Throughout the interviews, the researcher follows up on topics that have been raised by asking specific questions, encourages the informant to describe experiences in detail, and constantly presses for clarification of the informant's words.

In qualitative interviewing you have to probe for the details of people's experiences and the meanings they attach to them. This is where in-depth interviewing departs from everyday conversations. Unlike most people, the interviewer is interested in mundane events, a person's day-to-day struggles and experiences, as well as the highlights of a person's life. Further, in contrast to natural conversation, interviewers cannot assume that they understand exactly what people mean. *The interviewer cannot take for granted common sense assumptions and understandings other people share.* Deutscher (1973:191) explains how seemingly objective words can have different cultural meanings:

> When an American truck driver complains to the waitress at the diner about his "warm" beer and "cold" soup, the "warm" liquid may have a temperature of 50° F., while the "cold" one is 75° . . . The standard for the same objects may well vary from culture to culture, from nation to nation, from region to region and, for that matter, within any given social unit—between classes, age groups, sexes, or what have you; what is "cold" soup for an adult may be too "hot" to give a child.

Qualitative interviewers have to force themselves to constantly ask informants to clarify and elaborate on what they have said, even at the risk of appearing naive. Spradley (1979) comments that the interviewer has to teach the informants to be good informants by continually encouraging them to provide detailed descriptions of their experiences.

During the interview, you should continue to probe for clarification until you are sure what exactly the informant means: rephrase what the person said and ask for confirmation; ask the person to provide examples of what he or she means; tell the person when something isn't clear to you. You should also follow up on your informant's remarks until you have a clear picture in your own mind of the people, places, experiences, and feelings in his or her life. Ask a lot of specific questions:

Can you tell me what the place looked like?

How did you feel then?

Can you remember what you said then?

What were you doing at the time?

Who else was there?

What happened after that?

The skillful interviewer comes up with questions that will help jar a person's memory. Many past events lie hidden deep within a person's memory and remote from daily life. Try to think up questions that will bring back some of these memories; for example:

How does your family describe you at that time?

Do your parents ever tell stories about how you were when you were growing up?

What kinds of stories do you tell when you get together with your brothers and sisters?

Just as the participant observer can become more aggressive in the later stages of the research, the interviewer's questioning can become more directive as he or she learns about informants and their perspectives. It is not uncommon to find that informants are unwilling or unable to talk about certain things that are obviously important to them. In our interviewing with Ed Murphy, for example, he was reluctant to talk in personal terms about being labeled mentally retarded. Instead, he talked about how the label unfairly stigmatized other "mentally retarded" people. In order to get him to speak about the experience of being labeled retarded, we came up with questions that allowed him to maintain an identity as a "normal" person: "You're obviously a bright guy, so why do you think you wound up at an institution for the retarded?" and, "A lot of kids have problems learning, how did you do in school?" There were also times during our interviewing with Ed Murphy that we confronted him with his tendency to avoid certain topics. We tried to impress upon him the importance of talking about these experiences. When he was reluctant to talk about his family, we told him something like the following:

> I think it's important to know about your family life. A lot of families don't know how to deal with disabled children. I think you should try to talk about your feelings and experiences.

Although Ed continued to be uncomfortable with some topics, he eventually talked about many of those he had avoided.

Like the participant observer, the interviewer also can use what Douglas (1976) calls the "phased-assertion tactic" and other aggressive questioning techniques. As discussed earlier, the phased-assertion tactic involves acting as if you are already "in the know" in order to gain more information.

CROSS CHECKS

While qualitative interviewers try to develop an open and honest relationship with informants, they have to be alert to exaggerations and distortions in their informants' stories. As Douglas (1976) points out, people hide important facts about themselves in everyday life. Anyone may "lie a bit, cheat a bit," to use Deutscher's (1973) words. Further, all people are prone to exaggerating their successes and denying or downplaying their failures.

As emphasized throughout this book, the issue of "truth" in qualitative research is a complicated one. What the qualitative researcher is interested in is not truth per se, but rather perspectives. Thus the interviewer tries to elicit a more or less honest rendering of how informants actually view themselves and their experiences. Shaw (1955:2–3) explains this quite well in his introduction to *The Jack-Roller*:

It should be pointed out, also, that the validity and value of the personal document are not dependent upon its objectivity or veracity. It is not expected that the delinquent will necessarily describe his life-situations objectively. On the contrary, it is desired that his story will reflect his own personal attitudes and interpretations. Thus, rationalizations, fabrications, prejudices, exaggerations are quite as valuable as objective descriptions, provided, of course, that these reactions be properly identified and classified.

After writing these words, Shaw quotes W. I. Thomas' (1928:572) famous dictum, "If men define situations as real, they are real in their consequences."

In contrast to participant observers, interviewers lack the first-hand knowledge of how people act in their day-to-day lives. This can make it difficult to sort out the difference between purposeful distortions and gross exaggerations, on the one hand, and genuine perspectives (which are necessarily "subjective" and "biased"), on the other.

If you know a person well enough, you can usually tell when he or she is evading a subject or "putting you on." In in-depth interviewing, you spend enough time with people to "read between the lines" of their remarks and probe for sufficient details to know if they are fabricating a story. In his discussion of Shaw's *The Natural History of a Delinquent Career,* Ernest Burgess (in Shaw, 1931:240) argues that the validity of a life history depends on the manner in which it was obtained:

> The validity of the statement of attitudes in the life-history seems, in my judgment, to be closely dependent upon the following conditions: (a) a document reported in the words of the person; i.e., a written autobiography or a verbatim record of an oral narrative; (b) a document representing a free, spontaneous, and detailed expression of past experiences, present aspirations, and future plans; (c) a document secured in a favorable situation where the tendencies to deception or prejudice are absent or at a minimum.

The researcher also has the responsibility for imposing *cross checks* on the informants' stories. You should examine an informant's statements for consistency between different accounts of the same event or experience (Klockars, 1977). In the research with Jane Fry, for example, the researcher checked her story for inconsistencies. Jane frequently skipped from one topic to another. Since she covered the same events several times over the course of the interviews, the researcher could compare different versions given at different times.

You should also draw on as many different sources of data as possible

to check out informants' statements. In the early work of the Chicago
School, the researchers regularly compared informants' stories with official records maintained by police and social work agencies. Sutherland
(1937) submitted the life history of a professional thief to other professional thieves and detectives to get their views on the veracity of the
story. In our research, we held our informants' stories up against accounts by other knowledgeable persons and our own observations and
experiences. For example, we had conducted extensive participant observation at the institutions at which Ed Murphy and Pattie Burt had
been placed. In constructing Jane Fry's life history, the researcher interviewed others who had been through similar experiences. For instance,
he questioned a former Navy officer on the accuracy of her account of
life in the Navy. In his conclusion to her life story, he juxtaposed her
accounts of experiences with psychiatric records, although his purpose
was less to check out her story than to compare competing ideologies of
transsexualism.

Probably the best way to deal with contradictions and internal inconsistencies is to raise the issue directly. Gently confront the person with
the evidence:

> Maybe you could explain something for me. One time you told me this, but
> what you said at another time doesn't go along with that. I don't get it.

What are suspected lies and deceptions often turn out to be misunderstandings or sincere changes in a person's perspective. It is also important
to point out, as Merton (1946) notes, that people sometimes hold logically
contradictory views.

RELATIONS WITH INFORMANTS

The interviewer–informant relationship is largely one-sided. Through
the relationship, the interviewer has the opportunity to conduct a study
and, with it, to gain the status and rewards that come with receiving a
degree or publishing books or articles. It is unclear what, if anything,
informants stand to gain from the relationship, other than the satisfaction that someone thinks their lives and views are important. Although
informants have few tangible rewards to gain, they are asked to devote
considerable time and energy to the endeavor.

Due to the one-sided nature of the relationship, interviewers often have to work hard at maintaining informants' motivation in the interviewing. The best way to do this is to relate to informants as people and not mere sources of data.

Since informants are expected to open up completely—to bare their souls, as it were—there has to be some exchange in terms of what interviewers say about themselves. *It is probably unwise for interviewers to hold back their feelings completely.* Obviously, the interviewer should not express an opinion on any subject that comes up, especially during initial interviews. Somewhere between total disclosure and total detachment lies the "happy medium" that the interviewer should try to meet. The best advice is to be discreet in the interview, but to talk about yourself in other situations.

You should be willing to relate to informants in terms other than interviewer–informant. Interviewers can serve as errand-runners, drivers, babysitters, advocates, and whether or not they intend, Rogerian therapists (if you're an effective interviewer, you're bound to elicit painful memories and feelings and you have to be prepared to deal with these). In our life history interviewing, we occasionally had lunch or dinner with our informants. This contact strengthened our relationship with them, in addition to enabling us to talk with them informally and learn about their everyday lives. With both Jane Fry, a transsexual, and Ed Murphy, a man labeled retarded with minor physical disabilities, we learned a lot by just observing how people reacted to them and how they reacted in turn.

In many interviewing projects the informants are one of society's "underdogs" (Becker, 1966), powerless by virtue of their economic or social status. Researchers, in contrast, are likely to be secure in their status at universities. For this reason, researchers are in a good position to help them advocate for their rights. When Jane Fry was discriminated against by a community college, the researcher found a lawyer for her and put her in touch with a mental health rights group.

As with any relationship, tensions can arise between you and your informants during the course of the interviewing. It is not uncommon for rapport to wane during extended projects (Johnson, 1975). Informants can get tired of answering questions or begin to see the interviewing as an imposition on their lives. You can begin to get impatient when informants are reluctant to address questions or skirt certain topics. Either of you can become bored with the endeavor.

You should try to be sensitive to your informants' low spots and feelings. When you think something is wrong, try to clear the air by expressing your concerns. Sometimes it is a good idea to take a break from the interviewing altogether.

A common problem in large-scale projects is cancelled or missed appointments. In the family study a sizeable number of parents cancelled interviews at the last minute or failed to be at home at the agreed upon time. The research team came up with a set of tactics to prevent cancellations, including phone calls on the day preceding the interviews, appointment cards, buying calendars for some families, arriving an hour early on the scheduled day, and leaving notes expressing bewilderment when families were not home. When parents repeatedly missed appointments, they were asked directly whether they wanted to continue in the study. Although these tactics reduced the number of cancellations, it became obvious that some parents simply did not want to participate in the study, but were reluctant to say so, for whatever reason. There was disagreement within the research team over what to do about these families, with some members arguing that they should be left alone if they did not want to participate and others advocating continued attempts to obtain the data. As it turned out, the study dropped many of these families from the research when continued attempts over time to schedule appointments failed.

TAPE RECORDING INTERVIEWS

In the chapter on participant observation we advised researchers to rely on their memories to record data, at least until they had developed a feel for the setting. Recording devices, we argued, can make people self-conscious.

Although tape recording can alter what people say in the early stages of the research, interviewers can usually get by with taping interviews. In interviewing informants are acutely aware that the interviewer's agenda is to conduct research. Since they already know that their words are being weighed, they are less likely to be alarmed by the presence of a tape recorder. The interviewer also has an extended period of time in which to get informants to relax and become accustomed to the tape recorder. In participant observation researchers interact with a number of people, some of whom never get to know, let alone trust, them.

A tape recorder allows the interviewer to capture so much more than he or she could relying on memory. The interviewer's data consist almost entirely of words. Unlike participant observers, interviewers cannot sit back for a while and observe during lapses in conversations. It is possible that many of the most important life histories in the social sciences would never have been written without the use of electronic recording devices. Oscar Lewis (1963:xii) writes in his introduction to *The Children of Sanchez*, "The tape recorder, used in taking down the life histories in this book, has made possible the beginning of a new kind of literature of social realism."

The remarks should not make us lose sight of the fact that most people's memories are better than they suspect. Although we have used tape recorders in most of our interviewing, we have relied on our memories to record the substance of brief, one-hour interviews. Some researchers, such as Thomas Cottle (1972), regularly conduct interviews without tape recorders.

Obviously, you should not record interviews if it makes informants ill at ease (Klockars, 1977). Wait until the person has related sufficiently before raising the idea. Even if informants do not mind taping the interviews, try to minimize the recorder's presence. Use a small recorder and place it out of sight. The microphone should be unobtrusive and sensitive enough to pick up voices without having to speak into it. Find a recorder that will accommodate long-playing tapes so the conversation won't be interrupted so often.

A few final words of caution: label each tape clearly and make sure your equipment is functioning properly before each interview. In one of our studies we forgot to check out the tapes and recorder before some of the interviews. When we listened to the tapes later, they were barely audible. Our typist would not even try to transcribe them and we ended up spending many hours playing and replaying them to pick up all of the data.

THE INTERVIEWER'S JOURNAL

It is a good idea to maintain a detailed journal during your interviewing. The interviewer's journal can serve several purposes. First of all, the journal should contain an outline of topics discussed in each interview. This will help you to keep track of what has already been covered in the interviewing and to go back to specific conversations when you want to follow up on something that the informant has said. In our interviewing with Ed Murphy we neglected to do this and wasted quite a bit of time listening to tapes and reading transcripts looking for specific things.

Second, the journal takes the place of "Observer's Comments" recorded in participant observation field notes. Like the observer, you should make note of emerging themes, interpretations, hunches, and striking gestures and nonverbal expressions essential to understanding the meaning of a person's words. The following are examples of the kinds of comments that should be included in the journal:

> By the faces she was making, I think she was being sarcastic when she talked about her mother. She didn't seem to want to say anything really negative about her mother though.

> That's the third time she's raised that topic on her own. It must be important to her. I'll have to look into this in the future.

> Somehow we were both bored tonight. We just wanted to get the interview over with. Maybe this was because of the topic or maybe we were both tired today.

> I think I was a bit too aggressive tonight. I wonder if he just said those things to keep me off his back. I'll have to keep this in mind when I go over the conversation.

Notes like this will assist in guiding future interviews and interpreting data at a later time.

Finally, the journal is a good place to keep a record of conversations with informants outside of the interview situation. Ed Murphy often talked at length about important things in his life during breaks in the interviewing and informal contacts with the researchers. Such data are clearly important and should be analyzed along with those collected during the interview.

You should try to force yourself to write journal entries after each contact with informants, in addition to other times when you think of something important to record. Every once in a while look through your journal to get a sense of what you have covered and what you have learned.

In the past several chapters, we have presented the strategies and tactics of the predominant qualitative research methods: participant observation and in-depth interviewing. In the next chapter, we present examples of other ways in which qualitative research can be conducted. We shift our focus in this chapter from a "how to" approach to a descriptive one. Our goal in this chapter is to encourage creativity and innovation in research.

NOTES

1. We also refer the reader to the chapters on participant observation since many of the points in these chapters, such as those dealing with establishing rapport, apply to in-depth interviewing as well.

2. One can study how people act in interview situations. Strictly speaking, this would be participant observation research, rather than interviewing.

3. Many of the classic life histories prepared by the Chicago School of sociology were actually based on written documents solicited by the researchers, rather than in-depth interviewing. We discuss this later in the chapter. Also, in the Chicago School, the phrase "personal documents" was used to refer to both written materials and narratives based on in-depth interviewing.

4. In addition, many of the authors or subjects of the life histories prepared by the Chicago School were paid to write their stories (see Shaw et al., 1938; Sutherland, 1937).

5

Montage

──── DISCOVERING METHODS ────

In 1966 a team of social scientists published a book entitled *Unobtrusive Measures: Nonreactive Research in the Social Sciences* with which they hoped to "broaden the social scientist's current narrow range of utilized methodologies and to encourage creative and opportunistic exploitation of unique measurement possibilities (Webb et al., 1966:1)."[1] They went on to write:

> Today, the dominant mass of social science research is based upon interviews and questionnaires. We lament this overdependence upon a single, fallible method (Webb et al., 1966:1).

Although the authors of *Unobtrusive Measures* align themselves with quantitative research methods, their plea for creativity and innovation should be heeded by qualitative researchers as well. We must guard against the overdependence cited by these researchers; that is, we must be careful not to be boxed in by a limited repertoire of research approaches.

We have concentrated thus far in this book on two research approaches: participant observation, the mainstay of qualitative methods, and in-depth interviewing, less commonly used than participant observation but familiar to most researchers. Moreover, we have adopted a "how to do it" approach in describing these methods. There is a danger in what we have done. We may have given the impression that these are the only ways to pursue subjective understanding and inductive analysis.

With this thought in mind, we shift our focus in this chapter to a discussion of studies based on innovative methods. What is to be learned from these studies is that social scientists must *educate* themselves on ways to study the social world. We use the term "educate" as opposed to "train" because there is an important difference between the two. As Irwin Deutscher (1973) notes, one can only be trained in something that already exists. To be educated is to learn to create anew. *We must constantly create new methods and approaches.* We must take to heart the words written by C. Wright Mills (1959:224) in his conclusion to *The Sociological Imagination*:

> Be a good craftsman: Avoid a rigid set of procedures. Above all seek to develop and to use the sociological imagination. Avoid fetishism of method and technique. Urge the rehabilitation of the unpretentious intellectual craftsman, and try to become a craftsman yourself. Let every man be his own methodologist. . . .

These methods are not to be copied, but rather emulated. They do not determine the range of possibilities; only our thoughts do.

The studies that follow exemplify the ideal of researcher-as-innovator. Some of them have serious weaknesses; we mention them because of their strengths.

We do not discuss the ethical implications of the following approaches. Ethical issues have been explored in previous chapters. Some of the methods we describe kindle the fires of long-standing ethical feuds. By describing these studies, we do not necessarily endorse the ethical stances taken by the researchers.

DISRUPTING THE "COMMON SENSE WORLD OF EVERYDAY LIFE": HAROLD GARFINKEL

One hundred and thirty-five people wander into stores and attempt to bargain over the prices of such common items as cigarettes and magazines. Others go out and find unsuspecting partners to play tick-tack-toe: when it is their turn they casually erase their opponent's mark and move it to another square before they make their own. One person engages another in conversation and nonchalantly brings his face so close to the other's that their noses are almost touching. After all of these activities, the "tricksters" go home to write detailed notes on their encounters. All of these are strategies used by Harold Garfinkel (1967) in his influential studies in ethnomethodology. Garfinkel seems to ask himself: "What can be done to make trouble?" By producing confusion, anxiety, bewilderment, and disorganized interaction, he attempts to discover what is otherwise hidden: taken-for-granted rules of social interaction.

Let us discuss some of the other strategies Garfinkel has used to accomplish this goal. In one exercise people are asked to write down on one side of a sheet of paper actual conversations they have had with a friend or relative. On the other side they are asked to write what they understood the other person to have meant by each sentence. The relationships between the two are then examined for what they reveal about what is taken for granted, underlying assumptions, and shared meanings.

In a more provocative exercise people are told to engage others in conversation and to insist that the others clarify the meanings of commonplace remarks. One person asked one of the experimenters, "How are you?" To this, the experimenter replied, "How am I in regard to what? My health, my finances, my school work, my peace of mind, my . . . ?" The partner, red-faced and out of control, shot back, "Look! I was just trying to be polite. Frankly, I don't give a damn how you are."

Another tactic used by Garfinkel is to ask people to look at an ordinary and familiar scene in their own lives from a stranger's perspective. Thus undergraduate students are instructed to go to their families' homes and to act like boarders. Through this exercise people become aware of things they never notice in their everyday lives, such as table manners, greetings, and other subtle conventions. In a slightly different experiment the emphasis is placed on the reactions of others to students behaving like boarders in their own homes.

Garfinkel has created a series of strategies that allow him to explore those areas of social interaction in which he is interested. He uses his experimenters to uncover what is seen but usually unnoticed: the common sense world of everyday life.

THE IMPOSTORS: D. L. ROSENHAN AND OTHERS

An article published by D. L. Rosenhan (1973)* begins with the following question: "If sanity and insanity exist, how shall we know them?" Rosenhan reflects on that question with the use of data he and his cohorts collected in 12 mental hospitals.

Rosenhan and his co-workers conducted their research as impostors. They were "sane" or "normal" people, who had never been defined by themselves or others as "mentally ill," and they misrepresented themselves to the staffs of the hospitals under study. These "pseudopatients," three women and five men, included three psychologists, a pediatrician, a psychiatrist, a painter, a homemaker, and a psychology graduate student. The latter, a man in his early twenties, was the youngest of the group.

With the exception of Rosenhan, who forewarned the administrator and chief psychologist of the hospital of his plans, the pseudopatients conducted their experiment without the knowledge of the staffs of the institutions. All of the impostors used pseudonyms. Those who worked in the field of mental health lied about their occupations in order to avoid any special treatment which might be given them. The procedures that the impostors followed are best described in Rosenhan's (1973) own words:

> After calling the hospital for an appointment, the pseudopatient arrived at the admissions office complaining that he had been hearing voices . . .

> Beyond alleging the symptoms and falsifying name, vocation, and employment, no further alterations of person, history, or circumstances were made. The significant events of the pseudopatient's life history were presented as they had actually occurred. Relationships with parents and sib-

lings, with spouse and children, with people at work and in school, consistent with the aforementioned exceptions, were described as they were or had been. Frustrations and upsets were described along with joys and satisfactions . . .

Immediately upon admission to the psychiatric ward, the pseudopatient ceased simulating any symptoms of abnormality. In some cases, there was a brief period of mild nervousness and anxiety, since none of the pseudopatients really believed that they would be admitted so easily. Indeed, their shared fear was that they would be immediately exposed as frauds and greatly embarrassed. Moreover, many of them had never visited a psychiatric ward; even those who had, nevertheless, had some genuine fears about what might happen to them. Their nervousness, then, was quite appropriate to the novelty of the hospital setting, and it abated rapidly.

Apart from that short-lived nervousness, the pseudopatient behaved on the ward as he "normally" behaved. The pseudopatient spoke to patients and staff as he might ordinarily. Because there is uncommonly little to do on a psychiatric ward, he attempted to engage others in conversation. When asked by staff how he was feeling, he indicated that he was fine, that he no longer experienced symptoms. He responded to instructions from attendants, to calls for medication (which was not swallowed), and to dining-hall instructions. Beyond such activities as were available to him on the admission ward, he spent his time writing down his observations about the ward, its patients and the staff. Initially these notes were written "secretly," but as it soon became clear that no one much cared, they were subsequently written on standard tablets of paper in such public places as the dayroom. No secret was made of these activities.

The pseudopatient, very much as a true psychiatric patient, entered a hospital with no foreknowledge of when he would be discharged. Each was told that he would have to get out by his own devices, essentially by convincing the staff that he was sane. . . . They were, therefore, motivated not only to behave sanely, but to be paragons of cooperation.

As indicated by Rosenhan, the pseudopatients were all successfully admitted to the hospitals. All but one of the impostors were initially diagnosed as "schizophrenic" and were discharged with a diagnosis of "schizophrenia in remission." The length of hospitalization averaged 19 days with a range from 7 to 52 days.

Rosenhan's work is exciting in a variety of ways. It allowed the impostors to collect data on and, what is most important, to actually experience hospitalization for "mental illness." Rosenhan's pseudopatients were able to examine through first-hand knowledge the process by which people are perceived and categorized as "sane" and "insane." These researchers also had the opportunity to observe the unguarded behavior of the staff.

Although Rosenhan's researchers could have gained many of the same insights through the use of overt participant observation techniques, their impostor status enabled them to live through the experience themselves. They thus developed a depth of understanding that would have been difficult to achieve through other methods.

Of course, Rosenhan and his colleagues are not the first to conduct covert observational studies (see, e.g., Dalton, 1961; Festinger et al., 1956; Humphreys, 1975). The ethical issues raised by covert research were discussed earlier. In an especially innovative study of the world of a "deaf, blind, severely retarded" young girl, Goode (1980) gained the subjective understanding that comes with assuming the role of an impostor, while avoiding the ethical dilemmas raised by covert observation. Goode used a number of strategies in an attempt to enter into this young girl's subjective world: intensive observation for periods of 24 hours or longer; videotaping; wearing a blindfold and earplugs on the institutional ward on which she lived; and "interactional procedures," including mimicking her behavior and letting her organize activities for the two of them by remaining "obediently passive." Through these techniques Goode (1980:195) tried to "intuit, while interacting with her, what purposiveness or rationality her activities might have from her perspective." We also know several professors, including Bill English and Steve Murphy, who have sent their students to public places feigning different disabilities in order to give them a personal understanding of the perspectives of people who are disabled.

GROUP INTERVIEWS

One method that has been used sparingly in the past but offers great potential is the group interview. Here interviewers bring together groups of people to talk about their lives and experiences in free flowing, open ended discussions. Like in-depth interviewing, the researcher uses a nondirective approach. However, in group interviews the researcher probably never gains the depth of understanding that comes with one-to-one interviews.

Two geographers, Rowan Roundtree and Barry Gordan, creatively employed the group interview approach to study how people define geographical space, specifically, forests.[2] Initially, they intended to conduct observations in the "field"; that is, wooded areas. This plan contained its drawbacks. Since most people go to forests to get away from things, including others, it would be difficult for them to find people willing to be studied. They were also interested in the definitions of people who might never have been in forests.

What the researchers decided to do instead was to assemble groups of people, show them a set of 10 slides of forest areas, and encourage them to talk about what they had seen. Their research was directed toward understanding how different people view and use forest areas.

Other insightful group interviews have been conducted by Thomas Cottle and a group of researchers at the University of Michigan School of Social Work. Cottle (1973c) describes the interviewing on which his excellent paper, "The Ghetto Scientists," is based:

> It is difficult to say how many of us were speaking that afternoon in the little park near the hospital. So much was going on, like a colossal basketball game and boys darting after girls, or a pretend fight, that our population kept shifting. Still, there were always four or five young people about ten years old, who joined me on the grass alongside the basketball court, and the conversation tumbled along so that we all could follow it and the newcomers could be cued in easily. The girls and boys were speaking about school, their studies, teachers, parents, and brothers and sisters, although there was an unusual side trip into politics. In times like these I wish I could be totally free to say anything to young people, young black people, in this case. It is not that I am thinking anything particular about them as much as holding back ideas that for one reason or another I feel should remain hidden. Maybe it has to do with the laziness of the day or the fact that none of the young people seem especially eager to latch onto some topic. Maybe it is the way some of us do research; entering poor areas of cities and just speaking with people, letting conversations run on without interpretation or analysis. Maybe too, some of us have a strong desire to know what these people think of us and the work we do.

The Michigan group was concerned with how mothers receiving public assistance define welfare (Glasser and Glasser, 1970). In this study, the mothers were invited to form discussion groups to discuss the welfare program. Each group focused on a single area, such as employment opportunities, incapacitated fathers, child-rearing, and school problems, and met weekly for 6 to 12 sessions.

PERSONAL DOCUMENTS

The use of personal documents has a proud history in social science research stemming back to the heyday of the Chicago School (Allport, 1942;
Dollard, 1935; Gottschalk, 1945 et al.; also see Becker, 1966 and Frazier,
1978). Many of the classic life histories in sociology were based largely on
personal documents.

The phrase *personal documents refers to individuals' written first-
person accounts of the whole or parts of their lives or their reflections
on a specific event of topic.* The *diary* is probably the most revealing
and private type of personal document. In her introduction to her
famous diary Anne Frank (1952) wrote, "I hope I shall be able to con-
fide in you completely, as I have never been able to do in anyone else
before." The diary is an excellent source of data because of its intimacy
and self-reflection on one's immediate experiences.

The diary conjures up the image of the adolescent girl who withdraws
to the privacy of her room to remove her diary from its hiding place and
to bare her soul. However, there are other types of valuable ongoing
records. Travelers often maintain *logs* on their trips. Many professionals
and business people keep *calendars* that contain reflections on events in
addition to schedules. Some parents keep ongoing *developmental records*
of the progress of their children (see Church, 1966). *Photo albums* and
scrapbooks are other important forms of personal documents.

Private letters are a good source of information on specific events and
experiences in people's lives. The soldier on the battlefield, the grand-
parent thousands of miles away from his or her family, the immigrant—
all share their sadness and joys through letters. The classic study by
Thomas and Znaniecki (1927), *The Polish Peasant in Europe and America,* was based largely on letters written to relatives overseas.

One form of private correspondence that has received considerable
attention in social science research is *suicide notes* (Douglas, 1967; Jacobs,
1967). These notes are important for understanding not only why people
decide to take their lives, but also what they intend to communicate to
others by doing so.

As noted in the chapter on in-depth interviewing, *solicited narratives*
have been used extensively in qualitative studies. The research of Shaw
(1931, 1966) and his colleagues, Sutherland (1937), and others was based
on life histories actually written by delinquents and criminals. For a

study of the life histories of German refugees, Gordon Allport (1941) ran a competition for the best essay on "My life in Germany before and after January 30, 1933." He received 200 manuscripts averaging 100 pages in length in response. In comparison with other personal documents, solicited narratives yield a relatively small amount of irrelevant and unusable data at the cost of sacrificing spontaneity.

Although there are literally millions of personal documents "waiting to be found," *the researcher will almost always have to search them out imaginatively and aggressively*. Libraries, archives maintained by organizations, and historical societies are good places to start. One of the best ways to obtain documents is by placing ads in newspapers and newsletters. This is how Thomas and Znaniecki located letters for their study. Newspaper editors, columnists, celebrities, and others who receive a large volume of mail may also be willing to share it for research purposes. Finally, friends and acquaintances may be able to provide a supply of documents. Many people would rather put their letters and memorabilia to some useful purpose than burn them. Diaries are sometimes written with the expectation that someone will read them at some future time.

Personal documents are perhaps most valuable when used in conjunction with interviewing and first-hand observation.[3] While acknowledging their value, Herbert Blumer (1969) criticizes the exclusive use of personal documents on the grounds that they lend themselves more readily to diverse interpretations than other forms of data. As the recent Hitler diaries hoax illustrates, documents are relatively easy to fabricate, although in most social science research there is no real reason to do so.[4]

WORDS AND PICTURES: MICHAEL LESY

The word montage is both a verb and a noun. As a verb it refers to the process of making a composition from pictures and words that are closely arranged as in a still picture or presented in short intervals as in a movie; as a noun it refers to the product of such activities. It is not often used to refer to research activities or the products of such enterprises. Yet the word fits very well Michael Lesy's (1973) book, *Wisconsin Death Trip*.[5]

Lesy's work is an arrangement of photographs and quotations collected in and around the town of Black River Falls, Wisconsin, and treats the period 1890 to 1910. Using over 30,000 glass plate negatives from the files of the State Historical Society of Wisconsin and quotations and records from the Badger State Banner newspaper, Mendota State Mental Hospital, and other sources, Lesy attempts to capture "the structure of the experience of the people themselves, especially that aspect of the structure that might be regarded as pathological."

Wisconsin Death Trip contains hundreds of quotations and photographs, interspersed with Lesy's own commentary. He uses these materials to look at people as others have not and to implicitly, if not explicitly, challenge our traditional views of the period. In order to give you a flavor of the nature of the work, let us present some of the quotations found in the book:*

> Milo L. Nicholas, sent to the insane hospital a year or two ago after committing arson on Mrs. Nicholas' farm is now at large . . . and was seen near the old place early last week . . . He has proven himself a revengeful firebug.

> Henry Johnson, an old bachelor of Grand Dyke, cut off the heads of all his hens recently, made a bonfire of his best clothes and killed himself with arsenic.

> The motto of the high school class of 1895 was "Work is the Law of Life."

> John Pabelowski, a 16 year old boy of Stevens Point, was made idiotic by the use of tobacco.

> George Kanuck, a laborer, is alleged to have sold his 7 year old boy to Italian peddlers who have been working at Manitowoc. The sale is said to have taken place at Kanuck's house during a drunken orgy in which all participated. The Italians, 2 women and a man, left town next day with the boy.

> Billie Neverson's wife was a wierdie. They took over the old Creston place at the other end of the valley. No one knows what really happened. Some say it went back to Billie finding out about her having a kid before they got married. Anyway, she just stayed by herself. Once a year, maybe, someone would see her in town, but she wouldn't even nod her head to say hello. Acting like that nobody ever bothered to visit them either.

> Admitted Nov. 21st, 1899. Town of Franklin, Norwegian. Age 50. Married. Two children, youngest 3 years of age. Farmer in poor circumstances . . . Has an idea that people are taking what little he has—that they will come

* Michael Lesy, *Wisconsin Death Trip*, copyright 1973, Pantheon Books, a Division of Random House, Inc. Used by permission of the publishers.

to his house even when he is there. Is not homicidal . . . Poor physical condition . . . January 24th, 1900.: Died today. Exhaustion . . .

Lesy does not have much to say about his methods. After all, his task
was confined to the process of reading through and sorting the materials
for presentation to the reader. What is of greater importance than his
methodology, moreover, is the perspective and understanding he brings
to his data. He reminds us, for example, that none of the pictures he
presents were snapshots: since it was necessary to pose to permit the required half-second exposure, people had an opportunity to think about
how they wanted to appear.

In his introduction Lesy elaborates on the meaning of the materials
he has assembled:

> Neither the pictures nor the events were, when they were made or experi-
> enced, considered to be unique, extraordinary, or sensational . . . The
> people who looked at the pictures once they were taken weren't surprised,
> and the people who read about the events after they were printed weren't
> shocked.

In reference to those who write the newspaper he writes:

> They didn't question events; they confirmed them. Eventually they may
> have become particularly sensitive to appearances, but they never doubted
> their meaning. Charley took hundreds and hundreds of pictures of horses
> because he was asked to; he took dozens and dozens of pictures of houses and
> their owners because he'd been offered the job. The Coopers [the editors
> and writers for the local paper] vilified the Pullman strikers because every-
> one was Republican; they noted a departure, an arrival, or a visit because
> everyone always departed, arrived, or visited; they devoted a weekly column
> to abstinence because it was a Christian duty to remain temperate. Each of
> them said yes to what he was supposed to and no to what he was supposed
> to refuse. They were prosaic chroniclers of a conventionalized universe.

Finally, Lesy discusses the process by which he put the book together.
He suggests that he was more of an artisan than a technician:

> The text was constructed as music is composed. It was meant to obey its
> own laws of tone, pitch, rhythm, and repetition. Even though now, caught
> between the two covers of this book, it accompanies the pictures, it was not
> meant to serve them the way a quartet was intended to disguise the inde-
> corous pauses in eighteenth-century gossip. Rather, it was meant to fill the

space of this book with a constantly repeated theme that might recall your attention whenever it drifted from the faces and hands of the people in the pictures.

Lesy is an artist, an historian, and a social scientist *par excellence.* By illuminating a particular town, region, and country at a particular historical period, he illuminates our world now. He enables us to enter the past and to imagine what people in the future will know of us. Historical works like Lesy's lead us to examine our own common sense understanding of the world from a more detached perspective.

UNOBTRUSIVE METHODS

In their book *Unobtrusive Measures,* Webb et al. (1966) present a series of research approaches designed to minimize or eliminate the researcher's effects on the people and settings being studied. This is what they mean by *nonreactive research.*

The methods Webb et al. describe include analysis of physical traces people leave behind, archives, "simple" (noninteractive) observation, and contrived observation (including covert observation and mechanical recording devices). In their introduction, they offer some tantalizing examples of the kinds of methods surveyed in their book:

> The floor tiles around the hatching-chick exhibit at Chicago's Museum of Science and Industry must be replaced every six weeks. Tiles in other parts of the museum need not be replaced for years. The selective erosion of tiles, indexed by the replacement rate, is a measure of the relative popularity of exhibits.

> The accretion rate is another measure. One investigator wanted to learn the level of whisky consumption in a town which was officially "dry." He did so by counting empty bottles in ashcans.

> The degree of fear induced by a ghost-story-telling session can be measured by noting the shrinking diameter of a circle of seated children.

> Chinese jade dealers have used the pupil dilation of their customers as a measure of the client's interest in particular stones, and Darwin in 1872 noted this same variable as an index of fear.

> Library withdrawals were used to demonstrate the effect of the introduction of television into a community. Fiction titles dropped, nonfiction titles were unaffected.

The role of rate of interaction in managerial recruitment is shown by the overrepresentation of baseball managers who were infielders or catchers (high-interaction positions) during their playing days.

Sir Francis Galton employed surveying hardware to estimate the bodily dimensions of African women whose language he did not speak.

The child's interest in Christmas was demonstrated by distortions in the size of Santa Claus drawings. (Webb et al., 1966:2)

Ironically, the strength of unobtrusive methods is also their weakness: since researchers do not interact with people, they not only eliminate reactive effects, but fail to learn how people see and experience their world. Denzin (1978) criticizes unobtrusive methods for their extreme behaviorist bias and failure to reveal the subjective side of social life.[6] For the qualitative researcher, unobtrusive methods seldom can stand alone as a sole source of data. However, *Unobtrusive Measures* is an important book for sensitizing qualitative researchers to things that usually go unnoticed.

PHOTOGRAPHY AND METHODOLOGY

As Lesy's study so aptly demonstrates, photographs can provide an excellent source of data for qualitative analysis. Like personal documents, the pictures people take lend insight into what is important to them and how they view themselves and others. This is not the only way photography enters into qualitative research, however.

The camera is becoming an increasingly popular research tool in the social sciences (Dabbs, 1982; Stasz, 1979). Just as a tape recorder can aid in recording data, film and videotape equipment can capture details that would otherwise be forgotten or go unnoticed.[7] As Dabbs (1982:38) notes:

I have two reasons for liking these media. First, they are faithful and patient observers. They remember what they see and they can record steadily for long periods of time. Second, . . . they allow us to expand or compress time and make visible patterns that would otherwise move too slowly or too fast to be seen.

The ethnomethodologists seem especially enamored with electronic recording devices for studying the mundane and taken-for-granted aspects of everyday life. Thus Ryave and Schenkein (1974) studied the "art of walking," how people navigate in public places, by filming eight-minute segments of videotape on a public pavement. Commenting on their use of videotape equipment, Ryave and Schenkein (1974:266) write:

> It is plain enough that the use of videotape affords us the opportunity to review a given instance of the phenomenon innumerable times without relying on a single observation of an essentially transitory phenomenon. In addition, . . . we require intimate study of actual instances of walking and cannot be satisfied with the study of reports *on* those instances.

William H. Whyte (1980) has used time-lapse photography to study small urban spaces such as parks and plazas.[8] By filming for entire days, he examines what makes people use some spaces and not others. His research shows that time-lapse filming is an especially fruitful research approach.

Photographs and films also can be used as a mode of presenting and illustrating findings. Pictures take the place of words or at least convey something that words cannot. Certainly, for the reader of a qualitative study, pictures give a sense of "being there," seeing the setting and people first-hand. There have also been some pieces published in sociological journals such as *Qualitative Sociology* that consist *solely* of pictures without commentary or analysis (see, e.g., Jackson, 1978). Stasz (1979:36) points out that "visual sociologists" can either mimic art, letting the images speak for themselves, or "aim toward the ideals of visual ethnography, where texts would accompany photographs to provide features of description and abstract generalization which cannot be handled by images alone."

Dabbs (1982) describes studies by Ziller and his colleagues (Ziller and Lewis, 1981; Ziller and Smith, 1977) that demonstrate yet another way in which photography can be creatively used to study people's perspectives. In one study Ziller and Lewis (1981) gave people cameras and asked them to take pictures that tell who they are. They found that students with high grade averages produced more photographs in which books were prominently displayed, whereas juvenile delinquents took more pictures of people and fewer of school and home than others. In another study Ziller and Smith (1977) found that when asked to describe their university, new students brought back pictures of buildings and old students turned in photos of people.

Photographers, artists, and others have long produced media forms
rich in sociological understanding. Frederick Wiseman's films, *Titticut
Follies, High School, Hospital,* and others, get beneath the surface of
places we often visit but never really see.[9] The photos of Diane Arbus
(1972) and the photographic essays of institutions for the "mentally retarded" by Blatt and Kaplan (1974) and Blatt, Ozolins, and McNally
(1980) are notable for portraying the human condition.

OFFICIAL RECORDS AND PUBLIC DOCUMENTS

There is, for all practical purposes, an unlimited number of official and
public documents, records, and materials available as sources of data.
These include organizational documents, newspaper articles, agency records, government reports, court transcripts, and a host of other materials.

Of course, researchers have analyzed official records and statistics since
the beginnings of the social sciences. Durkheim's (1951) classic study of
suicide is a notable case in point. There have been countless studies of
crime based on police records and suicide based on coroner's reports.
However, the qualitative researcher brings a different perspective to
reports and documents than has been common in the social sciences.

The qualitative researcher analyzes official and public documents to
learn about the people who write and maintain them. Like personal
documents, *these materials lend insight into the perspectives, assumptions, concerns, and activities of those who produce them.* Kitsuse and
Cicourel (1963) point out that official statistics tell us about organizational processes rather than criminals, deviants, or others on whom they
are kept. Similarly, Garfinkel (1967) argues that organizational records
are produced for the purpose of documenting satisfactory performance
of the organization's responsibilities towards its clients. Concerning
psychiatric records, Garfinkel (1967:198) writes:

> In our view the contents of clinic folders are assembled with regard for the
> possibility that the relationship may have to be portrayed as having been in
> accord with expectations of sanctionable performances by clinicians and
> patients.

In slightly different veins, Douglas (1967, 1971) examined common sense
understandings of why people kill themselves by analyzing coroner's
records, and Platt (1969) looked at definitions of juvenile delinquency

around the turn of the century by reviewing official reports of charitable organizations, government reports, and other historical documents.

Popular media forms, such as newspapers, magazines, television, movies, and radio, provide another important source of data. For example, researchers have studied societal stereotypes of the "mentally ill" in comic strips (Scheff, 1966), images of the disabled in newspapers, books, and movies (Bogdan and Biklen, 1977), and portrayals of sex roles in children's books.

Most official records and public documents are readily available to researchers. Public libraries, organizational archives, and historical societies are good sources for these kinds of materials. Police and agency records are usually accessible through the same means that participant observers gain entrée to these settings. Many government reports and documents are public information and available under the Freedom of Information Law. Taylor et al. (1981) obtained survey reports of Medicaid-funded institutions for the "mentally retarded" through a Freedom of Information request to the federal government.

The qualitative analysis of official documents opens up many new sources of understanding. Materials that are thought to be useless by those looking for "objective facts" are valuable to the qualitative researcher precisely because of their subjective nature.

In this chapter we have highlighted innovative approaches to the study of social life. The spirit of the studies described here is captured by Nobel Prizewinning scientist P. W. Bridgeman (quoted in Dalton, 1964:60):

> There is no scientific method as such . . . The most vital feature of the scientist's procedure has been merely to do the utmost with his mind, no holds barred . . .

The preceding chapters have discussed a broad range of ways to collect qualitative data. In the next chapter we devote attention to data analysis in qualitative research.

NOTES

1. This book has been revised and published as *Nonreactive Measures in the Social Sciences* by Webb, Campbell, Schwartz, Sechrest, and Grove (1981).
2. Their ideas were inspired, in part, by Craig (1970).

3.   This is because of what Denzin (1978) refers to as the "reality-distance problem." In analyzing personal documents the researcher is several times removed from the phenomenon in which he or she is interested. Of course, there are many instances in which it is impossible to analyze documents in conjunction with face-to-face research approaches.

4.   Denzin (1978) provides a review of criteria for judging the validity and authenticity of personal documents.

5.   Also see Lesy's more recently published *Real Life: Louisville in the Twenties* (1976).

6.   See Dabbs (1982) for a defense of unobtrusive methods on this basis.

7.   See Dabbs (1982) for a good overview of the kinds of film and videotape equipment that can be used in research.

8.   Whyte has also produced a film entitled *The Social Life of Small Urban Places* which has been shown on public television.

9.   For a brief discussion of Wiseman's films, see "Viewpoint: Shooting the institution," *Time: The Weekly Newsmagazine* (December 9): pp. 95–98, 1974. Wiseman describes his documentaries as "reality fictions: reality in that the people are real and the events unstaged; fictions, in the sense that I have condensed and ordered those events in a fashion they did not have in real life."

6

Working with Data

DATA ANALYSIS IN QUALITATIVE RESEARCH

In the preceding chapters we discussed a variety of ways to collect qualitative data including participant observation, in-depth interviewing, written documents, and a number of creative approaches. In this chapter we turn to a discussion of how qualitative researchers can make sense out of and analyze data. We offer strategies and techniques that we have used and that you may find helpful in getting the most out of the data you have collected. We begin with a discussion of the different kinds of qualitative studies.

DESCRIPTIVE AND THEORETICAL STUDIES

All qualitative studies contain rich descriptive data: people's own written or spoken words and observable activities. In participant observation studies researchers try to convey a sense of "being there" and experiencing settings first-hand. Similarly, in studies based on in-depth interviewing they attempt to give readers a feeling of "walking in the informants' shoes" and seeing things from their points of view. Thus qualitative research should provide "thick description" of social life (Geertz, 1983). As Emerson (1983:24) writes, "Thick descriptions present in close detail the context and meanings of events and scenes that are relevant to those involved in them."

However, we can distinguish between purely descriptive studies, sometimes referred to as *ethnographies,* and theoretical or conceptual studies. In ethnographic description the researcher tries to render a "true to life" picture of what people say and how they act; people's words and actions are left to speak for themselves. Descriptive studies are marked by minimal interpretation and conceptualization. They are written in such a way as to allow readers to draw their own conclusions and generalizations from the data.

In sociology the classic studies of the Chicago School probably provide the clearest examples of descriptive ethnography. While motivated by a keen interest in social problems, the Chicago School researchers sought to describe in graphic terms the fabric of urban life. Nels Anderson's (1923) *The Hobo* is a notable case in point. Building on his own experiences as a hobo, participant observation (before the approach was even called that), and documents, Anderson described the hobo way of life as experienced by hobos themselves: their language, favorite haunts, customs, pursuits, personalities, and ballads and songs.

Life histories, as produced by members of the Chicago School and other researchers, represent the purest form of descriptive studies. In the life history the person tells his or her story in his or her own words: "The unique feature of such documents is that they are recorded in the first person, in the boy's own words, and not translated into the language of the person investigating the case" (Shaw, 1966:1).

It would be misleading to suggest that descriptive studies write themselves. In all studies researchers present and order the data according to what they think is important. For example, in life histories they decide on what to include and exclude, edit the raw data, add connecting passages between remarks, and place the story in some kind of sequence. Further, in conducting their studies researchers make decisions about what to observe, ask about, and record that determine what they are able to describe and how they describe it.

Most qualitative studies are directed toward developing or verifying sociological theory. The purpose of theoretical studies is to understand or explain features of social life beyond the particular people and settings studied. In these studies researchers actively point out what is important to their audience. They use descriptive data to illustrate their theories and concepts and to convince readers that what they say is true.

Glaser and Strauss (1967) distinguish between two types of theory: substantive and formal (see Chapter 2). The first relates to a substantive area of inquiry; for instance, schools, prisons, juvenile delinquency, and patient care. Formal theory refers to a conceptual area of inquiry, such as stigma, formal organizations, socialization, and deviance. In qualitative research most studies have focused on single substantive areas.

DEVELOPING AND VERIFYING THEORY

Since the publication of Glaser and Strauss' (1967) influential book, *The Discovery of Grounded Theory*, qualitative researchers have debated whether the purpose of theoretical studies should be to *develop* or *verify* social theory, or both (see, e.g., Charmaz, 1983; Emerson, 1983; Katz, 1983). Glaser and Strauss are probably the strongest proponents of the view that qualitative (and other) sociologists should direct their attention to developing or generating social theory and concepts (also see Glaser, 1978). Their *grounded theory approach* is designed to enable researchers to do just that. Other researchers take the position that qualitative research, just like quantitative studies, can and should be used to develop and verify or test propositions about the nature of social life. The procedure of *analytic induction* has been the principal means by which researchers have attempted to do this (Cressey, 1953; Katz, 1983; Lindesmith, 1947; Robinson, 1951; Turner, 1953; Znaniecki, 1934). Although most researchers adopt elements of both approaches in their studies, it is useful to distinguish between theory generation and verification and the respective approaches, grounded theory and analytic induction, in discussing qualitative data analysis.

The grounded theory approach is a method for discovering theories, concepts, hypotheses, and propositions directly from data, rather than from a priori assumptions, other research, or existing theoretical frameworks. According to Glaser and Strauss (1967:6–7), social scientists have overemphasized testing and verifying theories and neglected the more important activity of generating sociological theory:

> Description, ethnography, fact-finding, verification (call them what you will) are all done well by professionals in other fields and by laymen in various investigatory agencies. But these people cannot generate sociological theory from their work. Only sociologists are trained to want it, to look for it, and to generate it.

Glaser and Strauss propose two major strategies for developing grounded theory. The first is the *constant comparative method* in which the researcher simultaneously codes and analyzes data in order to develop concepts. By continually comparing specific incidents in the data, the researcher refines these concepts, identifies their properties, explores their relationships to one another, and integrates them into a coherent theory.

The second strategy proposed by Glaser and Strauss is *theoretical sampling,* which was described earlier in this book. In theoretical sampling the researcher selects new cases to study according to their potential for helping to expand on or refine the concepts and theory that have already been developed. Data collection and analysis proceed together.

By studying different substantive areas, the researcher can expand a substantive theory into a formal one. Glaser and Strauss explain how their grounded theory of the relationship between nurses' estimation of the social value of dying patients and their care of patients can be elevated to a theory of how professionals give service to clients based on social value.

In generating grounded theory researchers do not seek to prove their theories, but merely to demonstrate plausible support for them. Glaser and Strauss (1967:3) argue that key criteria in evaluating theories are whether they "fit" and "work":

> By "fit" we mean that the categories must be readily (not forcibly) applicable to and indicated by the data under study; by "work" we mean that they must be meaningfully relevant to and able to explain the behavior under study.

Ultimately, for Glaser and Strauss, readers must judge the credibility of qualitative studies.

Analytic induction is a procedure for verifying theories and propositions based on qualitative data. As formulated by Znaniecki in 1934, analytic induction was designed to identify *universal* propositions and causal laws. Znaniecki contrasted analytic induction with "enumerative induction" that provided mere correlations and could not account for exceptions to statistical relationships. The procedure was refined by Lindesmith (1947) and Cressey (1950, 1953) in their respective studies of opiate addiction and embezzlers and used by Howard Becker (1963) in his classic study of marijuana users. More recently, Katz (1983) has characterized analytic induction, which he refers to as analytic research, as a rigorous qualitative method for arriving at a perfect fit between the data and explanations of social phenomena.

The steps involved in analytic induction are relatively simple and straightforward (see Cressey, 1950; Denzin, 1978; Katz, 1983):

1. Develop a rough definition of the phenomenon to be explained.
2. Formulate an hypothesis to explain that phenomenon (this can be based on the data, other research, or the researcher's insight and intuition).
3. Study one case to see the fit between the case and the hypothesis.
4. If the hypothesis does not explain the case, either reformulate the hypothesis or redefine the phenomenon.
5. Actively search for negative cases to disprove the hypothesis.
6. When negative cases are encountered, reformulate the hypothesis or redefine the phenomenon.
7. Proceed until one has adequately tested the hypothesis (established a universal relationship according to some researchers) by examining a broad range of cases.

Using this approach, Cressey (1953:30) arrived at the following explanation of trust violators (a revised formulation of embezzlers):

> Trusted persons become trust violators when they conceive of themselves as having a financial problem which is non-sharable, are aware that this problem can be secretly resolved by violation of the position of financial trust, and are able to apply to their own conduct in that situation verbalizations which enable them to adjust their conceptions of themselves as trusted

persons with their conceptions of themselves as users of the entrusted funds or property.

Analytical induction has been criticized for failing to live up to the claims of its early proponents as a method for establishing causal laws and universals (Robinson, 1951; Turner, 1953). Turner (1953) suggests that analytic induction is fundamentally a method of producing definitions of social phenomena; hence explanations based on analytic induction may be circular.

However, the basic logic underlying analytic induction can be useful in qualitative data analysis. By directing attention to negative cases, analytic induction forces the researcher to refine and qualify theories and propositions. Katz (1983:133) argues:

> The test is not whether a final state of perfect explanation has been achieved but the *distance* that has been traveled over negative cases and through consequent qualifications from an initial state of knowledge. Analytic induction's quest for perfect explanation, or "universals," should be understood as a strategy for research rather than as the ultimate measure of the method.

In contrast to the grounded theory approach, analytic induction also helps researchers address the question of generalizability of their findings. If researchers can demonstrate that they have examined a sufficiently broad range of instances of a phenomena and specifically looked for negative cases, they can assert greater claims regarding the general nature of what they have found.

ONGOING ANALYSIS

It is perhaps misleading to have a separate chapter on working with data, since *data analysis is an ongoing process in qualitative research.* Data collection and analysis go hand-in-hand. Throughout participant observation, in-depth interviewing, and other qualitative research, researchers keep track of emerging themes, read through their field notes or transcripts, and develop concepts and propositions to begin to make sense out of their data. As their studies progress, they begin to focus their research interests, ask directive questions, check out informants' stories, and follow up on leads and hunches. In many studies researchers hold off on selecting additional settings, people, or documents for study until they have conducted some initial data analysis. Both grounded theory's strategy of theoretical sampling and analytic induction's search for negative cases require this.

Of course, it is toward the end of the research, when all of the evidence is in so to speak, that the researcher concentrates most on data analysis and interpretation. Many of the steps outlined in the following sections, such as cutting up data, occur after the data have been collected.

Some researchers prefer to distance themselves from the research prior to engaging in intensive analysis. Practical considerations may also force the researcher to postpone analysis. For example, people sometimes underestimate the amount of time it takes to have taped interviews transcribed.

It is a good idea to begin intensive analysis as soon as possible after you have completed the fieldwork or collected the data. The longer you wait, the more difficult it will be to go back to informants to clarify any points or tie up loose ends. Some researchers maintain casual contact with informants throughout data analysis and even after the data have been analyzed and the study written (see Miller and Humphreys, 1980). Researchers also may have informants read draft reports as a check on validity (Douglas, 1976).

WORKING WITH DATA

All researchers develop their own ways of analyzing qualitative data. In this section we describe the basic approach we have used to make sense out of descriptive data gathered through qualitative research methods.

Our approach is directed toward *developing an in-depth understanding of the settings or people under study*. This approach has many parallels with the grounded theory method of Glaser and Strauss (1967). As the following discussion indicates, insights are grounded in and developed from the data themselves. In contrast to Glaser and Strauss, though, we are less concerned with developing concepts and theories than with understanding the settings or people on their own terms. We do this through both description and theory. Thus sociological concepts are used to illuminate features of the settings or people under study and to aid understanding. Further, our approach places greater emphasis on analyzing "negative cases" and the context in which data are collected than Glaser and Strauss' method, although it falls short of imposing the systematic search for generalizations and universals entailed in analytic induction. Our basic analytical approach is compatible with both the grounded theory approach and analytic induction.

In qualitative research researchers analyze and code their own data. Unlike quantitative research, qualitative research lacks a division of labor between data collectors and coders. Data analysis is a dynamic and creative process. Throughout analysis, researchers attempt to gain a deeper understanding of what they have studied and continually refine their interpretations. Researchers also draw on their first-hand experience with settings, informants, or documents to make sense out of the data.

Data analysis, as we see it, entails certain distinct phases. The first is an ongoing discovery phase: identifying themes and developing concepts and propositions. The second phase, which typically occurs after the data have been collected, entails coding the data and refining one's understanding of the subject matter. In the final phase, the researcher attempts to discount his or her findings (Deutscher, 1973); that is, to understand the data in the context in which they were collected.

Discovery

In qualitative studies, researchers gradually make sense out of what they are studying by combining insight and intuition with an intimate familiarity with the data. This is often a difficult process. Most people inexperienced in qualitative research have difficulty recognizing patterns that emerge in their data. *You must learn to look for themes by examining your data in as many ways as possible.* There is no simple formula for identifying themes and developing concepts, but the following suggestions should get you on the right track.

1. Read and reread your data. Collect all field notes, transcripts, documents, and other materials and read through them carefully. Then read through them some more. By the time you are ready to engage in intensive analysis, you should know your data inside out. Some researchers spend weeks or even months poring over their data prior to engaging in intensive analysis.

As suggested in the chapter on fieldwork, *it is always a good idea to have someone else read through your data.* An outside reader can sometimes notice subtle aspects that elude the researcher.

2. Keep track of themes, hunches, interpretations, and ideas. You should record any important idea that comes to you as you read through and think about your data. In participant observation, researchers sometimes use "Observer's Comments" to note themes and record interpretations, whereas in in-depth interviewing the researcher can use an interviewer's log for this purpose. As you read through your data, you can also make notations in the margins.

Some researchers write memos to themselves as they come across themes in their data or think of concepts that might apply to what they are studying. For example, Charmaz (1983) describes a process of writing, sorting, and integrating memos for developing grounded theories. Of course, in team research memo-writing helps keep researchers on top of what their team members are learning and thinking. Spradley (1980) uses elaborate worksheets, lists, charts, and diagrams to discover underlying patterns.

3. Look for emerging themes. You must force yourself to search through your data for emerging themes or patterns: conversation topics, vocabulary, recurring activities, meanings, feelings, or folk sayings and proverbs (Spradley, 1980). *Do not be afraid to list tentative themes at this stage in the process.* Just don't develop a stake in any particular idea until you have had a chance to hold it up to experience and check it out.

Some patterns will stand out in your data. In the institutional study, "physical restraints," "pay," "cleaning the ward," "medications," and "programming" were frequent conversation topics. The attendants' vocabulary included terms such as "low grade," "working boy," and "tripping time."

Other patterns will not be so apparent. You will have to look for deeper meanings. In his study, *Stigma*, Goffman (1963) quotes a fictitious letter which is rich in sociological understanding and compassionate in human terms. This letter can be used to demonstrate how themes can be identified in data:

Dear Miss Lonelyhearts—

I am sixteen years old now and I dont know what to do and would appreciate it if you could tell me what to do. When I was a little girl it was not so bad because I got used to the kids on the block makeing fun of me, but now I would like to have boy friends like the other girls and go out on Saturday nites, but no boy will take me because I was born without a nose—although I am a good dancer and have a nice shape and my father buys me pretty clothes.

I sit and look at myself all day and cry. I have a big hole in the middle of my face that scares people even myself so I cant blame the boys for not wanting to take me out. My mother loves me, but she crys terrible when she looks at me.

What did I do to deserve such a terrible bad fate? Even if I did do some bad things I didn't do any before I was a year old and I was born this way. I asked Papa and he says he doesn't know, but that maybe I did something in the other world before I was born or that maybe I was being punished for his sins. I dont believe that because he is a very nice man. Ought I commit suicide?

Sincerely yours,
Desperate

Quite a few themes may be seen here. The first is despair. "Desperate" says she looks at herself and cries and asks whether she should commit suicide; the signature itself reflects this state of mind. The next theme relates to trying to find an explanation for her situation. "What did I do," she asks, "to deserve such a terrible bad fate?" She goes on to speculate about what she did in "the other world" and her father's sins. A third theme, which is somewhat more subtle, has to do with the meanings of physical stigma at different times in a person's life. "It was not so bad" when she was a little girl, but now that she has reached adolescence, when other girls have boyfriends and go out on Saturday nights, it is unbearable. A final theme relates to how "Desperate's" other qualities do not overcome the fact that she does not have a nose. That she may be a good dancer, have a nice shape, and wear pretty clothes does not get her any dates.

4. **Construct typologies.** Typologies, or classification schemes, can be useful aids in identifying themes and developing concepts and theory. One kind of typology relates to how people classify others and objects in their lives.[1] The researcher in the institutional study constructed a typol-

ogy of how attendants classify residents by listing the terms they used to refer to them. They used terms such as "hyperactives," "fighters," "spastics," "pukers," "runaways," "pests," "dining room boys," "working boys," and "pets."

The other kinds of typology are based on the researcher's own classification scheme. Thus in the institutional study, the researcher wanted to look at whether attendants said and did different things based on the length of time they worked at the institution. Conventional wisdom would suggest that "old-line" employees would be more entrenched in their perspectives. By classifying attendants according to old and new employees, he could examine whether this seemed to make a difference. He concluded that this common sense distinction between old-line and new-line employees had little to do with their perspectives and practices.

5. **Develop concepts and theoretical propositions.** It is through concepts and propositions that the researcher moves from description to interpretation and theory. *Concepts* are abstract ideas generalized from empirical facts. In qualitative research concepts are sensitizing instruments (Blumer, 1969; Bruyn, 1966). *Sensitizing concepts,* according to Blumer (1969:148), provide a "general sense of reference" and suggest "directions along which to look." He proceeds to explain that sensitizing concepts are communicated by "exposition which yields a meaningful picture, abetted by apt illustrations which enable one to grasp the reference in terms of one's own experience." Concepts are used to illuminate social processes and phenomena that are not readily apparent through descriptions of specific instances. *Stigma* is a powerful example of a sensitizing concept. When we think of stigma as a blot on one's moral character, and not merely a physical abnormality, we are better able to understand what "Desperate," quoted by Goffman (1963), experiences and to relate her experiences to those of others.

Developing concepts is an intuitive process. It can be learned, but not formally taught. However, here are some places to start. First, look for words and phrases in informants' own vocabularies that capture the meaning of what they say or do. Concepts from informants are referred to as *concrete concepts*: ". . . the concrete concept is derived indigenously from the culture studied; it takes its meaning solely from that culture and not from the scientist's definition of it" (Bruyn, 1966:39). Attendants frequently talk about the need to *control* residents. By examining themes in his data in light of this concept, the researcher found that a broad range of attendants' everyday activities could be interpreted as control measures: constant supervision of residents, restrictions on residents' freedom of movement, limiting residents' access to objects and possessions, physical restraining devices, drugging, offering residents rewards and privileges, physical force, work duty, and others.

Second, as you note a theme in your data, compare statements and acts with one another to see if there is a concept that unites them. Glaser and Strauss (1967:106) point out that this comparison can usually be done from memory. Attendants take precautions to avoid "getting caught" violating institutional rules. For example, they place a "watchdog" at the door to warn them of the arrival of supervisors or visitors and hit residents in such a way as not to leave marks. The researcher came up with the concept of evasion strategies to refer to these activities. Once he developed this concept, he noticed that other activities, such as "fudging" records, were related to these other strategies.

Third, as you identify different themes, look for underlying similarities between them. When you can relate the themes in this manner, see if there is a word or phrase that conveys how they are similar. Thus Goffman's (1959, 1961) concept of fronts applies equally to themes related to how institutional officials maintain grounds and how they manage media relations.

A *proposition* is a general statement of fact grounded in the data. The statement that "Attendants use evasion strategies to avoid getting caught violating institutional rules" is a proposition. Whereas concepts may or may not "fit," propositions are either right or wrong, although the researcher may not be able to prove them.

Like concepts, propositions are developed by poring over the data. By studying themes, constructing typologies, and relating different pieces of data to each other, the researcher gradually comes up with generalizations. In the institutional study the researcher developed a proposition that attendants define residents according to whether they help or hinder their own custodial work. Whereas teachers may view the mentally retarded according to their learning ability and physicians according to their medical conditions, attendants' definitions of residents reflect their concern with ward order and cleanliness.

This proposition was derived from attendants' own typology of residents. By looking at attendants' terms for and comments about residents, the researcher discovered that attendants classify residents according to seven broad categories: control problems ("troublemakers," "fighters"); custodial problems ("wetters," "pukers"); supervisory problems ("run aways," "self-abusers"); authority problems ("wise guys," "smart alecs"); special processing ("school boys"); helpers ("working girls," "bucket boys"); pets and no problems ("dopes," "dummies"). The common thread running through these categories relates to the problems residents create for attendants' day-to-day work; hence the proposition.

6. Read the literature. Qualitative researchers begin their studies with minimal commitment to a priori assumptions and theory (Glaser and Strauss, 1967). By the time you are ready to engage in intensive analysis, however, you should be familiar with the sociological literature and theoretical frameworks relevant to your research.

Other studies often provide fruitful concepts and propositions that will help you interpret your data. It is not uncommon to find that the best insights come from studies of a totally different substantive area. For instance, in the study of institutions, the observer drew on the literature on deviance to understand many of the attendants' perspectives and practices.

If you are inexperienced in qualitative research, you should take a look at some qualitative studies to see how researchers analyze and present their data. The articles in Part II of this book should give you an idea of how to write up a qualitative study. Books such as *Street Corner Society* by Whyte (1955), *Tally's Corner* by Liebow (1967), *Making the Grade* by Becker, Geer, and Hughes (1968), *Timetables* by Roth (1963), and *Tearoom Trade* by Humphreys (1975) are examples of insightful, clearly written studies.

Even if you have been exposed to qualitative studies, you should review the literature to relate your study to what others have done. Most good research builds on what has been done before.

You should be careful not to force your data into someone else's framework. If concepts fit your data, do not be afraid to borrow them. If they do not, forget about them.

How one interprets one's data depends on one's theoretical assumptions. It is important to expose yourself to theoretical frameworks during the intensive analysis stage of the research. Our own theoretical framework, symbolic interactionism, leads one to look for social perspectives, meanings, and definitions. Thus the symbolic interactionist is interested in questions such as the following:

How do people define themselves, others, their settings, and their activities?

How do people's definitions and perspectives develop and change?

What is the fit between different perspectives held by different people?

What is the fit between people's perspectives and their activities?

How do people deal with the discrepancy between their perspectives and activities?

Although most researchers align themselves with a specific theoretical framework, it is standard to borrow from diverse frameworks to make sense out of data.

7. Develop a story-line. It is sometimes useful to develop a "story-line" to guide analysis. The story-line is the analytical thread that unites and integrates the major themes in the data. It is an answer to the question, "What is this a study of?"

Perhaps the best way to develop the story-line is to come up with a sentence or phrase that describes your study in general terms. The titles and subtitles to qualitative studies sometimes do this. For instance, the title *Making the Grade: The Academic Side of College Life* (Becker et al., 1968) tells us about the importance of grades to students; the title *Cloak of Competence: Stigma in the Lives of the Mentally Retarded* (Edgerton, 1967) tells us that people labeled mentally retarded try to conceal their stigma.

Coding

In qualitative research coding is a systematic way of developing and refining interpretations of the data. The coding process involves bringing together and analyzing all the data bearing on themes, ideas, concepts, interpretations, and propositions. What were initially vague ideas and hunches are refined, expanded, discarded, or fully developed during this stage of analysis. Here is one way to code qualitative data.

1. **Develop coding categories.** Start by listing every theme, concept, interpretation, typology, and proposition identified or developed during the initial analysis. Be as specific as possible in writing down your ideas. You should have some sense of what kinds of data will fit into each category. However, some of your ideas will be tentative and vaguely formulated. For example, a coding category might relate to a recurring conversation topic. These should be listed also.

Once you have identified the major coding categories, go over the list once more. You will find that some categories overlap one another and can be collapsed.

The number of coding categories you develop will depend on the amount of data you have collected and the complexity of your analytical scheme. In the job training study the researcher coded his data according to approximately 150 categories. In the institutional study the researcher used roughly 50 coding categories. The coding scheme included well-developed propositions ("attendants discount IQ as an indicator of intelligence") and conversation topics ("programming").

Assign a number or letter to each coding category. You may want to indicate which ideas are logically related in assigning symbols. For example, "17" might refer to attendants' typology of residents, whereas letters might refer to specific types: "17a" custodial problems, "17b" control problems, and so on.

2. **Code all the data.** Code all field notes, transcripts, documents, and other materials by placing the assigned number or letter corresponding to each category in the margin. *You should code both positive and negative incidents related to a category.* In analyzing the proposition that attendants discount IQ as an indicator of intelligence, the research coded both supportive ("You can't trust IQ") and nonsupportive ("You can't teach him that much because his IQ is too low") statements.

As you code your data, refine the coding scheme; add, collapse, expand, and redefine the categories. The cardinal rule of coding in qualitative analysis is *make the codes fit the data and not vice versa.* Record any refinements in your master list of categories.

You will notice that some pieces of data fit into two or more coding categories. These should be coded according to all of these categories.

3. **Sort the data into the coding categories.** Sorting data is a noninterpretative, mechanical operation (Drass, 1980). Here the researcher as-

sembles all the data coded according to each category. We do this manually: cut up field notes, transcripts, and other materials and place data relating to each coding category in a separate file folder or manila envelope. When sorting data in this manner, you include enough of the context to understand the data fully. For example, you would include your own questions as well as the informants' answers. It is also a good idea to write down the specific set of materials from which the data were taken, although this is time-consuming. This will enable you to go back to the entire set of notes, transcripts, or documents to clear up any loose ends. *Be sure to keep a set of materials intact.*

Drass (1980) and Seidel and Clark[2] have developed computer programs to handle the mechanical phase of qualitative data analysis. Drass' program is called LISPQUAL and Seidel and Clark's is called THE ETHNOGRAPH. Both programs are designed to store, sort, and retrieve qualitative data. Drass notes that LISPQUAL also can be used to prepare "quasi-statistics," such as the frequency of positive and negative incidents bearing on a proposition. Either program can be used on home or microcomputers. The purpose of both programs is to serve as a "mechanical clerk." Drass and Seidel and Clark recognize that computers cannot be used as a substitute for the researcher's insight and intuition in interpreting data.[3]

4. See what data are left out. After you have coded and sorted all your data, review the remaining data that are left out of the analysis. Some of these data will probably fit into existing coding categories. You may also come up with new categories that are related to those you have already developed and the underlying story-line. It should be noted, though, that *no study uses all the data that are collected.* Do not try to force all the data into your analytical scheme if they do not fit.

5. Refine your analysis. By coding and sorting data, you will be able to compare different "pieces" of data relating to each theme, concept, proposition, and so on, and hence refine and tighten up your ideas. You will find that some themes that were once vague and obscure will be clearly illuminated. You are also likely to find that some concepts do not fit the data and some propositions do not hold true. You should be prepared to discard these and develop new ones to accommodate the data.

There are almost always contradictions and negative cases in the data. If you are using an approach such as analytic induction, you will want to modify your interpretations to account for each and every one of these. Most researchers do not do this. In most studies the researcher tries to come up with reasonable conclusions and generalizations based on a preponderance of the data. This is because of the complexity of social life. It is to be expected that people will sometimes say and do things that run counter to what they believe.

You should analyze negative cases to deepen your understanding of the people you are studying. Negative cases are often fruitful sources of insight. Attendants view residents as severely limited in their potential for learning. "These here are all low grades" and "You can't teach them nothing" are typical comments. In reviewing the data the researchers came across a number of statements that countered this perspective. One attendant, who usually denigrated residents' intelligence, commented on one occasion, "Yeah, they're dumb like a fox," implying that residents were smarter than they looked. The researcher explored the meaning of these statements. He discovered that attendants described residents as "smarter than they look" when it came to scolding or punishing them. They were saying that residents "know better" than to cause problems and should be punished for their behavior. These statements were made to account for or justify their treatment of residents. What appeared to be a contradiction initially was resolved through the analytical distinction between perspectives—how people view their world—and accounts—how people justify their actions to themselves and others. Although attendants may genuinely view residents as severely intellectually limited, they express an opposite view when convenient to do so.

There are no guidelines in qualitative research for determining how many data are necessary to support a conclusion or interpretation. This is always a judgment call. The best insights sometimes come from a small amount of data. Glasser and Strauss (1967) argue that a single incident is sufficient for developing a conceptual category for grounded theory.

Some researchers provide quasi-statistical evidence for their conclusions when they write up their findings. In their study of the academic side of college life, Becker, Geer, and Hughes (1968) provide a statistical breakdown of statements and activities supportive of their major thesis on the importance of grades to students. Proof is elusive in qualitative research, though. The qualitative researcher can probably demonstrate plausible support for conclusions and interpretations, but never truly prove them.

Discounting Data

The final phase in qualitative analysis is what Deutscher (1973) and Mills (1940) call *discounting* the data: interpreting them in the context in which they were collected. As Deutscher (1973:5) points out, all data are potentially valuable if we know how to assess their credibility:

> We do, of course, routinely discount history or biography according to what we know about the author . . . We do not discard reports merely because of biases or flaws of one sort or another. If we did, there would be no history. It is all presented by men who have some sort of stake in the matters of which they write, who are located somewhere in their own society (and tend to see the world from that perspective), and whose work is more or less open to methodological criticism. This same observation can be made of all discourse, including social science research reports.

All data must be discounted in this sense. You have to look at how the data were collected in order to understand them. You do not discard anything. You just interpret the data differently depending on the context. There are a number of considerations.

1.   **Solicited or unsolicited data.**   Although qualitative researchers usually try to let people talk about what is on their minds, they are never totally passive. They ask certain kinds of questions and follow up on certain topics. By doing so, they solicit data that may not have emerged on their own.

You should look at whether people say different things in response to your questions as opposed to when they are talking spontaneously. As a check on their data, Becker, Geer, and Hughes (1968) systematically compare volunteered and directed statements from informants. However, a quick review of your data is usually sufficient.

2.   **Observer's influence on the setting.**   Most participant observers try to minimize their effects on the people they are studying until they have grasped a basic understanding of the settings. In the chapter on fieldwork we urged observers to "come on slow" during the early stages of

the research. As we noted in that chapter, participant observers almost always influence the settings they study.

Especially during the first days in the field, informants may be cautious in what they say and do. They may even try to "put the observer on." Attendants admitted to the participant observer that they did many things differently when he first started to visit the ward. One attendant explained how they reacted to outsiders:

> We usually know when someone's comin'—an hour or so beforehand. They let us know when someone's comin' so we can put some clothes on 'em— make sure they're not bare-assed or jerkin' off when someone comes up here. I had some visitors up here today . . . They asked me a bunch of questions. I answered em, but I wasn't gonna overdo it. You know? I wasn't gonna tell 'em everything.

It is important to try to understand one's effects on a setting. As Emerson (1981:365) writes, the participant observer must try "to become sensitive to and perceptive of how one is perceived and treated by others." One way to do this is to look at how people reacted to you at different times in the research. In the institutional study the observer distinguished between these phases in his research according to his acceptance by attendants: (1) Outsider: treated cautiously; (2) Frequent visitor: attendants spoke freely, but remained somewhat guarded in their actions; (3) Casual participant: attendants seemed to speak and act freely; (4) Participant: attendants accepted the observer as "one of their own." Of course, this scheme oversimplifies the fluid nature of field relations. However, by comparing data collected at different phases in the research, the researcher is better equipped to examine how informants' reactions to his or her presence may have influenced what they said and did.

3. Who was there? Just as an observer may influence what an informant may say or do, so too may other people in a setting. For example, attendants act differently around supervisors than they do among themselves; teachers may say something among themselves that they would not say to their principal. You should be alert to differences between what people say and do when they are alone as opposed to when others are around. Becker, Geer, Hughes, and Strauss (1961) tabulate statements and activities according to this dimension as a way of assessing the credibility of evidence in participant observation.

4.   **Direct and indirect data.**   When you analyze your data, you code both direct statements and indirect data bearing on a theme, interpretation, or proposition. The observer concluded that attendants were oriented toward controlling residents, rather than teaching them skills by examining what they say about residents ("You have to control them") and how they act toward them (attendants seldom interact with residents except to tell them what to do). The more you have to read into your data, to draw inferences based on indirect data, the less sure you can be about the validity of your interpretations and conclusions (Becker and Geer, 1957).

5.   **Sources.**   There is a danger of generalizing about a group of people based on what one or a few of them say or do. Some participant observers are so taken in by "key informants," so dependent cn them for information, that they end up with a selective view of a setting. One talkative person can produce reams of data that appear throughout the field notes or transcripts.

For this reason, you should pay attention to the sources of the data on which you base your interpretations. It is all right to look to key informants for critical insights, but you had better be able to distinguish between perspectives held by one person and those of a broader group of people. This is why we usually try to give readers a sense of who said and did what ("one informant," "some people," "most informants," and so on) when we write up our findings.

6.   **Your own assumptions and presuppositions.**   In qualitative methods, as we have described them, the researcher begins the study with a minimum of assumptions and presuppositions. It is impossible to avoid one's own commitments and biases, however. Data are never self-explanatory. All researchers draw on their own theoretical assumptions and cultural knowledge to make sense out of their data.

Probably the best check on the researcher's bias is critical self-reflection. An understanding of one's data requires some understanding of one's own perspectives, logic, and assumptions. As we indicated in the chapter on fieldwork, some researchers record their own feelings and assumptions in "Observer's Comments" throughout their studies as a check on themselves.

Colleagues and even informants who are willing to read draft reports also can assess the validity and credibility of your analysis.

CONSTRUCTING LIFE HISTORIES

The life history contains a description of the important events and experiences in a person's life or some major part of it in his or her own words. In constructing life histories analysis is a process of editing and putting the story together in such a way that it captures the person's own feelings, views, and perspectives.

As a sociological document, the life history should be constructed to illuminate the socially significant features of the person's life. The concept *career* probably provides the most fruitful way of doing this. *The term career refers to the sequence of social positions people occupy through their lives and the changing definitions of themselves and their world they hold at various stages of that sequence.* The concept directs our attention to the fact that people's definitions of themselves and others are not unique or ideosyncratic but, rather, follow a standard and orderly pattern according to the situations in which they find themselves (Goffman, 1961). In putting together the life history, one tries to identify the critical stages and periods in a person's life that shape his or her definitions and perspectives. For example, we can see how the meaning of being labeled mentally retarded changes as people move through infancy, early childhood, secondary age, and adulthood.

In the life history of Jane Fry, her story was organized around her career as a transsexual; that is, the chronology of experiences related to the development of her social identity as a transsexual. The story winds through her family life, high school years, life in the Navy, marriage to a woman, institutionalization as a mental patient, starting out a new life as a woman, and reflections on the future.

All analysis in qualitative research starts with becoming intimately familiar with the data. Read through all transcripts, notes, documents, and other data. Identify the major stages, events, and experiences in the person's life. The life history is constructed by coding and sorting the data according to these stages. Each stage becomes a chapter or section in the life history.

You will not be able to incorporate all the data into the life history. Some stories and topics will not be relevant to your research interests and can be set aside. However, you should try to include all of your data that could change any interpretation of the person's life and experiences (Frazier, 1978).

The final step in assembling the life history is editing the person's accounts of his or her experiences to produce a coherent document. Since people vary in their ability to express themselves clearly, different stories will require different amounts of editing. In our interviewing with people labeled retarded Ed Murphy was much more prone to engage in small talk and going off on tangents than Pattie Burt and hence his story required much more editing.

As a rule, *you should make the life history readable without putting words in the person's mouth or changing the meaning of his or her words.* You can omit repetitious phrases and words, but should include the person's characteristic speech patterns, grammatical constructions, and mispronunciations (if you have the life history published, you will have to be firm with copy editors in this regard). You will have to add connecting passages and phrases to make the person's words understandable. Your questions will sometimes have to be incorporated into the person's answers. For example, the question, "When was the first time you heard about the state school?" and the answer, "It was about a week before I was sent there," can be combined to form the statement, "The first time I heard about the state school was about a week before I was sent there."

In most life histories, the researcher's own comments and interpretations are relegated to the introduction or conclusion. Some researchers such as Sutherland (1937) have used footnotes to clarify and explain their informants' words.

The preceding chapters have dealt with the logic and procedures of qualitative research methods: designing studies, collecting data, and data analysis. After researchers have collected and made sense out of their data, they must decide on how to present their findings and understandings to others. Part 2 of this book is intended to aid the researcher in this endeavor. Chapter 7 provides some general guidance on writing up findings, and Chapters 8 through 11 contain articles based on qualitative research.

NOTES

1. Social scientists sometimes distinguish between the *emic* and the *etic* approach and between *first-order* and *second-order* concepts (Emerson, 1983; Patton, 1980). According to the emic approach, social behavior should be studied in terms of the categories of meaning (concepts, typologies, etc.) of the people under study. These categories of meaning are first-order concepts. In the etic approach, researchers apply their own concepts

to understand the social behavior of the people being studied. These are called second-order concepts, since they are "constructs of the constructs made by actors on the social scene" (Schutz, 1962:6). The first kind of typology we describe relates to the emic approach and first-order concepts; the second relates to the etic approach and second-order concepts. As our discussion indicates, these approaches may be used in a single study.

2. Information on Seidel and Clark's program, THE ETHNOGRAPH, may be obtained from John Seidel (7700 W. Glasgow 14-D, Littleton, CO 80123) or Jack Clark (1020 13th St., Boulder, CO 80302).

3. By contrast, Stone, Dunphy, Smith, and Ogilvie (1966) have developed a computer program that analyzes qualitative data statistically according to a predetermined conceptual framework. This approach is more aligned with traditional quantitative research than with qualitative methods.

Part 2

Writing Up Findings

7

The Presentation of Findings

This chapter deals with the culmination of the research process: the presentation of findings.[1] The purpose of research is not only to increase your own understanding of social life, but also to share that understanding with others.

Many qualitative studies result in dissertations, theses, research reports, and books. There is also a growing number of outlets for research articles based on qualitative methods. In sociology and anthropology, journals such as *Urban Life, Qualitative Sociology,* and *Human Organization* are devoted to studies based on participant observation, in-depth interviewing, and other qualitative approaches. Similarly, *Social Problems* and *Sociological Quarterly* publish a large number of qualitative studies. Professional journals in applied fields such as education, human services, child care, mental retardation, mental health, psychology, and geography are increasingly receptive to qualitative research. Unfortunately, some of the "mainline" sociological journals such as the *American Sociological Review* and the *American Journal of Sociology* serve primarily as outlets for quantitative research and theoretical essays and publish few qualitative studies (Faulkner, 1982). It is ironic to note that the *American Journal of Sociology* is published by the University of Chicago which can rightfully be considered the birthplace of qualitative research in America. However, even journals oriented to "hard-core" quantitative research occasionally publish works based on qualitative methods. The article, "The Judged, Not the Judges," which is reprinted in Chapter 8, originally appeared in *The American Psychologist,* a journal known for its emphasis on "hard science."

This is not the place to discuss how to publish books or articles. Suffice it to say, there are many forums available for publishing qualitative studies. Whether you are able to publish your findings depends on the quality of your work, your perseverence in tracking down an interested publisher or journal, and an element of luck. Keep in mind that even the most productive and insightful researchers have had their works rejected at some time or another.

In the remainder of this chapter we offer some guidelines for writing up qualitative studies and introduce the articles contained in the chapters that follow.

WHAT YOU SHOULD TELL YOUR READERS

As a researcher, *you owe it to your readers to explain how you collected and interpreted your data.* You should give readers enough information about how the research was conducted to enable them to *discount* your findings; to understand them in context (Deutscher, 1973). There is a tendency among many researchers to gloss over the specifics of their methodology. When we read these studies, we have no way of knowing whether the findings came from cultural knowledge, prior theoretical frameworks, direct personal experience, or actual fieldwork and interviewing (and if so, what kind of fieldwork or interviewing). Hence we do not know how to judge the credibility and validity of the researcher's account.

The controversy surrounding the popular writings of Carlos Castenada (1968, 1971, 1972, 1974, 1977) and his dissertation approved for a PhD in anthropology (1973) illustrates why it is so important for researchers to provide sufficient details about how their studies were conducted. Writer, psychologist, and self-taught anthropologist Richard de Mille (1976, 1980), joined by numerous social scientists, makes a convincing case that Castenada's wonderfully entertaining and in many ways insightful works are a hoax. By identifying internal inconsistencies in Castenada's books, comparing his writings to those in philosophy and religion, and examining factual inaccuracies in his stories, de Mille concludes that what Castenada passes off as ethnographic fieldwork is actually fiction based on library research. Castenada offers little with which to defend himself against these charges. Not only does he fail to describe how his fieldwork was conducted, but has not produced the evidence, such as detailed fieldnotes, that would support his story.

Some of Castenada's defenders take the position that his writings teach important lessons about the nature of reality and knowledge systems. There may be an element of truth in this. Popular fiction can also contain sociological insights. Yet there is a difference between telling a good sociological story, on the one hand, and accurately describing a way of life, on the other. Readers have a right to know which is which. That is enough said about this controversy.

Although few researchers fabricate their research, it is probably true, as Jack Douglas (1976:xiii) argues, that most or perhaps all research reports are laundered: ". . . authors choose to leave certain important parts of the context out, certain details about what really happened, how they really got their data or failed to do so." We can only hope that researchers will be as candid as possible in giving us the details we need to understand and interpret their findings. John Johnson's (1975) intimate account of his field of research is exemplary in this regard.

We can outline some basic points researchers should cover in reporting their studies that, although not covering the full story, will help readers begin to assess the credibility of the findings. All the following points should be addressed in a full-length book or research report. For shorter pieces and journal articles, space limitations probably preclude covering all these points, at least in detail. You must always ask yourself whether you have explained all that readers need to know.

1. *Methodology.* You should inform your readers of the general methodology (participant observation, in-depth interviewing, documents,

etc.) and specific research procedures (covert or overt research, mechanical recording devices) used in your study. Since the phrases "participant observation" and "in-depth interviewing" mean different things to different people, you should be as specific as possible in explaining your methods. If you identify with a particular approach, such as Douglas' (1976) investigative research paradigm, you should tell this to your readers.

2. *Time and length of study.* Your readers should know how much time you spent with informants and over what time frame.

3. *Nature and number of settings and informants.* What kinds of settings did you study? How many were there? Who were the informants? How many did you interview?

4. *Research design.* You should explain how you identified and selected settings, informants, and documents. Did theoretical sampling or analytic induction guide your selection? Did you know the settings or informants beforehand?

5. *Your own frame of mind.* What was your original purpose? How did this change over time? How did you come to understand the setting or informants?

6. *Your relationship with informants.* You should discuss how and to what extent you established rapport with people. How did informants see you? How did your relationship with them change over time?

7. *Checks on your data.* How did you analyze your data? What checks did you impose on informants' statements? Did informants review your findings? What did they say?

A NOTE ON WRITING

Some have joked that to be a social scientist is to be a poor writer (Cowley, 1956). Many important ideas are obscured and many trivial ones made to sound profound through jargon and excessive verbiage (Mills, 1959).

The ability to write clearly and concisely is an important skill. Like the many other skills discussed in this book, it is learned through practice, discipline, and exposure to exemplary works. There are no quick and easy ways to become a good writer, but the following suggestions may be useful when writing up your findings.

1. *Outline your thoughts on paper before you begin to write.* What you have learned in your research—your concepts, interpretations, and propositions—should provide a structure for your writing. Decide on a story-line, the major point you want to make in the piece, and show how each specific point relates to it. Remember that you cannot include all of your interpretations and data in any single writing. Treat the outline as a flexible working model, something that can be revised as you write.

2. *Decide what audience you want to reach and adjust your style and content accordingly.* It is useful to have a specific audience or type of reader in mind when you write. One writes differently for qualitative sociologists, a general sociological audience, professionals in applied fields, and so on. Try to put yourself in the role of the reader: "Will he or she understand what I'm saying?"

This is not to say that you should skew your findings to please readers. It is true, as Warren (1980) argues, however, that researchers take into account the anticipated reactions of colleagues, friends, journal editors, informants, and others when they prepare research reports and this influences "the cumulation of knowledge we call science."

3. *Let your readers know where you are going.* Help your readers by telling them your purpose early in the writing and explain how each topic relates to this along the way. This will also help you keep on track.

4. *Be concise and direct.* Use short sentences and direct words as much as possible. Social scientists have been accused of using complicated words when there are simple ones available. Malcolm Cowley (1956) brings home this point with the following example:

> A child says "Do it again," a teacher says "Repeat that exercise," but the sociologist says "It was determined to replicate the investigation." Instead of saying two things are alike or similar, as a layman would do, the sociologist describes them as being either isomorphic or homologous. Instead of saying that they are different he calls them allotropic. . . .
>
> . . . A sociologist never cuts anything in half or divides it in two like a layman. Instead he dichotomizes it, bifurcates it, subjects it to a process of binary fission, or restructures it in a dyadic conformation—around a polar foci.

5. *Ground your writing in specific examples.* Qualitative research yields rich descriptions. Illustrative quotations and descriptions convey a deep understanding of what settings and people are like and provide

evidence that things are the way you report them to be. Your research report should be filled with clear examples. These should be short and to the point, however. Most readers find it tedious to read through long quotes.

You should resist the temptation to overuse colorful data. No single quote or description should be used more than once. If you cannot find alternative examples, the point you are trying to make may not be as important as you thought. Irwin Deutscher tells us in a personal communication that he marks "used" across materials after they have been quoted to make sure he does not repeat anything.

6. *Get something down on paper.* Some people experience "writer's block" the moment they sit down to type or write something. The only way to overcome this is to get something, *anything,* down on paper. Concentrate on expressing your ideas. You can edit later.

Most writers write several drafts of a paper. Let the first draft flow freely. After you have completed this draft, leave it for a day or two to gain some detachment. When you go back for a second try, eliminate unnecessary words, sentences, phrases, and paragraphs. For most writers, the first draft can be reduced by as much as one-quarter without a loss in content. Some people can write one draft which only needs minor editing the second time around. One of us labors over writing an initial draft, but what results is usually close to the final version.

7. *Have colleagues or friends read and comment on your writing.* Even if someone is not familiar with your field, he or she can critique your writing in regard to clarity and logic. A good reader is someone who is not afraid to provide you with critical comments and gets around to reviewing your work within a couple of weeks.

THE PRESENTATION OF FINDINGS: SELECTED STUDIES

Chapters 8 through 12 contain articles written by ourselves and colleagues based on the methods described in this book. They are examples of some of the ways in which qualitative studies can be presented. Of course, they reflect our own interests, values, and theoretical framework.

"The Judged, Not the Judges: An Insider's View of Mental Retardation" is an abbreviated version of a life history (Ed Murphy's full life history, as well as Pattie Burt's, is contained in the book, *Inside Out*).

The life history itself represents pure description: Ed's own story in his own words, as told during tape-recorded in-depth interviews and edited and compiled by us. However, in the introduction and conclusion of this piece, we outline our own perspective on the social meaning of mental retardation and comment briefly on the general lessons to be learned from Ed's story.

When first published in 1976, "The Judged, Not the Judges" sparked numerous reactions and requests for reprints from qualitative researchers, psychologists, and professionals in the field of mental retardation. Many readers viewed the article as a sensitive and moving account of the experiences of a person who had been subjected to societal prejudice and discrimination. The story stood as an indictment of the treatment of the so-called retarded in our society. However, some readers tried to dismiss what we say are the lessons from Ed's story by viewing his situation as an unfortunate case of misdiagnosis. In other words, they assumed that because Ed is perceptive and articulate, he could not be retarded. Yet we can assure readers that Ed is "mentally retarded" by any definition. If the concept does not fit, it is not because of misdiagnosis, but because the concept is defective.

Chapter 9 contains an article entitled "Be Honest But Not Cruel: Staff/Parent Communication on a Neonatal Unit," co-authored by Robert Bogdan, Mary Alice Brown, and Susan Bannerman Foster. The article is based on participant observation and interviewing. Although it cannot be considered a pure ethnography, the article is largely descriptive. The authors focus on hospital staff members' perspectives on and typologies of premature and fragile infants and their families. The title of the article comes from the hospital staff and conveys their perspective on communicating with parents.

The article in Chapter 10, "Let Them Eat Programs: Attendants' Perspectives and Programming on Wards in State Schools," was based on participant observation research at three different institutions for the mentally retarded. It is co-authored by Bogdan and Taylor and Bernard deGrandpre and Sandra Haynes. The article falls halfway between a descriptive and theoretical piece. After describing common perspectives among attendants at the institutions, the authors link these perspectives to the implementation of "innovative programs" designed by supervisory and professional staff. They show how attendants watered down or altered the programs in line with their perspectives on superiors and professionals, their work, and residents. The title is meant to capture the irony of programming at institutions which by their nature isolate, desocialize, and dehumanize those they are designed to serve.

The article in Chapter 11, "National Policy and Situated Meaning," looks at the impact of a national mandate on local programs from a symbolic interactionist perspective. Based on participant observation and informal interviews conducted by researchers at 30 Head Start centers, the study examines what happened when these programs were mandated to serve 10 percent children with disabilities. This study is an example of qualitative evaluation or policy research (Patton, 1980). In contrast to other forms of evaluation research, a qualitative approach directs attention to *how* things work and not whether they work. After an indepth look at how the national mandate affected the perspectives, meanings, and practices of local Head Start personnel, the article moves to a general sociological analysis of the effects of "counting," the production of official statistics, and labeling of clients.

Like "Let Them Eat Programs," "Defending Illusions: The Institution's Struggle for Survival" focuses on the substantive area of total institutions for the "mentally retarded." However, this article is more oriented toward sociological theory: how institutional "standard bearers," or spokespersons, symbolically manage the discrepancy between formal goals and actual practices and conditions. By citing studies of other types of organizations, the authors attempt to expand their theoretical insights to apply to how organizations in general legitimate themselves.

"Defending Illusions" is based largely on data from participant observation and interviewing at 15 separate institutions. The authors also draw on a range of other sources of data, including written materials from institutions, newspaper accounts, court cases, and casual contacts with institutional officials.

NOTE

1. For a critique of styles of reporting qualitative research, see Lofland (1974). See Davis (1974) and Roth (1974) for researchers' accounts of how they reported their findings.

8

The Judged, Not the Judges

AN INSIDER'S VIEW OF MENTAL RETARDATION

If one wishes to understand the term holy water, one should not study the properties of the water, but rather the assumptions and beliefs of the people who use it. That is, holy water derives its meaning from those who attribute a special essence to it (Szasz, 1974).

Similarly, the meaning of the term mental retardation depends on those who use it to describe the cognitive states of other people. As some have argued, mental retardation is a social construction or a concept that exists in the minds of the "judges" rather than in the minds of the "judged" (Blatt, 1970; Braginsky and Braginsky, 1971; Dexter, 1964; Hurley, 1969; Mercer, 1973). A mentally retarded person is one who has been labeled as such according to rather arbitrarily created and applied criteria.

Retardate and other such clinical labels suggest generalizations about the nature of men and women to whom that term has been applied (Goffman, 1963). We assume that the mentally retarded possess common characteristics that allow them to be unambiguously distinguished from all others. We explain their behavior by special theories. It is as though humanity can be divided into two groups, the "normal" and the "retarded."

Robert Bogdan and Steven Taylor. This article was originally published in the *American Psychologist*, Vol. 31, No. 1, January 1976, 47–52.

To be labeled retarded is to have a wide range of imperfections imputed to you. One imperfection is the inability to analyze your life and your current situation. Another is the inability to express yourself—to know and say who you are and what you wish to become.

In the pages that follow we present the edited transcripts of some of the discussions we have had over the past year with a 26-year-old man we will call Ed Murphy. (For methodology, see Bogdan, 1974, and Bogdan and Taylor, 1975.) Ed has been labeled mentally retarded by his family, school teachers, and others in his life. At the age of 15 he was placed in a state institution for the retarded. His institutional records, as do many professionals with whom he has come into contact, describe him as "a good boy, but easily confused; mental retardation—cultural–familial type." Ed currently works as a janitor in a large urban nursing home and lives in a boarding house with four other men who, like himself, are former residents of state institutions.

AN INSIDER'S VIEW

When I was born the doctors didn't give me six months to live. My mother told them that she could keep me alive, but they didn't believe it. It took a hell of a lot of work, but she showed with love and determination that she could be the mother to a handicapped child. I don't know for a fact what I had, but they thought it was severe retardation and cerebral palsy. They thought I would never walk. I still have seizures. Maybe that has something to do with it too.

My first memory is about my grandmother. She was a fine lady. I went to visit her right before she died. I knew she was sick, but I didn't realize that I would never see her again. I was special in my grandmother's eyes. My mother told me that she had a wish—it was that I would walk. I did walk, but it wasn't until the age of four. She prayed that she would see that day. My mother told me the story again and again of how, before she died, I was at her place. She was on the opposite side of the room and called, "Walk to grandma, walk to grandma," and I did. I don't know if I did as good as I could, but I did it. Looking back now it makes me feel good. It was frustrating for my parents that I could not walk. It was a great day in everybody's life.

The doctors told my mother that I would be a burden to her. When I was growing up she never let me out of her sight. She was always there with attention. If I yelled she ran right to me. So many children who are handicapped must be in that position—they become so dependent on their mother. Looking back I don't think she ever stopped protecting me even when I was capable of being self-sufficient. I remember how hard it was to break away from that. She never really believed that after I had lived the first six months that I could be like everybody else.

I remember elementary school; my mind used to drift a lot. When I was at school, concentrating was almost impossible. I was so much into my own thoughts—my daydreams—I wasn't really in class. I would think of the cowboy movies—the rest of the kids would be in class and I would be on the battlefield someplace. The nuns would yell at me to snap out of it, but they were nice. That was my major problem all through school—that I daydreamed. I think all people do that. It wasn't related to retardation. I think a lot of kids do that and are diagnosed as retarded, but it has nothing to do with retardation at all. It really has to do with how people deal with the people around them and their situation. I don't think I was bored. I think all the kids were competing to be the honor students, but I was never interested in that. I was in my own world—I was happy. I wouldn't recommend it to someone, but daydreaming can be a good thing. I kind of stood in the background—I kind of knew that I was different—I knew that I had a problem, but when you're young you don't think of it as a problem. A lot of people are like I was. The problem is getting labeled as being something. After that you're not really a person. It's like a sty in your eye—it's noticeable. Like that teacher and the way she looked at me. In the fifth grade—in the fifth grade my classmates thought I was different, and my teacher knew I was different. One day she looked at me and she was on the phone to the office. Her conversation was like this, "When are you going to transfer him?" This was the phone in the room. I was there. She looked at me and knew I was knowledgeable about what she was saying. Her negative picture of me stood out like a sore thumb.

My mother protected me. It wasn't wrong that she protected me, but there comes a time when someone has to come in and break them away. I can remember trying to be like the other kids and having my mother right there pulling me away. She was always worried about me. You can't force yourself to say to your mother: "Stop, I can do it myself." Sometimes I think the pain of being handicapped is that people give you so much love that it becomes a weight on you and a weight on them. There is no way that you can break from it without hurting them—without bad feelings—guilt. It is like a trap because of the fact that you are restricted to your inner thoughts. After a while you resign yourself to it. The trap is that you can't tell them, "Let me go." You have to live with it and suffer. It has to do with pity. Looking back on it I can't say it was wrong. She loved me. You do need special attention, but the right amount.

One time maybe when I was 13, I was going to camp and had to go to the place where the buses left. My mother kept asking me if I had everything and telling me where my bags were and if I was all right. It is similar to the way other mothers act, but it sticks out in my mind. I was striving to be a normal boy so it meant more to me. After my mother went back to the car the other kids on the bus kidded me. They said things like, "Momma's boy." That's the one that sticks out in my memory.

I liked camp. The staff and counselors were good. I had this thing with my legs. They weren't very strong. When I fell back from the group on a hike I was light enough so that they could give me a ride on their backs. I had the best seat on the hike. Looking back on being carried, they would have lost me if they didn't. I was glad that I was light because it was easier for them. I needed help and they helped. I didn't mind being carried. The important thing was that I was there and that I was taking part in the events like everybody else.

I remember the day the press came. It was an annual award day. They came to write up the story. The best camper got his picture in the paper. My name was in the paper. I got a patch for being a good camper. It was something that I had accomplished and felt pretty good about. My mother kept the article and the neighbors knew too.

In January of 1963, without any warning, my father died. A couple months later, Ma died too. It was hard on us—my sister and me. We stayed with friends of the family for a while, but then they moved. They told us we had to go. So they sent us to an orphanage for a few months, but eventually we wound up at the State School. I was 15 then.

Right before they sent me and my sister to the State School, they had six psychologists examine us to determine how intelligent we were. I think that was a waste of time. They asked me things like, "What comes to mind when I say 'Dawn'?"—so you say, "Light." Things like that. What was tough was putting the puzzles together and the mechanical stuff. They start out very simple and then they build it up and it gets harder and harder.

If you're going to do something with a person's life you don't have to pay all that money to be testing them. I had no place else to go. I mean here I am pretty intelligent and here are six psychologists testing me and sending me to the State School. How would you feel if you were examined by all those people and then wound up where I did? A psychologist is supposed to help you. The way they talked to me they must have thought I was fairly intelligent. One of them said, "You look like a smart young man," and then I turned up there. I don't think the tests made any difference. They had their minds made up anyway.

Another guy I talked to was a psychiatrist. That was rough. For one thing I was mentally off guard. You're not really prepared for any of it. You don't figure what they're saying and how you're answering it and what it all means—not until the end. When the end came, I was a ward of the State.

I remember the psychiatrist well. He was short and middle-aged and had a foreign accent. The first few minutes he asked me how I felt and I replied, "Pretty good." Then I fell right into his trap. He asked if I thought people hated me and I said "Yes." I started getting hyper-nervous. By then he had the hook in the fish, and there was no two ways about it. He realized I was nervous and ended the interview. He was friendly and he fed me the bait. The thing was that it ended so fast. After I got out I realized that I had screwed up. I cried. I was upset. He came on like he wanted honest answers but being honest in that situation doesn't get you any place but the State School.

When the psychiatrist interviewed me he had my records in front of him—so he already knew I was mentally retarded. It's the same with everyone. If you are considered mentally retarded there is no way you can win. There is no way they give you a favorable report. They put horses out of misery quicker than they do people. It's a real blow to you being sent to the State School.

I remember the day they took me and my sister. We knew where we were going, but we didn't know anything specific about it. It was scary.

To me there never was a State School. The words State School sound like a place with vocational training or you get some sort of education. That's just not the way Empire State School is. They have taken millions of dollars and spent them and never rehabilitated who they were supposed to. If you looked at individuals and see what they said they were supposed to do for that person and then what they actually did, you would find that many of them were actually hurt—not helped. I don't like the word vegetable, but in my own case I could see that if I had been placed on the low grade ward I might have slipped to that. I began feeling myself slip. They could have made me a vegetable. If I would have let that place get to me and depress me I would still have been there today.

Actually, it was one man that saved me. They had me scheduled to go to P-8—a back ward—when just one man looked at me. I was a wreck. I had a beard and baggy State clothes on. I had just arrived at the place. I was trying to understand what was happening. I was confused. What I looked like was P-8 material. There was this supervisor, a woman. She came on to the ward and looked right at me and said, "I have him scheduled for P-8." An older attendant was there. He looked at me and said, "He's too bright for that ward. I think we'll keep him." To look at me then I didn't look good. She made a remark under her breath that I looked pretty retarded to her. She saw me looking at her—I looked her square in the eye. She had on a white dress and a cap with three stripes— I can still see them now. She saw me and said, "Just don't stand there, get to work."

Of course I didn't know what P-8 was then, but I found out. I visited up there a few times on work detail. That man saved my life. Here was a woman that I had never known who they said was the building supervisor looking over me. At that point I'm pretty positive that if I went there I would have fitted in and I would still be there.

I remember the day that Bobby Kennedy came. That was something. All day long we knew he was coming and he walked around. I got a look at him. He told everybody what a snake pit the place was so it was better for a few days. At least he got some people interested for a while. I really admired that man. You take a lot of crusaders though, like local politicians, they go over to the State School and do a lot of yelling. They only do it when someone forces them to, like when someone gets something in the paper about someone being beaten or is overdosed bad. The newest thing at Empire was someone yelled sodomy. Some parent found out about it and called the legislator. Big deal. If they knew what was going on it wouldn't be that big a deal—one incident of sodomy. Hell, for that matter they ought to look around them and see what the people on the outside are doing sexually.

It's funny. You hear so many people talking about IQ. The first time I ever heard the expression was when I was at Empire State School. I didn't know what it was or anything, but some people were talking and they brought the subject up. It was on the ward, and I went and asked one of the staff what mine was. They told me 49. Forty-nine isn't 50, but I was pretty happy about it. I mean I figured that I wasn't a low grade. I really didn't know what it meant, but it sounded pretty high. Hell, I was born in 1948 and 49 didn't sound too bad. Forty-nine didn't sound hopeless. I didn't know anything about the highs or the lows, but I knew I was better than most of them.

Last week was the first time I went into a state school since I was discharged as a ward of the state—which makes it about three years. I just went up to visit. I purposely avoided going there. I have been nervous about it. There are good memories and bad memories. The whole idea of having been in a state school makes you nervous about why you were ever put there in the first place. I'm out now, but I was on that side of the fence once. It has less to do with what I am doing than with how the game is played. Being in a state school or having been in a state school isn't fashionable and never will be. Deep down you want to avoid the identification. If I could convince myself that in the end they are going to be cleaned up I might feel better about it. You have got to face the enemy and that's what it is like.

I have come from being a resident of a state school to being on the other side saying they're no good. It has been brought up to me—"Where the hell would you be if it wasn't for the State School." That holds water, but now the dam is drying up as I am on this side. Sure I had a need, but they kind of pitched you a low pitch. There wasn't anything better. I needed a place to go, but unfortunately there was no choice of where to go. When it's all said and done there were those at the school that helped me so I'm grateful, but still some other place would have been better.

I guess the State School wasn't all that bad. It was tough to leave though. You had all your needs taken care of there. You didn't have to worry about where your next meal was coming from or where you were going to sleep.

I don't have it that bad right now. I have my own room and I get my meals at the house. The landlord is going to up the rent though—$45 a week for room and board. I'll be able to pay it, but I don't know what Frank and Lou across the hall will do. They wash dishes at the steak house and don't take home that much.

It's really funny. Sunday I got up and went for a walk. All of a sudden

Joan's name came to my mind. She's sort of my girlfriend. I don't know why, but I just thought of her moving in next door to the place where I live. That would be something.

Is there still any magnetism between that woman and me? I haven't seen her in three months, but there is still something, I can tell. We had a good thing going. I opened her up a lot mentally. I saw a very different person there than others see. I saw a woman that could do something with her life. If she could wake up one morning and say to herself, "I am going to do something with my life," she could. I don't think that retardation is holding her back so much as emotional problems. If she had confidence that would make the difference. I know she could build herself up.

The family had respect for me, at least to a point, but they don't think she should marry. We got pretty close psychologically and physically— not that I did anything. They don't have programs at the Association for Retarded Children that say to adults you are an adult and you can make it. She has been at the ARC for a long time now. She was a bus- aide, so in one way they showed her that she could work but on the other hand they didn't build her confidence enough to feel that she could go out to work.

The last time I saw her she didn't say a word. When she is pissed off at the world she is pissed off. That's the Irish in her. In my opinion she doesn't belong at the ARC. But one thing is her parents don't want to take chances. Like a lot of the parents, they send their 30-year-old kids with Snoopy lunch pails. They are afraid financially and I can't blame them. If she went out on her own they are afraid that her Social Security would stop and then if she could continue they wouldn't have anything. She could lose her benefits.

I first met Joan in 1970. It was when I started working at the ARC workshop. I sat there and maybe the second or third day I glanced over and saw her there. The first time I noticed her was in the eating area; I was having lunch. I looked around and she was the only one there that attracted me. There was just something about her. At first she wasn't that easy to get along with. She put on the cold shoulder and that made me think about her more.

One time I had a fight with one of the boys in the workshop. He was her old boyfriend. This day I was getting off the bus and he said that I pushed him. He pushed me and then when we went to the locker room

it got rougher. I yelled to him, "Get away from me." I started cursing
and we started swinging. I guess he was jealous that Joan was spending
so much time talking to me. He was a big guy and he hit me in the
mouth and cut it. The staff came and broke it up. They treated it like
the whole thing was a joke. They thought it was cute, the two of us
fighting over Joan. They ribbed us about it like they always rib about
boyfriends and girlfriends.

It took a while for her to understand how she felt. She didn't want
to be too friendly. She didn't like me putting my arm around her. We
went for walks during lunch and she got pretty fond of me and I got
pretty fond of her. One day I asked her, "Well, how about a movie?"
She said, "All right," but she had to get her mother's permission. Then
one day she said she could go. It was a Saturday matinee gangster movie.
We arranged to meet at the bus stop downtown. I remember that I got
down there early and bought the tickets before she came. I met her at
the stop and then I went up to the ticket office with the tickets in my
hand. I was a little fuzzy, nervous, you might say. Of course, you were
supposed to give the tickets to the man inside. The ticket woman looked
at me—sort of stared and motioned with her finger. It was kind of funny
considering our ages. I was 22 and she was 28. It was like teenagers going
on our first date.

Being at the State School and all you never have the chances roman-
tically like you might living on the outside. I guess I was always shy
with the opposite sex even at Empire. We did have dances and I felt
that I was good looking, but I was bashful and mostly sat. I was bashful
with Joan at the movie. In my mind I felt funny, awkward. I didn't know
how to approach her. Should I hug her? You can't hug the hell out of her
because you don't know how she would take it. You have all the feeling
there, but you don't know what direction to go in. If you put your arm
around her she might scream and you're finished. If she doesn't scream
you're still finished.

I never thought of myself as a retarded individual but who would
want to. You're not knowledgeable about what they are saying behind
your back. You get a feeling from people around you; they try to hide
it but their intentions don't work. They say they will do this and that—
like they will look out for you—they try to protect you but you feel sort
of guilty. You get the feeling that they love you but that they are looking
down at you. You always have that sense of a barrier between you and the

ones that love you. By their own admission of protecting you you have an umbrella over you that tells you that you and they have an understanding that there is something wrong—that there is a barrier.

As I got older I slowly began to find myself becoming mentally awake. I found myself concentrating. Like on the television. A lot of people wonder why I have good grammar. It was because of the television. I was like a tape recorder—what I heard I memorized. Even when I was 10 or 12 I would listen to Huntley and Brinkley. They were my favorites. As the years went by I understood what they were talking about. People were amazed at what I knew. People would begin to ask me what I thought about this and that. Like my aunt would always ask me about the news—what my opinions were. I began to know that I was a little brighter than they thought I was. It became a hobby. I didn't know what it meant—that I had a grasp on a lot of important things—the race riots, Martin Luther King in jail—what was really happening was that I was beginning to find something else instead of just being bored. It was entertaining. I didn't know that that meant anything then. I mean I didn't know that I would be sitting here telling you all this. When you're growing up you don't think of yourself as a person but as a boy. As you get older it works itself out—who you are deep down—who you ought to be. You have an image of yourself deep down. You try to sort it all out. You know what you are deep inside but those around you give you a negative picture of yourself. It's that umbrella over you.

What is retardation? It's hard to say. I guess it's having problems thinking. Some people think that you can tell if a person is retarded by looking at them. If you think that way you don't give people the benefit of the doubt. You judge a person by how they look or how they talk or what the tests show, but you can never really tell what is inside the person.

Take a couple of friends of mine, Tommy McCann and PJ. Tommy was a guy who was really nice to be with. You could sit down with him and have a nice conversation and enjoy yourself. He was a mongoloid. The trouble was people couldn't see beyond that. If he didn't look that way it would have been different, but there he was locked into what the other people thought he was. Now PJ was really something else. I've watched that guy and I can see in his eyes that he is aware. He knows what's going on. He can only crawl and he doesn't talk, but you don't know what's inside. When I was with him and I touched him, I know that he knows.

I don't know. Maybe I used to be retarded. That's what they said anyway. I wish they could see me now. I wonder what they'd say if they could see me holding down a regular job and doing all kinds of things. I bet they wouldn't believe it.

CONCLUSION

Ed's story stands by itself as a rich source of understanding. We will resist the temptation to analyze it and reflect on what it tells us about Ed. Our position is that at times and to a much greater extent than we do now, we must listen to people who have been labeled retarded with the idea of finding out about ourselves, our society, and the nature of the label (Becker, 1966).

There are specifics that can be learned from stories such as Ed's (for discussion, see Allport, 1942; Becker, 1966; Bogdan, 1974). For example, his story clearly illustrates that mental retardation is a demeaning concept that leads to a number of penalties for those so labeled. These penalties include lowered self-image and limited social and economic opportunity. Also, his story shows the profound effect of early prognosis on how people are treated and on the way that they think about themselves. It clearly demonstrates how segregated living environments and facilities such as state schools severely limit basic socialization for skills that are needed to participate in the larger society. His story also illustrates how being institutionalized is a function of a variety of social and economic contingencies—family difficulties, lack of alternatives—more than the nature of the person's disability or treatment needs. It also touches on the difficulties faced by people who are "protected." We can more accurately assess the resentment and the restrictions this protection imposes. We can also see the profound effects of simple words of praise and rejection on the person's self-concept. Ed's story points to how some people who work "with" the so-called "retarded" develop joking styles that minimize the real and normal problems and conflicts that the labeled is attempting to deal with and how the object of them feels about this. Although his story mentions all these specifics, there are two general points that we should remember.

The first point is simple but is seldom taken into account in conducting research or planning programs. People who are labeled retarded have their own understandings about themselves, their situation, and their experiences. These understandings are often different from those of the professionals. For example, although cure and treatment might dominate the official views of state schools and rehabilitation centers and programs, boredom, manipulation, coercion, and embarrassment often constitute the client's view. In our own work interviewing labeled people (Bogdan, 1974), and in Ed's story, the vocabulary of the therapist often contradicts that of the patient. The handicapped—the so-called "retarded"—respond to therapy and services according to how they perceive it, not according to how the staff sees it. Devaluing an individual's perspective by viewing it as naive, unsophisticated, immature, or a symptom of some underlying pathology can make research one-sided and service organizations places where rituals are performed in the name of science.

The second area that his story points to has to do with the lack of alternative ways that those who are "different" have to conceptualize their situation.

The present state of such fields as mental retardation is controlled by powerful ideological monopolies. As Ed's story suggests, there is a dearth of definitions in our society and few divergent agencies that provide individuals who are mentally and physically different and struggling and suffering with ways of conceptualizing themselves other than the demeaning vocabulary of "sickness," "handicapped," and "deviant," of which "retardate" is a part.

The categories available to place individuals cannot help but affect how we feel about them and how they feel about themselves. When we present "subjects" or "clients" as numbers or as diagnostic categories, we do not engender in others a feeling of respect for or closeness to the people being discussed. Such views of human beings are not evil or unnecessary, but they comprise only a single view. Overemphasis on this view without presenting the subjective side distorts our knowledge in a dangerous way. (Social scientists presenting the alternative view include Coles, 1971; Cottle, 1971, 1972, 1973; Lewis, 1962; Shaw, 1966; Sutherland, 1937.)

Traditionally, social scientists have studied the retarded as a separate category of human beings, and by doing this they have accepted common sense definitions. It is assumed that the retardate is basically different from the rest of us and that he or she needs to be explained by special theories distinct from those used to explain the behavior of "regular" people. By taking this approach, social scientists have contributed to and have legitimized common sense classifications of individuals as "normal" and "retarded." We have told the world that there are two kinds of human beings. Ed's own words are a form of data and a source of understanding that permit us to know a person intimately. By sharing his life we can approach the concept of intelligence in its more human dimensions. It is through this intimacy that we learn how the subject views himself or herself, and what he or she has in common with all of us becomes clear. Differences take on less importance. The person's own words force us to think of subjects as people, and categories of all kinds become less relevant.

9

Be Honest but Not Cruel

STAFF/PARENT COMMUNICATION ON A NEONATAL UNIT

INTRODUCTION

The second time we visited an intensive care ward for infants (neonatal unit) we witnessed an event that foreshadowed the focus of the research reported here. A couple had come to visit their three-quarter kg critically ill, premature son. They were rural poor, in their early twenties, and had driven 128 km that morning for the visit. They taped the carnation they bought at the hospital gift shop onto the heavy steel pole that held a heater over the open plastic box in which their child lay. Both stood near the child talking to each other and to the fragile infant, "You be home soon fella," the father said to his son. His mother added, "Everything's all ready for you." A nurse, standing within hearing distance, approached the couple and said, "Now, you have to be realistic, you have a very sick baby." That night the baby died. When the parents were told they were overpowered with grief. The mother said that the news took her completely by surprise. Staff/parent communication became the focus of our field research study of neonatal units. Specifically, we became interested in developing an understanding of: Who talks to parents about their child's condition? What do they say? What do parents hear?

Robert Bogdan, Mary Alice Brown, and Susan Bannerman Foster. This article originally appeared in *Human Organization*, 41(1): 6–16, 1982.

What physicians tell patients (Cartwright, 1964, 1967; Waitzkin and Stoeckle, 1972) and parents of juvenile patients (F. Davis, 1960, 1963; Korsch, 1974; Skipper and Leonard, 1968) has been the subject of social science investigation for as long as there has been a social science of medicine (Parsons, 1951). Of special interest has been the communication of bad news (McIntosh, 1979), of pending death (Friedman et al., 1963), of chronic disease (Glaser and Strauss, 1965, 1968), and of disabling physical and mental abnormalities (Jacobs, 1969; Taichert, 1975).[1]

Most discussions of doctor/patient relationships start with Parsons (Parsons, 1951) and his social system model, which posits a stable and complementary interaction between physicians and patients. Some studies are based on these functionalist assumptions (Fox, 1959; Merton, 1957). Others have challenged these assumptions (Emerson, 1970; Friedson, 1962, 1970; Jacobs, 1971; Stimson, 1974; Voysey, 1972a, 1972b, 1975). Friedson (1962, 1970) suggests a clash of perspectives inherent in the doctor/patient relationship. There are studies that show that patients tend to be more dissatisfied about the information they receive and how they receive it than any other aspect of health care (Cartwright, 1964; Duff and Hollingshead, 1968; Korsch, 1974; Korsch et al., 1968). Roth (1958), in his study of tuberculosis treatment, emphasizes the negotiation between the physician and patient about the "timetable" of treatment and the miscommunication of news. F. Davis (1960, 1963) has studied polio victims and their families and provides a typology of what physicians tell and do not tell parents under conditions of medical uncertainty.

The study reported here lies within the interactionist tradition (also see Glaser and Strauss, 1967). Rather than focusing on communication with patients with particular diseases, or on adults who have terminal illness, we look at parents of infants with a variety of life-threatening and potentially disabling conditions (Duff and Campbell, 1973; Jonsen and Lister, 1978). In addition, researchers often study a topic such as professional/parent communication as an isolated occurrence, that is, without an understanding of the setting in which it occurs (e.g., Clyman et al., 1979; Wiener, 1970), whereas our emphasis here is the context of communication on neonatal units, stressing how the staff perceives the units and highlighting aspects of the units that relate to staff/parent communication. We deal with the staff's way of categorizing infants, parents, and each other. In addition, we describe perspectives they share that relate to talking to parents about their children. Then we introduce the parents' world—how they experience the unit and what influences what they hear when the staff speaks. We conclude with a discussion of the implications of our findings for theory, method, practice, and social policy.

Neonatal Unit

High technology neonatal units became a part of the medical scene during the past decade. The particular units we are concerned with are part of recently developed perinatal systems. They provide level III care, which means they have the highest level of trained personnel, the most sophisticated equipment, and treat the most severely involved infants in the regions they serve. They receive referrals from hospitals with level II and level I units. Special transport teams using chartered planes carry some patients over 160 km. The units we have studied have a maximum capacity of 35 to 64 infants each (600 to 1200 patients per year) and employ 80 to 100 full-time nurses, 3 to 6 full-time neonatologists, a large number of technical and other staff, plus 6 to 10 house officers who serve the unit in conjunction with their medical training.

Most of the patients are premature infants, the smallest weighing as little as 500 gm. Others have life-threatening birth defects. Approximately 15% of the infants die; some are so premature that they need prolonged treatment on which they may become dependent or which may cause them irreparable damage (blindness, brain tissue destruction, chronic lung conditions). Although most of the children leave the unit to live relatively normal lives, these units are a place where many are at high risk of being part of the next generation of mentally retarded and otherwise handicapped people.

The newcomer to a unit is struck by the pace of activity, the long intense hours the staff works, the sophisticated technology, and the life and death struggle that is a regular part of the routine. As one spends time on these units, all of those factors, plus the awesome sight of tiny infants with a substantial portion of their bodies covered with tape, attached to respirators, oxygen dispensers, IVs, monitors, under heaters and bilirubin lights, with monitors beeping warnings of heart arrest, soon become the details of everyday life.

METHOD AND PROCEDURES

The data reported were collected during a one-year period on and with people related to neonatal intensive care units in urban teaching hospitals. Our work began under the auspices of a funded service delivery project in which physical therapists, educators, social workers, and other professionals acting in teams were to provide services to infants who were at high risk of becoming developmentally delayed. Service providers were to go into the homes of the infants who had been on the unit and involve parents in the "intervention." We were to give information to the teams about the fit between what they planned to do and the service system as we observed it in operation. It seemed important for them to understand what parents experience on the unit and what parents understood about their childrens' conditions. Our interests soon expanded beyond the project, and our data collection was enlarged so that we could explore the broader issues presented here.

We started our research doing participant observation (Bogdan and Taylor, 1975) on the unit the project served. We visited for four months, two to four times a week for one to three hours, taking extensive fieldnotes after each visit. In conjunction with these observations we interviewed physicians, nurses, and parents in addition to reviewing official documents. After the initial four months we increased our interviews with parents but decreased our observations on the unit. In addition, we expanded our observations to three other units; one in a neighboring state, and two in other cities but in the same state as the project unit. Our purpose in these visits was to explore generalizability and enlarge our emerging model. The visits to the other units were only for a day each and consisted of interviews with key personnel as well as observations.

During our observations on the project unit we went on rounds, attended case conferences, sat in on orientation sessions for new staff, and observed day-to-day activities including discussions between staff and parents about the condition of their children. (We observed similar activities on the other units but on a more limited basis.) We completed more than 40 tape recorded interviews 35 minutes to 2 hours in length, plus the less formal interviews done in the course of our observations. Many of the professionals we talked to had worked or were trained on units other than those on which we observed. We questioned them about those units and concluded that they are substantially similar to the ones described in this paper. What we report here has, in various drafts, been presented to, discussed with, and, where warranted, modified in response to reactions from professional staff on the units.

THE CONTEXT OF COMMUNICATION ON NEONATAL UNITS

Patients as Seen by the Staff

Parents on neonatal units seek out the staff to ask about their child's condition. At certain times particular staff members pursue parents for the purpose of telling them news. Who talks to parents of a particular patient, and what is said, can only be understood by knowing how the staff thinks about their clients. Babies are not just babies. A particular baby fits into a loose typology that is part of the staff's way of seeing things.

Staff on the units studied share an informal classification system of their patients with statuses identified by a special vocabulary. (Similar classification schemes, although less detailed, are noted in H. Becker et al., 1961 and Duff and Hollingshead, 1968). Although there are differences in specific phrases used and other details, the classification schemes are consistent from hospital to hospital.

Figure 1 depicts the staff's conceptual scheme of patients. Words in quotes refer to those consistently used on the units. Those without quotes are our phrases. These represent categories that the staff do not have specific or consistent words for, but, by the way they talk (Take a baby LIKE this . . ." "This KIND of infant . . .") and act (e.g., the amount of time spent discussing the baby at rounds) they indicate that they do think of babies as belonging to that designation. Although all professional staff in all units studied use a scheme similar to the one presented, ours is an "ideal type" (in the Weberian sense) in that it neither captures perfectly nor seriously distorts any of the units' schemes. All staff on a particular unit do not see patients exactly the same way. Nurses, for example, use a slightly different system than physicians, but on any unit staff share a general common vocabulary and scheme. Although staff share the general typology, for any particular child there may be dis-

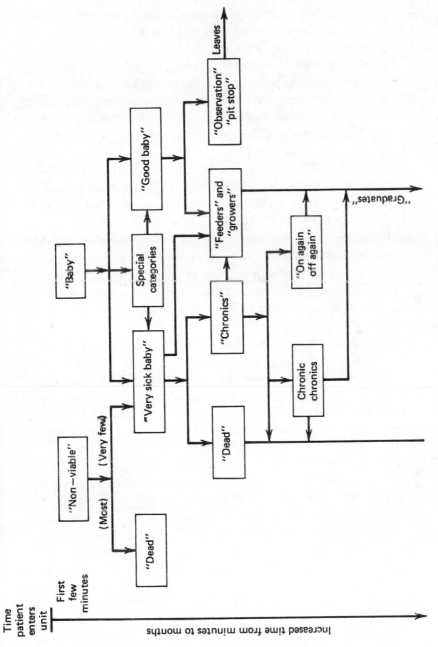

Figure 1. The staff's classification of infants.

175

agreement as to what "type" they are dealing with. As we will discuss, this can be a source of conflict over what is said and who talks to parents.

As the diagram suggests (see left-hand side), the classification system used by medical personnel is temporal. Those categories that are used early in the patient's career appear at the top of the diagram and those at the later stages further down the sheet. As we present in our discussion, the professional staff's classification system is related to timetables they hold regarding career patterns of patients on the unit (Davis, 1963; Roth, 1963).

During the first few minutes on the unit, the patient is either classified "baby" or "nonviable."[2] This judgment is made using a combination of gestation age, birth weight, apgar scores, other tests and findings, and, in extreme cases, the extent and nature of apparent or assumed physical and mental abnormalities. Although the staff of a particular unit has conventions to make such a decision, there is always an element of judgment. Conventions vary from unit to unit and over time. The size and gestation age of a patient considered viable has gone down drastically in recent years as a result of the development of technology and the growth of neonatology.

Nonviables, who are often referred to as "fetuses," may be placed in a special room or some other out of the way place on the unit, and given no treatment.[3] Babies are treated, often using heroic means. Once a baby is on a particular treatment (e.g., a respirator), it is rarely withdrawn, although with consultation from parents, additional potential life-saving intervention may be withheld. Infants may be "no coded," which means there are orders not to use additional treatment if the patient arrests.

Often parents of nonviables arrive after the death and are told immediately of the event by the physician assigned to the child or by the highest ranking staff member present. (Sometimes parents are told that their child is nonviable, only to arrive and find the infant under treatment with the possibility of life reopened.) When the parents arrive before death, the attending officer or a house officer assigned to the child or an available staff member discusses the condition with the parents, indicating that death is imminent and that the baby is not being treated. If the parent presses for treatment, there may be intervention. The great majority of nonviables are dead on arrival or die shortly after, but each unit has cases of the few who persevered and became babies. Occasionally, a new arrival defined by some staff as baby is defined by other staff as nonviable. Thus some infants under treatment are referred to in a critical way by some as fetuses. These and other situations where there is disagreement are stressful for staff because they are expected to present a united front to parents. For the staff members who are critical of a treatment decision, not speaking to parents about the matter may be difficult, especially if the staff member is a nurse who has come to know the parents.

During the first hours on the unit, most patients are held in the status of baby. Some are placed in categories other than baby and nonviable during the first few minutes, but for most, more specific designations are held in abeyance until the baby is observed, tested, and treated. During this period parents are provided with general information about the condition of their child, with an explanation of how difficult it is to know anything specific at this early stage and that more will be known in time. Professional staff often use a specific amount of time in discussions with parents: "We will know more in 48 hours" or in "72 hours."

The patient may remain an undifferentiated baby for a few minutes or a few days but eventually moves into one of three categories: "very sick babies," "good babies," and "babies with special problems." This latter type includes infants with such problems as heart defects, hydrocephaly, spina bifida, undifferentiated gender, special syndromes, and other birth defects. They either leave the unit within a few days or join those with the status of very sick baby or good baby with a special anomaly. Certain special category babies (e.g., children with meningomyeloceles) face the risk of having withheld exceptional procedures needed to keep them alive. Special category babies are, more than any type of baby, put up for adoption or are institutionalized. The most concentrated amount of time is spent talking to parents who are involved in these decisions, and the way the child's condition is presented can be critical in formulating parents' thinking.

Good babies are babies judged not to be at high risk of dying but who need support and observation either because of birth-related trauma or because of prematurity. Often, they need to grow in order to reach the weight required to be discharged from the unit, 1.8 to 2.3 kg. Good babies who are there for a day or less are called "observation babies" or "pit stops" like raceway automobiles; they need only a quick check, some minor fixing, and they're on their way. (As Figure 1 indicates, observation babies are not considered "graduates" of the unit. That designation is reserved for infants who spend longer periods of time on the unit.)

Good babies who are not there just for observation are "feeders and growers." This phrase is used because the professional staff see them as basically healthy except for their low weight and minor problems. All they need to do is feed and grow before they graduate. There is a number of subcategories under feeder and grower. There are "3-hour babies" and "4-hour babies," these names deriving from the time between feedings. There are also "nipplers," babies that are beginning to take food by sucking. Other categories also contain such elaborate subdivisions.

Very sick babies are those the staff sees as at high risk of dying. Most of these infants are of very low birth weight (1 kg or less) or have not spent enough time in utero to develop their lungs sufficiently to breathe on their own. Typically, they are on respirators and oxygen and are dependent on other life-support technology. Very sick babies may respond to treatment, be weaned from the machinery, and become feeders and growers. Other babies remain dependent on the life-supporting devices and become known as "chronics." Chronics whose condition deteriorates or who remain at the same high level of technological support, we refer to as chronic-chronics but the staff use a variety of epithets.[4] There are other babies under the heading of very sick babies whose reliance on life-support technology fluctuates. At times they appear to be weaned, only to have a serious setback. A patient with this kind of pattern fluctuates between being chronic and being a feeder and grower. Any very sick baby can die or change to a good baby. Feeders and growers can, though less often, change to very sick babies. The major thrust of the professional staff's work is to get patients to be feeders and growers.

A few patients from the chronic designation leave the unit with a low level of life-supporting devices, usually to a pediatric ward, but most who leave go through the feeder and grower route. Most of the ongoing communication between physicians and parents occurs in relation to new arrivals, very sick, chronic, chronic-chronic, and "on again–off again" babies. The long-term complication that may result from treatment, as well as disabilities, become of primary concern (and a topic of discussion) as the chronic baby spends more time on the unit and as children are prepared to go home. Feeders and growers are moved to one end of a unit (or a separate room) and receive relatively little attention from physicians, with nurses being more active in parent communication and patient care.

There are other factors related to how staff define patients that are important in communication between staff and parents. Infants arrive on the unit through a number of routes. The most common routes are being transported from another hospital (the hospital of birth; approximately 50%) and being transferred from the delivery room of the hospital of which the units are a part (the other 50%). Babies from other hospitals are called "transports," and those from within the hospital are called "our babies" or "from upstairs" or "downstairs" depending on where the delivery room is located. Transports come by the special transport team and do not arrive accompanied by a parent, who, all through the patient's career, has less access to the patient and staff because of the distance between the hospital and their home. Babies from inside the hospital are rushed to the unit immediately after delivery. Wherever the baby comes from, the father often follows close behind. When involved, fathers typically visit and speak to unit staff first. Although attendings often insist on talking to mothers either by phone or through visits to the maternity ward, fathers often convey information from the staff to the mother for the first few days and are most often the first person to explain the child's condition to the mother.

Who talks to the parents about the infant's condition and what is said depends on the different types of patients and where the patient is in his or her career on the unit. The designations and what they mean to the staff can only be understood within the timetables held for each status designation.

When a child first enters the unit, there is a tendency for physicians to talk to parents and to tell them that "it is too early to tell." As time progresses, nurses play a greater part in communication, due to their greater access to parents and contact with babies. At certain times and with certain categories death dominates communication; at other times it is the child's future. It is easier to talk to parents about good babies than about chronics and very problematic to talk about chronic-chronics and on again–off agains. With feeders and growers the content of information centers on progress.

Parent's Status as Seen by Staff

The typology of patients just presented is necessary to understand the context of who talks to parents about the condition of children and what is said. Patients are the subjects of professionals' diagnoses, prognoses, and treatments. But we have found that when the patient is a child, parents are assessed as well. On the basis of these assessments, judgments are made about who should talk to parents and what should be told regarding the child's condition and about parent participation in treatment. Physicians and nurses collect information from each other and from the parents and make judgments concerning what "type" parent they are dealing with. In encounters with parents, physicians and nurses "feel" parents out. Through observing them, hearing them talk, and most important, assessing their reaction to information given, staff make judgments about what to say, how to say it, and who should do the talking. Staff indicate that "you have to talk to parents at their level." They adjust their explanations to a level that allows the parent to grasp what it is they are trying to convey, given what the staff judge to be their intelligence, education, and emotional state.

Staff talk about three types of parents: "good parents," "not so good parents," and "troublemakers." [For a similar typology of adult patients, see Lorber's (1967, 1975) discussion of good and bad patients.] Although these terms are used, there is overlap in categories, disagreements as to which parent belongs where, and changes in parents' status over time.

As we discuss, what exactly is expected of a parent who is thought of as a good parent varies depending on the status of the child and the amount of time the child has spent on the unit. A good parent is defined by having a sufficient amount of the following characteristics.

1. *They understand.* As one physician put it when describing a good parent, "We communicate." Good parents ask questions the staff defines as appropriate. They recognize the seriousness of the condition of the child. They are tolerant of not knowing the final outcome of the child's condition. Their knowledge of the baby's condition and treatment increases over time. They are grateful for the level of care available to them. They understand and conform to the unit's practices and schedule.

2. *They care about the baby.* They visit regularly, touch the baby, call asking about its condition, and respond in what the staff deem as appropriate ways to good and bad news. The distance the pair lives from the hospital is taken into account in judging whether the frequency of visits indicates concern. Some staff use the terminology of "bonding" to discuss this dimension of a good parent.

3. *They show potential for giving the baby proper care if it leaves the hospital.* Babies who leave the unit are thought of as needing more care and more skilled care than typical babies. Good parents show they can provide the proper care in the proper environment.

Social class, age, and race are related to being a good parent, but they are not synonymous in the staff's minds. Although some teenagers, inner-city blacks, and single parents are thought of as being good parents, most people who are considered good are middle or upper middle class. The good parents are those that staff like to talk to and talk to the most. These parents are also free with their praise. They provide feedback concerning their understandings of how they and their child have been treated on the unit.

Not so good parents, some of whom are referred to as "doozies," or "one of those," are frustrating for the staff. The prototype of the not so good parent has characteristics opposite those of good parents.

1. *They are like talking to a brick wall.* Staff see them as not having the ability or refusing to show that they understand the condition of their baby. Most often this means, according to staff, that the parents do not acknowledge the seriousness of their child's condition. This lack of communication is attributed to the parents and is thought of as stemming from one of two possible causes. The first is that the parent is too uneducated or unintelligent to understand. The second is that the parent is experiencing a psychological state termed "denial." Some staff use denial indiscriminately to refer to parents who do not see the condition of the child as they do. Others use it in reference to more specific parent behavior, and, as we discuss later, in relation to a stage model of parents experiencing the crisis of an intensive care infant. For whatever reason, these parents ask what the staff see as inappropriate questions (i.e., "When will my baby come home?" or "When will he be circumcised?" when the child is close to death). This type of parent is seen as not hearing when told of impending death or long-term complications the child may have.

2. *Couldn't care less about the child.* They don't visit and don't call. When they do come, they stay a short time and do not touch or hold the child or in other ways show interest. There is special concern for some staff in this dimension of the not so good parent because it is seen as the source of potential "failure to thrive" and "neglect cases."

3. *Can't manage care.* They are seen as not having the skills, background, resources, or even a home to take care of the child. Staff typifies one variety of not so good parents (teenagers) with the phrase, "They think they have a baby doll," accompanied by, "They don't know the first thing about taking care of a baby." Many nurses express special frustration with parents exhibiting this dimension in that they see themselves giving one-on-one direct intensive care for long periods of time only to turn a child over to an environment in which inadequate care will be given.

Staff finds talking to not so good parents difficult. Although repeated efforts may be made to "reach" them and some change status to good parents, the frequency and length of contact declines after these parents have initial discussions with staff. Many not so good parents are poor, young, and culturally different from the staff.

There is a third category into which staff place parents—troublemakers. These are parents who pose special problems or make what the staff sees as unreasonable demands. Some who fall into this category are good parents in that they understand, they care, and they are competent, but they are not satisfied with the treatment their child is receiving. For example, they do not feel that their child's life should be supported and are assertive in pursuing that point of view, even though the staff may have a different view. Other parents are defined as overly critical or as "looking to sue." From the staff's perspective, these parents ask the same question to different staff in order to trip them up. Still others never seem to be satisfied. Rather than being grateful, they are always finding things wrong. Staff are extremely cautious in their communication with troublemakers.

According to staff, parents have to be understood in terms of their movement through the experience of having an intensive care baby. Some staff, borrowing from the professional literature on parental response to death or illness, think of parents as moving through specific stages in their response to the "crisis" (Culberg, 1972; Klaus and Kennell, 1976; Kubler-Ross, 1969). Some staff refer to five stages through which a parent is expected to pass in coming to grips with the fact that their newborn is not normal. These stages are anger, denial, bargaining, acceptance, and being practical. The typology of parents we presented (good parent, etc.) has to be understood in relation to the stage model. Some behaviors that we have pointed to as being associated with good, not so good, and troublesome parents are seen as typical at certain stages. It is when these behaviors are in excess of what the staff deems normal, or only when parents exhibit the behavior at a time that staff sees as inappropriate, that they are used to classify parents into the not so good or troublesome categories. It is important to point out that the staff does not uniformly or rigidly apply the stage model in evaluating parents; rather it is one way in which they explain and understand parents' behavior.

Staff take into account what type of parent they are talking to when they speak to them about their children. Complicating the matter is the fact that one parent of a child may be good and the other not so good or troublesome. Certain staff may be given the job of exclusive communication with particular parents.

With some exceptions, namely, good parents who have had children on the unit for months, the staff's assessment of parents and the parents' dispositions toward their babies and the degree to which parents are understanding what is being told to them is often inaccurate. Most assessments of parents are based on limited knowledge, derived mainly from short observations, limited conversations, or secondhand reporting of incidents and information. What is known is episodic, not informed by the context of the perinatal experience in the lives of the parents.

Staff is concerned with communicating with parents. They seek out parents regularly to talk with, and phone parents of transport babies daily in the early stages of the patient's career. The units have open door visiting policies for parents and grandparents. They can come to the unit any time, unannounced. They are encouraged to touch the baby and to call the unit as often as they want. In spite of this, and with some exceptions, staff, and physicians especially, spend relatively little time with parents. The priority is saving and mending the physical child. In general, staff know very little about what the parents are thinking and about their life outside the hospital.

The Staff

We described the patients and their parents as the staff see them. Now we turn to how the staff see themselves. There are six major categories of staff: attending physicians, house officers, nurses, technical specialists, social workers, and maintenance and cleaning. Attending physicians are usually the full-time neonatologists who work on the units, plus any other practicing physician who might have primary responsibility for a child on the unit. The house officers can include fellows and the pediatric interns and residents (PL1, PL2, and PL3s) who rotate on and off neonatal units as part of their pediatric training. Nurses include supervisors and staff nurses who work on rotating shifts. Technical specialists include physical therapists and inhalation therapists, and the units either have a full-time social worker or share a social worker with another department.

From the point of view of the professional staff, only the nurses, the social worker, the attending physicians, and the house staff officially talk to the parents about the child's condition. People in particular positions have responsibility for talking to parents under specific situations and about specific aspects of the child. Nurses know they should only discuss the patient's immediate condition, that is, if it has not taken a drastic turn for the worse. Nurses and social workers may discuss the child's larger diagnostic and prognostic picture, but only in an attempt to clarify what physicians have already told the parents. They ask the parent what they know, and then answer questions within that context, frequently referring them back to a physician for clarification. In two units, attendings have the major responsibility for talking to parents when the child first enters as well as updating the parents on significant changes in the child's condition. In the other two, the house staff assigned to the child fills this role. Staff try to assess what has been already told in deciding what will be said to parents. Although this is so, there is a shared perspective that parents should be given new information and answers to their questions as soon as possible. Thus house officers often talk to parents in lieu of attendings. Each intern is assigned a number of infants on the unit and they are most readily available to parents when parents visit the unit, thus at times they talk to parents. Nurses either practice primary care or are randomly assigned patients each day. Whatever nurse is in charge of the baby for the day usually talks to the parent. Although the social worker may have as a goal knowing the parents of every child and providing counseling, the case load is prohibitive. Social workers narrow their role to informing parents of financial aid that is available to help with the extraordinary expense of having a child in intensive care, referrals to other agencies, and to some personal counseling with a few parents. Social workers vary to the extent that they are active and involved with other unit staff. Although some generalizations can be made about who talks to parents, the pace and schedules of those who work on the unit change so often that such generalizations have only limited value.

We have discussed the staff positions on the unit. Nurses often refer parents to doctors for information, and the doctors' ability to communicate with the parents affects the nurses' relationship with the parents. One way nurses unofficially classify doctors is on the basis of their ability to talk to parents. Doctors are either "good doctors" or "bad." (They also classify them according to their technical skill and how they relate to nurses but these three dimensions are seen by nurses as often going hand in hand.) Good doctors are straightforward with parents. From the nurses' perspective, they make sure that parents understand what has been told to them by trying different methods of explaining and by going over the explanation in nontechnical language. Good doctors have regular (ideally daily) contact with parents and phone them at home if need be—most importantly, they never avoid parents. They seek out parents with information of progress in their child's condition as well as with bad news. Finally, good doctors involve the nurses in informing parents. This is seen as important because it ensures consistency in communication and it lessens the possibility that parents can "play off" nurses against doctors in efforts to get additional information.

In contrast, bad doctors are less straightforward with parents, and often fail to make sure that parents are clear about their baby's condition. They do not take the extra time to explain to parents and when they contact parents it is only with bad news. In addition, bad doctors do not tell nurses what they have told parents. Nurses observe doctors on the basis of their unofficial classification scheme and also determine what they say to parents on the basis of who the parents have talked to.

Staff's Perspectives on Talking to Parents

To some extent, exactly what is said to parents and how it is phrased is a function of who is saying it. Staff have different styles that they have developed. Some say they picked up their approach during training or since being on the unit. People are seldom coached on what to say and how to approach parents—it is not a formal part of training.[5] Knowing how to talk to parents is seen as an art. As our discussion has suggested, some staff are defined as being better at it than others. Some, especially house staff, may define themselves as poor at communication and defer to others when they might normally be expected to talk. Although some attendings are thought of as being better than others at communication, they are always expected to fulfill their parent-talking duties.

All staff would agree that they should be more systematic in their approach to parents. Some nurses in units where primary care is not followed advocate a primary care system in which the infants are assigned to the same nurses week after week, as a way to have more consistent communication. Others suggest that increased communication between doctors and nurses regarding what is to be said to a parent in a particular case would improve the situation. Although all agree that they should improve, they know that other aspects of their work are more pressing. Time is at a premium and keeping the many babies alive and helping them become "feeders and growers" dominates their long workdays. In addition, the work they do on the patient as a physical being is more visible than conversations with parents. The medical work is subject to regular discussion and careful review at rounds and during case conferences. Conversations with parents often occur in private and, when heard, are not subject to critiquing as is their other work. In addition, the staff receives positive feedback from "good parents," indicating to them they are successful in talking with parents. They can attribute the obviously poor communication with the "not so good parents" and the "troublemakers" to characteristics of the parents.

Some staff raise questions about the value of keeping infants with very low birth weights and severe impairments alive. They express reservations about aggressive medical procedures that save lives, after which parents take home a severely impaired child and a staggering hospital bill, or as a result of which the baby lives months under intensive care only to die a seemingly inevitable death. Some feel that even though parents may be involved in the decisions, they really cannot grasp the long-term complications. Although some staff members express reservations, they are put aside or countered by a shared perspective that "You can never really tell" how a child you are treating will turn out. Nurses keep scrapbooks and picture collections of children who are successful graduates. Parents of graduates visit the units bringing their child with them. One unit has a yearly get-together of ex-patients and their parents. Those who return are visibly grateful and the children who return are most often normal. They provide living teestimony to the value of the staff's work. Frequently you hear, "This child was once less than a thousand grams and look at her now."[6]

"You can never really tell" is an important theme in understanding what is said to parents. Staff tell stories of infants judged to be nonviable and who were put aside to die, only to live, and of children who had cerebral hemorrhages who grew to normal intelligence. Although staff make judgments about who they think will live and who will die, and speak among themselves about babies who "will never go home," this is always tempered with a comment that suggests that although they may judge who will die, "you can never really tell." In conversations with parents, unless there is very clear evidence of impending death or clear diagnosis of impairment, "You can never really tell" dominates the tone of communication.

The fact that "You can never really tell" dominates communication with parents, rather than more candid assessments, has to do with another understanding the staff share; that is, "Be honest, but not cruel." Although there is variation in the degree to which staff is optimistic rather than pessimistic in what they tell parents about their child's condition (Clyman et al., 1979), there is general agreement that you should not take away hope from the parent. It is cruel to be too negative; the parent may withdraw from the infant and, if it were to live, irreversible damage might be done to the relationship.[7] On the other hand, staff shares the perspective that it is bad to surprise parents with bad news; that it is important to foreshadow possible revelations and, if there is a chance of death, there should be some prior warning. The staff sometimes softens bad news by suggesting that a child's temperament or disposition provides reason for hope. One father was told that although his child was very ill, the child was a "fighter." Another parent was told that her child wasn't a quitter and that the staff wasn't giving up. Despite these children's poor medical health, the families were encouraged not to give up hope.

Another part of "Be honest, but not cruel" is not to burden the parent with too many of the problems that might be faced later in the child's career, not to be too pessimistic about the long-term prognosis. Some use the technique of normalizing the child's condition by saying something like, "I have seen children who were a lot worse than this who are now doing fine." On occasion some staff cite prognostic statistics, but statistics are generally thought to be inaccurate and to tend to mislead, as parents are prone to misinterpret the predictive potential for their child.

Another practice related to the perspective, "Be honest but not cruel," is the use of euphemisms and less than direct phrases in discussing the child's condition. Such expressions as "You have a very sick baby," or "Your baby is very immature," or "Your baby has some tough going," are used at times, instead of "We think your baby is going to die." "Developmentally delayed" and "learning disability" are sometimes substituted for "mentally retarded." The use of euphemisms is in line with "Don't be cruel," as well as "You can never really tell."

The Parents

Space does not permit us to fully discuss the parents. Parents do not know the staff's typology of patients, parents, and staff. Nor do they understand staff's perspective and rules on talking to parents. For the staff, the units and interactions with parents are part of the routine everyday life. For professionals, the unit is a place where they practice medicine; for parents, it is a place where THEIR CHILD is.

For most parents the neonatal unit is initially an unknown world— "neonatology" and even "intensive care for infants" are words that they have never heard before the birth of their child.[8] Similarly, some of the conditions that their child may have are completely outside their realm of experience. Further, many do not know the difference between an intern and a neonatologist. Parents process information they receive from the staff through the world as they understand it. What staff think they are communicating is often not what parents hear. For example, in a setting where death is a regular occurrence, "You have a very sick baby" may mean "Your baby is going to die," but in the context of parents' lives, it may mean their baby is going to be in the hospital for a few extra days. Much of the parents' early activity on the unit as well as their state of mind is consumed with trying to understand what has happened and what it means. Not having a set of understandings to draw on often leaves them confused and without a repertoire of consistent behavior.

Parents come from a variety of backgrounds and experiences. They are disproportionately young and poor, but middle-class and wealthy people are represented. Some have had no prenatal care and have kept the pending birth out of their minds until it happened. For others, the anticipated birth is the fulfillment of a dream. Some have had no prior warning that the birth would be unusual or the baby would be at high risk of death or of being developmentally disabled. Others had been seeing specialists because their pregnancy was known to be "high risk." Some parents have had medical training; others do not know what the heart does. For some it is their first child; for others it is one of many. Some are married; others have no partner with whom to share the events. Some have recently lost jobs; others have just started a new business. For some, grandmothers will be looked to for guidance; for others, the clergy; for still others, specialists. Others will depend entirely on the staff of the unit. Only by knowing the details of the many worlds of parents prior to and surrounding the neonatal experience can we begin to understand how they experience the unit and what they hear when staff talks to them.

Although what parents hear and understand is related to their world, their understanding is changed by the events of the birth and their experiences in and surrounding the unit. Mothers are often physically exhausted immediately after birth, if not unconscious. Many do not understand where their baby has gone. Fathers, on the other hand (if present), are torn between being with their partners and following their baby. Many of the mothers are on maternity wards where other mothers have their babies close by. This intensifies their sorrow of not having their baby with them. The first visit to the unit can be traumatic. The sight of the babies with their medical paraphernalia and the number of people and intensity of activity can be overwhelming. Some parents put complete confidence in the doctors, no matter what the doctors' status, and do not ask many questions. They leave the particulars up to them. Others learn the details of the child's condition and consult with various people, taking an active role in monitoring doctors and carefully listening and interpreting what is said. It can be misleading to generalize about stages parents go through in learning about the unit and their child. Having a child admitted to the unit may not be as traumatic an event as other events they may experience down the road—such as the realization of pending death or of permanent physical or mental disability.

Parents seek out information and receive it from a variety of sources in addition to the staff's words. They learn about the physical layout of the units and what a move from one place to another means in relation to their child's condition. They pay attention to staff members' gestures and tone of voice looking for unspoken information about the child's condition. They compare their child with others they have known and others on the unit. They talk to friends and relatives and make note of casual remarks made on the unit. In addition, they view the mass media with an eye to clues on how to understand their child. Although for the majority the stay on the unit is less than a month, some stay up to a year. Parents of long-term patients often develop a detailed knowledge of the setting, read their child's charts, and get to know the staff well. Although at first these parents think in terms of their child getting well soon, they change their timetable of their child's development and look for small signs of change. For some parents, particularly those of long-term patients, the experience on the unit seriously changes their relations with each other, with friends, and with family—it changes their lives. For some it is the start of a life of being the parent of a child with a disability. For the most part, parents leave the unit knowing their life has been changed but not knowing their child's condition and in most cases not very aware of what the future might bring.

CONCLUSION

When we first asked the physicians what they told parents about their children's condition they said, "We are completely honest." Similarly, during our first visits, when we asked nurses what they told parents, they said, "Everything." These phrases have a special and circumscribed meaning for those who work on neonatal units. Further, in our interviews with parents and through observations we began to see the other side of staff/parent communication. What physicians and other hospital staff thought they said to parents was often not what parents heard. Our research was guided by the questions: Who talks to parents? What do they say? What do parents hear? Our presentation reveals that there are no simple answers to these questions. Only through a description of salient aspects of the setting can we begin to grasp the meaning, process, structure, and entangled communication in such a complex environment. We have described the rudiments of an elaborate communication system, one which operates on several levels and from many perspectives. The phrases, "Be honest" and "Tell everything," for example, take on distinct meanings depending on who is talking to whom, about whom, under what conditions, and the nature of the information to be conveyed.

Neonatal units are more complex and intense than most other settings in which professionals talk to clients. The news that is to be communicated is unique too, but there are understandings to be derived that transcend the substantive focus of our description. In a study one of us conducted (Bogdan and Barnes, 1979) of programs for disabled students in elementary and secondary schools, we are discovering the complex typologies that school personnel have for students (beyond conventional classifications such as emotionally disturbed, mentally retarded, blind, etc.).[9] Also, teachers, in a manner similar to that described in this paper, size up and type parents, and on that basis decide what to say and how and if they will involve them in their child's educational program. Schools, like hospitals, develop conventions regarding who talks and what they say, and this affects what it is that parents hear. For parents seeking information, encounters with professionals in schools as well as hospitals are episodic and seldom with knowledge of the context from which professionals are operating. The way we have approached studying communication between professionals and parents has broad application and requires that we concentrate on seeing communication from the participants' point of view and that we understand the context of the setting in which communication takes place. Obtaining such information from a variety of settings will move us toward a grounded theory of professional/client communication.

Our research was sponsored by a state-funded service project that was to help neonatal unit graduates. Of what use are our findings to that effort? Our basic research interests took us beyond the confines of our narrowly conceived role in that project, but we were able to point to issues and warn project members of potential problems. For one, the project had to interface with a neonatal unit. Infants and their parents were referred to the intervention teams by hospital personnel. The grant proposal stipulated that services would be delivered to infants defined as "at high risk" of developing disabling conditions. As our discussion disclosed, the hospital personnel does not define babies that way—their typology is based on infants' present condition, not on projections. How they classify infants, as well as the perspectives "You can never really tell" and "Be honest but not cruel" had to be incorporated into the plans. In addition, in choosing families to participate in the project, priority was to be given to those of low socioeconomic status. As we pointed out in our discussion of hospital staff's definitions of parents, not so good parents tended to be poor, young, and culturally different from the white, middle-class staff. These were the parents who the staff were least effective in communicating with and who were thought to provide homes least conducive to infant development. Further, transport patients were seen by unit staff as those who needed follow-up the most because of the underdeveloped resources in rural areas—yet the resources of the project, according to the grant, were to be directed at the geographic area closest to the hospital. How the project staff might overcome barriers that stood in the way of serving those defined by the staff as being in the greatest need became an issue with which to grapple.

We raised other issues. Hospital personnel respond to the crises as they occur on the unit: when an infant needs attention everything else comes second. Further, the hours that hospital staff work are irregular compared to the nine-to-five workdays of some of the project staff. The logistics of meetings and reconciling the difference in life-style and priorities between hospital staff and project workers had to be faced. We could go on, but suffice it to say that our findings did have application to practitioners.

As we proceeded in our work, we made presentations outlining the contents of this paper to project staff as well as to people who worked on the unit we had concentrated on in data collection. Although the presentations evoked much discussion, we know that the nature of communication has not changed because of what we have done. The staff's priority is to save lives and they look at communication as an accessory to their major work. Their typifications of parents and patients as well as their perspectives on communication fit the logic of those priorities, and to change communication, if that were desirable, would take more than educating staff to how they presently behave.

We conclude this paper with a reminder of the weakness in our research. It is particularly important to point it out because our focus is a setting which is alive with human drama and saturated with moral and ethical dilemmas. On such units decisions are made concerning who should be treated. Communication between staff and parents affect such decisions, but the social policy and culture that created the situation in which staff and parents find themselves also have to be studied. Neonatal units were, in part, the United States' answer to its embarrassing position among other nations in rates of infant mortality. Why a technological solution to the problem was embraced rather than one that emphasized prevention has to be understood. As we cannot ignore the society and culture that created these settings, we would also be remiss if we did not point out that what is occurring in these settings can have a profound effect on the future of the society of which they are a part. By decreasing the birth weight and gestation age, by changing definitions of what is "a baby," we are witnessing events that may transform definitions of life itself.

NOTES

1. Patient and parent compliance with "the doctor's orders" as well as their satisfaction with treatment have also been discussed (H. Becker et al., 1972; M. Davis, 1968, 1971; M. Davis and Eichhorn, 1963; Elling et al., 1960; Cordis et al., 1969; Korsch et al., 1968; Svorstad, 1976).

2. Similar findings have been noted by Glaser and Strauss (1968) and Sudnow (1967). Glaser and Strauss note that admittance to the premature baby ward is sometimes delayed until the baby has lived at least an hour and a half after birth. "If the preemie demonstrates that possibly he can live, he is permitted to enter the ward . . ." (Glaser and Strauss, 1968:44–45). Sudnow notes that, "There is a system of definitions and weights intended to describe the status of the fetus. According to the weight, length, and period of gestation at the end of which it is delivered, a fetus is considered to be 'human or not' " (Sudnow, 1967:108).

3. We do not want to suggest that it is a daily occurrence on these units that severely deformed and brain damaged babies are left to die or that babies who might have lived are regularly not treated. The units we studied practice what some staff call "aggressive treatment."

4. Epithets used for chronic-chronics vary from unit to unit. Such benign phrases as "sad case" and "never going home" are sometimes used; "preemie trash" was used by some staff on one unit. Other phrases are used for other categories. Babies with severe problems on one unit are referred to as "trainwrecks." "Gork" is used on more than one unit to refer to infants who are severely neurologically impaired. Such terminology is generally not shared with outsiders, and never used around parents. Staff that do use such expressions explain the use by saying that work on such units is difficult and it is their way of venting frustration.

5. The only coaching that the physician does have is with reference to the medical interview. There has been increased concern that the physician does not have the necessary skills to communicate with patients and parents, especially those who have special needs; for example, those parents whose child has died. (See Bergman, 1974; David, 1975; Elliot, 1978; Fischoff and O'Brien, 1976; Gilson, 1976; and Mayerson, 1976.)

6. This is similar to the position advocated by Klaus and Kennell (1976) who note that if the infant lives and the physician was pessimistic, it is sometimes difficult for parents

to become closely attached after they "have figuratively dug a few shovelsful of earth" (ibid.:153).

7. This is similar to the position of Friedman (1963, 1974) who suggests that parents be given advance warning that their child will die so that they may go through a phase of anticipatory grieving. Parents who do experience such a phase are better able to cope with the child's death. The two positions place the staff in a dilemma; they must choose the information and the bias in terms of optimism and pessimism rather carefully. This applies not only to information regarding the child's death but also to information regarding possible handicaps such as brain damage and retardation.

8. There are occasional "repeaters" which is the staff's phrase for parents who have had more than one birth with the child being admitted to the unit. One 19-year old woman had children on the unit in all of her five births. "Repeater" is sometimes used derogatorily in that in some cases it is taken as an indication of being a not so good parent.

9. This research was funded under a grant from the National Institute of Education, grant #3532413.

10

Let Them Eat Programs

ATTENDANTS' PERSPECTIVES
AND PROGRAMMING ON
WARDS IN STATE SCHOOLS

Those who attempt to introduce therapeutic programs at "total institutions" (Goffman, 1961) often fail to take into account the invariable effects of the ward setting (Scheff, 1961). That is, new programs are planned and implemented without a sufficient understanding of the context into which they are being introduced. Many of those interested in change, for example, subscribe to a system of definitions and beliefs that they assume are shared by those in the setting they are attempting to change. Those within the setting, however, may act from totally different perspectives. The result is a poor interface between the change agent and the setting—a factor that inevitably circumscribes the potential effectiveness of the change.

The primary purpose of this paper is to present specific aspects of attendants' perspectives on their supervisors, their jobs, and residents, and to show how these relate to the implementation of "innovative" programs designed by supervisory and professional staff to serve the needs of the residents on the attendants' wards. Our discussion deals with a spe-

Robert Bogdan, Steven Taylor, Bernard deGrandpre, and Sondra Haynes. This article originally appeared in the *Journal for Health and Social Behavior*, 15(June): 142–151, 1974.

cific kind of total institution that is relatively unknown to social scientists: state schools for the "mentally retarded."

In the United States there are between 200,000 and 250,000 people residing in these often massive facilities which physically and administratively resemble state mental hospitals. (They generally operate through a rigid hierarchy and are dominated by the medical model.)

Although criteria for admission to state schools vary, an IQ of 75 or below makes one eligible in most states and so-called "maladaptive" behavior combined with the social contingencies of poverty, family crisis, or lack of community services completes the formula. "State School" is, in the institutions we have studied, a euphemism for the most barren kind of custodial care offered to any category of "client" in our society. Straitjackets, isolation cells, beatings, nudity, herding, medical neglect (i.e., skin burns from lying in urine), massive drugging, and unsanitary conditions (i.e., drinking from toilets) are characteristic of what has been termed the "back wards" of these facilities, but more subtle forms of dehumanization characterize the best of the wards. They chronically suffer from poor patient-to-staff ratios and other impediments to providing even decent custodial care.

The study reported here is based on data collected in intensive observation on three different wards in three different institutions plus supporting data from more casual fieldwork on other wards in the same facilities and in eight other institutions. All of these institutions are located within the Northeastern United States. The primary fieldwork was conducted by three of the authors. Supporting data collection was carried out by others over a three-year period. The three authors who conducted the fieldwork each spent a minimum of one year of at least weekly observations on one of the three wards. One lived at the institution for five months in addition to conducting observations prior and post. The observers, in participant observation style (Bogdan, 1972), spent large amounts of time with the attendants in the natural setting interacting with them as they went about their normal activities. They presented themselves as university students who were interested in mental retardation and were successful in developing a rapport characterized by trust and candor as the quotations cited throughout this paper suggest. The observers collected thousands of pages of field notes from which the quotations in the paper have been drawn to illustrate our points.

The three institutions on which this study concentrates are located on the edge of a middle-size city and in rural communities. One institution houses 400 residents, another 2500, and the third 3000. The wards were an infant/children's ward, a ward for adolescent girls of rather high ability, and a ward for "severely and profoundly retarded aggressive young adult males" (age range 14 through 44)—what we shall refer to as the back ward. The wards, as one can imagine from their brief introduction, vary as to the kind of residents and the nature of the environment and services provided. What we have attempted to do is to draw from our data the commonalities in attendants' perspectives that are directly related to understanding the implementation of programs. Although we do not maintain that the material we present represents the views of all attendants, we do take the position that it characterizes their dominant views.

"THEY DON'T KNOW WHAT IT'S REALLY LIKE": PERSPECTIVES ON SUPERIORS

Attendants share the view that their superiors, be they administrators, line professionals, or supervisors, misunderstand the needs of the residents and the nature of life and work on the wards. It is their belief that their own proximity to the residents and time spent on the ward provide them with a knowledge of ward life that is inaccessible to others. As an attendant from the back ward put it:

> They just sit in the office and tell us what to do; but they're not here. They don't know what we know.

An attendant on the infant/children ward expressed a similar point of view in reference to staff meetings at which decisions are made about residents' placements and from which attendants are excluded:

> We're the ones who spend most of the time with the children. We know what they can do and what they can't do. At the last meeting they had a teacher come who doesn't hardly have anything to do with any of the children. Somebody from O.T. (Occupational Therapy)—they have very little to do with the children. And then Dr. Erthardman[1] who doesn't even know the children. She might make a decision that a child needs another IQ test to see what he can do since the last test. I could tell her what they can do and what they can't do.

As this quotation begins to suggest, the perspective that attendants "know best" is also based on a skepticism of professionals and the procedures and approaches they employ. The attendants, many of whom have not completed high school, believe in direct observation and the application of "common sense," and tend to regard with tongue in cheek test scores, esoteric vocabularies and explanations, and the general approach some professionals use in treating "patients" (as the residents are often referred to). For example, attendants on the back ward as well as those on the adolescent ward hold a very dubious view of the advice of the institution's professionals:

> Let me tell you, those psychiatrists are all crazy. . . . They just don't know what they are doing. They tell you to sit down with 'em and talk to them when they start going at it (fighting). Christ, if I tried that I'd get my fuckin' brains kicked out.

And on all three wards attendants question the validity of IQ scores:

> That (score) can't be right. He ain't that dumb.

> I know they told us she was retarded, but after working with her a week I knew darn well she wasn't no matter what they said.

It is also clear that the attendants doubt the competence of the particular professionals working at the institutions. Attendants know and discuss the fact that professional work at the institution confers low status among professionals and that the professional departments encounter difficulties in recruiting trained and competent personnel. Thus the vast majority of physicians at the institutions have not met state certification requirements, and more than half are foreign born and trained, which in itself creates communication barriers. These characteristics are associated with inferiority in the attendants' minds. The following quotation illustrates the perspective we are describing:

> We have a foreign doctor and I don't think he knows what he is doing. All he does is put yellow salve on her feet and they get worse. I can't understand a word he says. We have another doctor that is even harder to understand. I think half of these kids are getting the wrong medicine. You would think they could get a decent doctor.

Attendants offer countless examples to support their view that professionals at the institution are incompetent, lazy, or lax in performing their duties. The remarks quoted below are typical of those commonly heard on the wards:

> (The professionals) read off the IQ and what the patient can do and the stuff isn't anywhere up to date. It will say the patient is blind and you'll find the patient running around the day room.

> The care these kids get is criminal. I don't know why they can't give them decent medical care. They have to be half dead before they will do anything. I remember sending one kid up to the hospital with a 102 fever and they wouldn't do anything about it.

> I haven't seen a psychiatrist up here since I started.

As the many quotations serve to indicate, attendants also resent most professionals, supervisors, and administrators at the institutions. They believe that they themselves have the "roughest" jobs, and that others are over-paid and underworked:

> Those whose jobs require them to sit down all day get the air conditioning while we run around like sweltering pigs.

> They're always off some place to a meeting or a conference. You would think we'd have a conference or something.

> Dr. Lee never came in today. Boy! It must be nice to come and go like that.

The attendants' skepticism and hostility extend to high state officials and legislators who are ultimately responsible for the institutions. Legislators, according to attendants, "won't give us what we need," and state officials, "don't give a shit." The attendants point to understaffing, the general ward conditions, the lack of basic supplies, and the inaccessibility of officials and legislators to buttress their view that nobody other than themselves cares. Witness the following comment which was offered by an attendant on the back ward, a ward on which the smell of feces and urine permeates the air:

> You tell them they don't give us antiseptic or clothes for the patients. You tell them we can't do nothin' cause they won't give us what we need.

Another attendant summarized his own and his co-worker's feelings about the state and the institution:

It's really bad here—no programs, no nothing. We sit here and watch bodies. I've been here 27 years—the state and the doctors—they're something else. The directors get big and fat salaries—they've never had experience on the wards—they don't know what's going on. After they pay them there's no money for the people and services here. When I retire I'm gonna tell my friends in the Capitol about the way things are being run.

PERSPECTIVES ON WORK: "A JOB IS A JOB"

Although attendants derive some satisfaction from the intrinsic aspects of their work (such as the companionship other attendants offer), they define their jobs primarily in terms of the extrinsic benefits these jobs provide. Thus they resemble unskilled workers in other settings in their definition of their work:[2]

It's a job—nothing more, nothing less.

As one attendant from the adolescent ward related:

If I didn't need the checks so bad I'd quit.

Attendants on the back ward place an equal importance on monetary rewards and fringe benefits:

Everyone is here for one reason and one reason only—money. That's right, they're all here for the money. That's why they took this job. That's why I took this job.

In accordance with this perspective, attendants see themselves not as "professionals" who are responsible for engaging the residents in programmed activities but, rather, as custodians who are responsible for keeping the ward clean and maintaining control and order among the residents (Taylor, 1973). Witness the following remarks offered by an attendant on the back ward:

We're supposed to feed 'em and keep an eye on 'em and make sure they're OK. They have people in recreation—psychologists and sociologists. They're the ones who are supposed to train 'em and work with 'em—not us.

This emphasis on custodial care is so strong that the well-being of the residents is often ignored or deliberately violated (Taylor, 1973). One attendant commented:

> We have no time to keep things as they should be let alone help the residents. We sometimes have to tie people up so that we can carry on with the work.

Another stated:

> By the time you're done with your work, you're too tired to do anything else.

Attendants develop routines to minimize their custodial work and develop methods of control to deal with troublesome residents. Those on the back ward use "brighter" residents (so-called "working boys") to do much of the custodial work and to control other residents. Attendants on all wards form work quotas and goldbrick, as do factory workers (Roy, 1952a, 1952b). Thus they spend much of their time "screwing off" despite the fact that they complain that they never have enough time. On back wards a resident is assigned to watch out for supervisors while the attendants pitch nickels, read the newspaper, harass residents, drink, or pass the time in idle conversation. On all wards the television, which is turned to stations of the attendants' choosing, provides diversions during the long breaks. On all wards each observer has been left single-handed to cover for the attendants while they left the wards for breaks.

The attendants resent those who disrupt their routines. They direct negative comments toward co-workers who do either too little work or who do too much, and they resent outsiders who come to help with the residents but interfere in other ways. The following comments were made in regard to a group of LPN trainees who were willing to help dress, feed, and bathe the children on the infant/children ward:

> They're a nuisance. Each of the girls was assigned to one of the children. They took so long bathing them that we got way behind on that. They got the laundry all mixed up.

For most attendants, then, work at the institution represents nothing more than a job, albeit a well-paying one. Some attendants are stoics in discussing their work. That is, work is not something that is to be liked or disliked; it is something that must be done. In their own words:

My husband always asks me how I can stay on this job. Well, I figure some-body has to do it. It has to be done.

Somebody's gotta do it. Somebody's gotta take care of the kids.

PERSPECTIVES ON RESIDENTS:
"LOW GRADES," "REJECTS," AND "DELINQUENTS"

In view of the importance attendants place on the custodial aspects of their work, it is hardly surprising that they define residents in terms of either their disabilities or the amount of trouble or work they cause. Thus attendants refer to residents with words that emphasize those characteristics: "puker," "regurgitator," "dummy," "biter," "grabber," "soiler," "headbanger," "low grade," "vegetable," "brat," "fighter."

Certain residents are sources of concern to attendants on all wards. "Hyperactive" residents and those who lack basic self-help skills are especially resented. On the infant/children ward women attendants complain about nonambulatory children who are heavy to lift. These children are transferred from the ward regardless of age despite the fact that they are supposed to stay on the ward until they reach the age of 12 years.[3] On the back ward the population is composed of what the attendants call "rejects" from other wards, residents who were placed there because they were too much trouble for other attendants. And on the adolescent ward attendants believe that about one-third of their residents were placed there not because they are "retarded," but rather, because they are incorrigible.

> This bunch of girls isn't retarded—they are just delinquents. They don't like school and their parents don't make them go. We get them back when the parents can't handle them.

Few attendants believe in the residents' potential to learn or to change. From their point of view, little can be done for the residents be-yond what is already being done. One attendant typified this perspective in her response to a question concerning the futures of the children on her ward:

> Eventually they'll go to another building. Most of them will be this way for the rest of their lives.

Attendants on the back ward remark that their residents are too "low grade" to learn despite the fact that some of them demonstrate competence in speech and spelling:

> I'd give anything to be able to help these kids, but you can't do it. They're too low grade.

On the adolescent ward attendants held similarly fatalistic views in regard to the innate capacities of the residents they called the "poor kids" or the "really retarded." And even the "delinquents" on this ward were seen as having been morally damaged by their families to the extent that it was difficult to teach them "new tricks."

Attendants also view residents as being susceptible to being "spoiled." This view is often used by attendants to justify their own inactivity in working or playing with residents. The attendants on the infant/children ward, for example, frequently allow the children to lay in their cagelike cribs and cry rather than pick them up under the reasoning that they have been spoiled in the past and further attention will only spoil them more. One of these attendants described the effect of the aforementioned group of LPN trainees who had spent a week on the ward and had held and fondled the children:

> It's really not fair to the children. They get used to all of this attention and then it's taken away. Some of them have been spoiled in only five days.

An attendant on the back ward revealed a similar point of view when he discussed the actions of attendants on another ward:

> These women attendants spoil these kids. They let 'em get away with anything. Jimmy used to be in that ward. He ran the place. They brought him up to us though—he was pulling out his cock and chasing women. When Jimmy came up here he was spoiled but that didn't last too long. He tried to steal food from the other kids and they let him have it. Man, he didn't pull that shit anymore.

Another attendant from this ward stated:

> You just can't give them everything they want or you won't be able to control them.

Finally, this same "give them an inch and they'll take a mile" view was expressed by an attendant on the adolescent ward:

> If the attendants don't keep things under control, it's their own fault. They have to show them who is the boss.

In the eyes of attendants, professionals, superiors, and state officials pose a challenge to their own "give them an inch" view. These persons, it should be remembered, "don't know what it's really like." Yet these persons also impose restrictions which attendants resent. Thus attendants regard them as threatening and resent rulings that allegedly affirm the rights of residents, superiors' concern with incidents of resident abuse, and new time demands and program ideas.

Although attendants underline the differences between their own perspectives and those of others, the institutions' administrative and professional staff often support attendants' perspectives. For example, physicians prescribe large dosages of tranquilizers to control residents, and the schools at the institutions provide educational services for a relatively small number of residents. Most significant in this regard, however, is the training all attendants receive in preparation for their jobs.

The focus of formal attendant training at the three institutions is on the etiology of "mental retardation" and the developmental characteristics of the "mentally retarded." Witness the following quotations:

> We learn about medications, how these people are different from you and I, how to care for them, how to treat them, what to expect, things like that.

> They teach you a lot about causes and things, but you can't use that here.

Such "facts" and the concept of "mental retardation" are reified through a series of lectures and charts that describe the limitations of the "retarded." One chart states that the "profoundly retarded" are "helpless." Attendants are trained, then, to concentrate on residents' innate limitations.

In addition to formal training sessions in which "retardation" is explained, newly employed attendants are taught first-aid skills and are informed of the rules and regulations of the institution. Perhaps a more important aspect of the three-week orientation program is the experience they get working on the wards as they are rotated from building to building. This orientation to the wards puts new attendants in contact with the "old timers" from the first day thus exposing them to the perspectives we have been discussing early in their careers as institution employees.

THE BROTHERHOOD AT THE BOTTOM

There are factors other than training that support, intensify, and validate attendants' perspectives. Although we do not discuss all of these at this point, an important concept to understand in this regard is what we might term "the brotherhood at the bottom." By this, we mean that attendants are both occupationally and socially isolated from supervisors, professionals, and administrators at the institution.

Attendants have little actual contact with others at the institution in the context of their work. They spend their time together on the wards and discuss the faults of this or that superior or professional and, in general, how "they don't know what it's really like." More than this, however, attendants share similar socio-economic and geographic backgrounds and have opportunities to see each other outside of work. Thus many attendants spend their free time together at local bars and clubs and many are related to each other through blood or marriage. On the back ward, for example, one attendant has eight relatives who are attendants at the institution.

Attendants' perspectives are reinforced through these on-the-job and off-the-job contacts. They also develop feelings of solidarity among themselves and of alienation from others.

INNOVATIVE PROGRAMMING

It should not be difficult to imagine what happened when supervisory and professional staff attempted to introduce "innovative" programs onto these wards. In this section, we briefly discuss the impact and outcomes of these attempts.

The program that was introduced in the back ward was what attendants and their supervisors referred to as a "motivation training" program. The attendants were never quite certain of the program's intended purpose, and, in fact, received their information about the program from fellow workers on other wards and shifts. In the following quotation, one "ward charge" (supervising attendant) described how he learned about the program:

> I was talking to another charge and he told me about it. You see, it's sup-
> posed to be from 6 to 8:30 every night. Then each guy will take 12 kids (age
> range of residents on this ward is 14 to 44) and sit around and teach 'em
> things—like how to take care of themselves and dress themselves. And then
> every ward is getting a popcorn popper and we'll give 'em popcorn every
> night as a reward.

Although some attendants were willing to give the program their guarded approval prior to its implementation, most viewed it with skepticism from its beginning. Some argued that they had too little time and too much other work to implement such a program:

> Now how are we supposed to motivate 'em and clean this place and every-
> thing? We don't have enough employees.

Others believed that the intellectual capacities of the residents precluded significant "improvement":

> You see, the patients we have are all rejects and we're supposed to do some-
> thing with them. You can teach them so much and that's it. They can't learn
> no more.

Although this ward's supervising attendant postponed the program's implementation for a period of four weeks after it was supposed to have begun, it was finally introduced with the aid of a "trained" attendant from another ward. The actual program consisted of two activities which were offered on alternative evenings: crayoning in coloring books and listening to children's records. The sessions lasted for periods of an hour to an hour and a half for the time the program was in operation.

How did the attendants see the program? Some viewed it as a means of keeping the residents occupied:

> I don't think it's doing any good. It gives them something to do—that's all.

There was some truth to this statement, for this was, for the great majority of the residents, the only "training" or recreation they received at the institution.

Most attendants, however, perceived the crayoning and the music as

some type of "training." In spite of the, at best, tenuous connection between these activities and training, the attendants viewed the activities
as the initial stage of a more comprehensive program:

> We're supposed to progress from here—start teaching them how to dress
> and things.

Yet the residents' performance in these most simple activities served to
further confirm the attendants' perspectives that training for these residents and on this ward was futile. Their general belief in the inability
of the residents to change was supported and specified. One attendant
explained:

> I've been trying to teach them how to color, but it doesn't work for most
> of them. They don't switch colors when they're coloring, and they won't
> stay in the lines. I've been trying to teach them, but they just scribble.

The program was unofficially terminated six weeks after its start. One
attendant related:

> It kinda fizzled out. We're not doin' it anymore.

And another stated:

> All the wards just about stopped doin' it. The whole institution was sup-
> posed to have it, but most of them stopped. I don't know—I haven't been
> here that long but I think that's the way it always goes . . . it's too hard
> keeping their attention.

Finally, one attendant summed up his own and his peers' fatalism when
he remarked:

> I bet you think we're just a bunch of lazy fat asses here. . . . Well, we do
> sit around a lot doin' nothing'. We read the paper and watch TV. But
> actually there isn't much we could do with 'em even if we wanted to.

The program on the adolescent ward lasted much longer than the program we have just reviewed, and, in fact, was still operating at last
knowledge. This program was designed by the Chief of Children's Services, Dr. Warner, who described the program as a "behavior modification program—token economy—designed to teach responsibility to the

girls." According to the plan, the girls were to be rewarded for doing assigned ward jobs and for satisfactory school work by receiving points which could be redeemed for merchandise. As Dr. Warner told one of the authors:

> This will reward them for good behavior. I really think it will make a differ-
> ence. We need a lot more behavior modification here. It's the answer.

Although skeptical of Dr. Warner, the attendants initially viewed the point system as a potentially effective way for them to control the residents' behavior and to make their work easier. One explained:

> The girls are snapping to it and doing what they are supposed to. If you tell
> them that they are going to lose some points, they pay attention to you now.

As this comment suggests, the program that was designed to reward residents for "appropriate behavior" was used to punish them for annoying behavior. Thus attendants took away points for insolence or vulgarity. Since residents could receive points from personnel other than themselves, this was one of the few means by which the attendants could retain control.

In the eyes of the attendants, Dr. Warner was far too permissive and misunderstood the girls. They claimed that the new system and other innovations would only serve to further spoil them. Witness the following comments offered by one of the attendants:

> Have you heard Dr. Warner's latest idea? He wants to let volunteers take
> the boys and girls with the most points out to dinner at some fancy place.
> These kids would probably beat up the volunteer.

The precise record-keeping which the point system entailed soon became "just a lot of trouble" for the attendants. At the end of the observation period, approximately six months after the program's implementation, the attendants were extremely lax in their point recording, and many of the girls had simply forgotten about the points they had accumulated.

A "range of motion" program was introduced onto the infant/children ward by the attending physician and the day shift ward charge, an R.N. It lasted the shortest period of time of the three programs we have reviewed, and, in fact, was never implemented for many of the residents.

The goal of this program was to provide children with the physical stimulation necessary to prevent physical regression and the development of spasticity and irreversible contractures. The program was developed in view of the fact that these conditions had already stricken many children and that, without some program, would strike many more.

The institution's lone physical therapist (institutional population: 2500) visited the ward, evaluated each child, and wrote a prescription describing the therapy that each was to receive. Each child was assigned to an attendant who had been instructed in the range of motion exercises to be employed daily.

Direct observation on the dorms revealed that few attendants ever provided their designated children with the range of motion therapy. At one point, the daytime charge, who was ultimately responsible for the program's implementation, became aware of the problem and mentioned it to her supervisor in the observer's presence:

> "The attendants aren't doing anything," said Mrs. Dey, the R.N. who was the daytime charge.
>
> "What kinds of things do you think they ought to be doing?" the observer asked.
>
> "I think they ought to be doing the range of motion," she responded.
>
> "Aren't they doing it?" asked Mrs. Dumas, the supervision nurse.
>
> "No," said Mrs Dey, shaking her head. "I go into the front dorm and all they're doing is sitting around."

When they were alone with the observer, the attendants articulated the reasons for their failure to pursue the program. They maintained, among other things, that the wrong children had been selected to participate and that they themselves were neither able (trained) nor willing (sufficiently paid) to do what was expected of them.

CONCLUSION

Our primary position in this study has been that institutional programs must be examined in the context of the ward settings on which they are introduced. We have studied one aspect of that setting, the way attendants define their supervisors, their jobs, and the residents under their charge.

In reading a paper such as ours, one might conclude that the problem of programming in total institutions lies only in attendants' attitudes and lack of training. Although this is a seductive way of defining the problem, walking through these isolated, massive facilities which are filled with unwanted human beings, one must question whether the problem is not the institutional model itself. Perhaps the feeble attempts at programming we have reported here represent the cruelest lies of this dehabilitating system. Perhaps attendants' reactions to programming are realistic adjustments to the truth of these facilities. To offer programming as a remedy to a system that by its very nature isolates, desocializes, and dehumanizes, reminds us of Marie Antoinette's remark when informed that her subjects were starving—that they had no bread. Her response was: "Let them eat cake."

NOTES

1. All proper names are pseudonyms.

2. The alternative to institutional employment for most attendants is lower-level factory or construction work.

3. This practice can have dire consequences for nonambulatory children. Those who cannot walk by the time they leave this ward are transferred to wards for nonambulatory adolescents or adults where they receive no training to walk. Many, therefore, never do walk.

11

National Policy and Situated Meaning

THE CASE OF HEAD START AND THE HANDICAPPED

In 1972, Congress required Head Start to increase through affirmative action the number of "handicapped" children to 10% of those served (P.L. 92–424, 1972). Local Head Start programs were directed to comply by the fall of 1973. Handicapped children were defined as

> . . . mentally retarded, hard of hearing, deaf, speech impaired, visually handicapped, seriously emotionally disturbed, crippled, or other health impaired children who by reason thereof require special education and related services (P.L. 92–232, 1965).

The intent of the mandate was to provide services to severely impaired youngsters in the regular Head Start setting (for a history of the legislation, see LaVor, 1972).

This paper discusses the consequences of that legislation on local programs during its first few months (Syracuse University, 1974). Data were collected by 16 site visitors who went out alone and in teams of two to spend one to three days at each of 30 Head Start programs. They used

Robert Bogdan. This article originally appeared in the *American Journal of Orthopsychiatry*, 46(2), 1976.

participant observation techniques (Becker, 1970; Bogdan, 1972; Bogdan and Taylor, 1975; Bruyn, 1966) and recorded detailed fieldnotes. A modified random sample technique was used in choosing most programs but other criteria were sometimes employed. A complete discussion of sample selection and methodology is available elsewhere (Syracuse University, 1974). The study was exploratory and designed to generate understanding of the effect of the mandate.

It has been more than 10 years since Kitsuse and Cicourel (1963) clarified the distinction between the study of the "causes" of rule breaking (the etiology of deviance) and the study of the organizational activity that produces a unit rate of deviant behavior (rate producing processes). Designation of particular people as deviant and production of official rates of deviance occur in specific situational contexts such as courts, hospitals, rehabilitation centers, and local Head Start programs. National policies that allocate resources and mandate services "for" particular categories of "clients" influence the defining process. It is important to understand how actions at the national level enter into the web of interaction in the everyday life of people. To get to the process by which labels are used, meaning negotiated, and rates of deviant behavior produced, a fieldwork approach is desirable; because of the cost and the nature of that kind of research (often these studies are unfunded and are carried out by one person), however, participant observation research has been limited in the number and diversity of settings explored in any given study. The research reported here offered a unique opportunity to explore, in a variety of settings, the effect of a national mandate on an area to which social scientists have paid relatively little attention, the large scale designating of children as handicapped (Beeghley and Butler, 1974; Edgerton and Edgerton, 1973; Mercer, 1973; Richardson and Higgins, 1965; Scott, 1969). The findings have broad policy, substantive, and theoretical implications.

PRIOR SURVEY

It is important to note, for purposes of contrast, that immediately prior to our visits, the Office of Child Development (OCD) mailed a questionnaire to all Head Start directors requiring them to report the number of handicapped children enrolled and the handicapping conditions involved. On the basis of that survey, it was stated:

Compared to last year, the number of handicapped children in Head Start approximately doubled (System Research, Inc., 1974).

A report based on those findings, submitted to Congress in April 1974, stated:

To date, children professionally diagnosed as handicapped account for at least 10.1 percent of the children enrolled. . . . In addition, 3.1 percent of the enrolled . . . are either partially diagnosed or reported possibly handicapped (U.S. Dept. of Health, Education, and Welfare, 1974, iii).

As the discussion of our data suggests, the impact of the mandate could not be understood by the figures in that report. The major difference between the approach of the survey and our field work approach was that the questionnaire took for granted matters of definition and quantification—it did not consider as problematic the ways in which handicaps were defined or counted, a skepticism central to our appoach.

OFFICIAL DEFINITIONS

Professionals dealing with the "handicapped" have continually engaged in debates about the definitions of diagnostic terms. Whereas at any given time a definition may be said to be "official" (the one accepted by the most influential professional organization), there is never a clear consensus as to the meaning of such terms as handicapped, or the specific diagnostic categories falling under that heading. A number of social scientists have pointed to the ambiguity of such terminology and the differential application of the terms in different contexts. Mercer (1973), Braginsky and Braginsky (1971), Hurley (1969), and Dexter (1964) have concurred in regard to the field of mental retardation. Scott (1969) pointed to the problem of meaning in the seemingly "objective" area of blindness. Szasz (1961, 1970), Bogdan (1974), and a host of others have noted the ambiguous and metaphorical terminology in the area of mental illness and emotional disturbance.

PERSONNEL REACTIONS

The directives given to Head Start personnel were not precise in defining handicapped or its various subcategories; nor could they be, given the nature of such terms and the controversies surrounding them. The great majority of people we talked to said they were initially confused by the mandate. "We weren't clear who they were talking about," and "It wasn't clear what 'kind' of child the mandate was referring to," were typical comments. Although staff indicated that they were initially unsure of the meaning of the mandate, they had understandings of what they *thought* it meant. Approximately half of the Head Start directors we talked to thought that the mandate referred to what they termed severely handicapped children. As one director put it: "Children who can't talk and walk." The others had broader definitions of handicapped. At the other end of the severity continuum were some who defined the mandate as referring to all the children in the Head Start programs. As one director said: "They want 10% handicapped. Hell, we have 100%." What the mandate initially meant, and what its specific charge conveyed, was a function of the common sense understandings held by project directors and their staffs.

IN SEARCH OF THE SEVERELY HANDICAPPED

Although a few program directors, acting on the broad definition of handicapped (i.e., all children in Head Start are handicapped), defined themselves as already in compliance with the mandate and did nothing to recruit, most programs made greater efforts to recruit and enroll severely handicapped children than they had prior to the mandate. Contacts were made with special agencies; advertising campaigns were launched using newspapers, radio, and flyers. In spite of these efforts, the great majority of children who became designated as handicapped were recruited through the regular Head Start recruitment procedures. These were the kinds of children Head Start had always served. Typically, the condition of "handicapped" was conferred upon children after they had entered the program.

We were told on a number of occasions: "We tried to find severely handicapped children, but they just weren't out there." The failure of special recruitment efforts can be understood in part by looking at how community agencies, which have traditionally provided services to the "handicapped" in segregated environments, reacted to the Head Start efforts. We visited representatives of these agencies as part of our field work. Many took the position that, although in general agreement with the idea of mixing handicapped children with typical children, they felt the needs of severely handicapped youngsters could not be met in Head Start. The inability of Head Start to recruit severely handicapped children seemed directly related to such perspectives, as well as to the monopoly that people with such views had in providing services.

Another important factor in the inability of Head Start programs to recruit severely impaired children is that the incidence of such conditions in the preschool population is very low. Such children are scarce, especially in communities in which other agencies have well-developed programs.

DRAWING THE LINE

As we have already pointed out, the overall nature of the population of children in Head Start changed only modestly, if at all, as a result of the mandate. Given that the characteristics of the population were the same as in the year previous, and that 10% had to be designated as handicapped, the problem became who was to be so designated.

According to directives issued to the programs, only those children who had been *professionally* diagnosed "handicapped" were to be counted as part of the required 10%. In attempting to fulfill the mandate, programs increased their use of professionals in the examination and evaluation of children. This helped Head Start staff deal with some of the ambiguities involved in diagnosing "handicaps" but it did not solve their dilemma. When examining a child, professionals made note on the record that the child had, for example, an umbilical hernia or an articulation problem or a heart murmur. But it was still up to the staff to decide whether these constituted a handicapping condition. Children were designated handicapped on the records by Head Start personnel, and it was ultimately their judgments that prevailed. Staffs in different programs developed their own definitions and applied them in order to meet the demands of the mandate. Variations in enrollment rates of the handicapped were thus meaningful only in relation to the varied concepts of "handicapped," which changed from program to program.

The nature and availability of community agencies serving handicapped children affected not only those who Head Start was able to recruit but also determined the categories in which children were placed. If, for example, a community had a well-developed speech and hearing clinic, there was a tendency for more children to be designated as having speech and hearing handicaps, since such a clinic was likely to be called upon to give special assistance to Head Start staff in assessment.

EFFECTS OF LABELING

Head Start staff in some programs were reluctant to label children as handicapped, out of concern over the long-lasting consequences of starting school careers with such a stigma. As one teacher told us: "It's bad enough that these children are known as the 'Head Start Kids.' You don't want them starting out with two strikes against them."

Although there may have been confusion and anxiety over designating youngsters, Head Start supervisors felt they had to do so in order to meet Washington's requirements. Some solved the dilemma of not wanting to stigmatize but needing to designate by not telling parents, other staff, and community agencies which children were on the handicapped list, and by not referring to a child as "handicapped." In these cases being handicapped was more an administrative matter than a programmatic concern or a stigmatizing label. In other programs, however, there was no such resolution, and certain youngsters who in the past would not have been so designated became known as handicapped. On visiting some centers, our observers found that personnel were not sure whether a certain child was on the list or not. In others, being on the list made a child the object of special attentions and made the staff more aware of special differences and needs the child might have. For some of these children, then, being "handicapped" meant receiving services they would not otherwise have had. For others, it meant being known as "hadicapped" yet receiving no special services. Thus being listed as handicapped had a variety of effects.

WHAT THE MANDATE CHANGED

We asked local Head Start directors whether they had served handicapped children prior to the mandate. Almost without exception they indicated that they had, but they did not necessarily see them as handicapped. When asked how many handicapped children they served last year, they said those figures were difficult if not impossible to estimate. The reasons given were: "children were not labeled handicapped last year," "we did not keep our handicapped separate before," "most were not professionally diagnosed until recently," and so on. Thus in retrospect it was difficult for staff to determine which of the children enrolled in the previous year would, if enrolled the year of the mandate, be classified as handicapped. There was a strong tendency to underestimate this number.

Most program personnel we talked with defined themselves as having met the regulations of the mandate: they were serving and had diagnosed 10% of their population as handicapped. For the most part, what our observers saw indicated that Head Start staff did not purposely misrepresent themselves in reporting the figures to Washington. These were people trying to come to grips with problems of meaning and definitions, attempting to evolve an operational definition of what they had been ordered to define and count. As already noted, some of the staff initially thought the mandate referred to severely impaired children, which indeed was its intent. But in attempting to recruit such children, they found few forthcoming and thus redefined handicapped so as to include more "typical" children. Those whose definition of handicapped had earlier been broader, developed definitions so as to make clearer distinctions. There was discussion about the moral implications of classifying children as handicapped. Staff sought professional advice to help clarify the concepts. Some threw up their hands in frustration. Others, and this became increasingly true over time, began to think differently about the children they were serving. We were told by one director: "We didn't know we had so many handicapped children until we started counting." Another said: "Now that the staff has an idea of how 'handicapped' is defined, they feel comfortable. They've had them all along—the definition changed them." Although the children might not have changed, staffs changed their definitions and their common sense understandings about children were altered. The official counts submitted by Head Start personnel to Washington represented those changes. Thus the mandate had a significant effect on the official rate of handicapped children enrolled without appreciably altering the characteristics of the population served.

CONCLUSION

As the mandate passed into the world of common sense understanding, its intent was lost or transformed in a complex process by which people discern, order, and reorder their own worlds. Our concern has not been focused on the effects of the mandate on children, although this is an important question, but on its implications for researchers, policy makers, practitioners, and academicians.

Specific findings of our study have general application. For one, the findings provide a clear illustration of how requiring an organization to serve specific "types" of clients makes those types more precious commodities, heightens competition for them, and increases official occurrence rates (Bogdan, 1973; Wallace, 1968). When an organization is required to recruit and count particular "types" of clients, there is a tendency for its personnel to broaden definitions so as to make more people eligible (Bogdan, 1971). The data reported here also demonstrate how a national mandate that requires counting particular "types" of clients can serve to reify and legitimize diagnostic categories, for example, children who had problems keeping still became emotionally disturbed and children who were slow became mentally retarded.

The study allowed us to see the wide variety of responses, definitions, and effects that could be generated by a particular national policy. Certainly, there is evidence in our study to suggest that requiring people to count "types" of clients resulted in "labeling" people. But the study makes clear that requiring counting has a variety of effects. Some people strongly resist applying labels and develop ways of meeting requirements of official rate production without stigmatizing. The study, then, presents a more complicated and diverse picture of the application of labels, the production of official statistics, and the relationship between the two. Although it has pointed to all these things, it makes one point that should be of paramount importance to those concerned with sociological theory and its relation to public policy.

Early in this paper we cited a report to Congress (U.S. Dept. of Health, Education, and Welfare, 1974) that 10.1% of the Head Start children had been professionally diagnosed as handicapped, and that the number of handicapped children enrolled had approximately doubled since the previous year. We have noted the great disparity between those findings and our own. The difference arises because the survey reported to Congress did not treat the terms handicapped and its various sub-categories as problematic or question the process of counting the "handi-capped," matters of central concern to us. Taking for granted the ter-minology and not being concerned about the social nature of the pro-duction of official rates of deviance led OCD to ask questions that forced Head Start staff to supply specific counts of handicapped children, some-times in spite of their better judgment.

Most studies of the impact of national or state policy decisions do not deal with the question of meaning or the manufacture of official statis-tics. This is particularly true of studies that focus on such categories as "the hard core unemployed," "the elderly," and, most recently, "child-abusing parents." Large sample size and "the facts" are what appear to be emphasized. Those interested in the effects of national policy, both on theoretical and applied levels, often have little understanding of how such policy enters into the web of interaction of their own activities, and influences the production of official rates of deviance. We have attempted to provide some understanding of that process, and to interest others in our approach.

12

Defending Illusions

By definition, all organizations have goals and formal structures. Following in the Weberian (1947) tradition, social scientists have until recently emphasized the instrumental elements of formal organization. Formal organizations have been conceptualized as rational structures oriented toward the pursuit of stated goals (Blau and Scott, 1962; Etzioni, 1962). Blau and Scott (1962:1), for example, define an organization as a social unit composed of people working together to accomplish common ends. When viewed from this perspective, goals define the purpose of an organization—its reason for existence—whereas formal structures represent the rational means used to accomplish those goals.

Increasingly, however, sociologists and anthropologists have begun to direct attention to the symbolic nature of organizational goals and formal structures (Bittner, 1964; Jacobs, 1969; Kamens, 1977; Meyer and Rowan, 1977). Organizational goals justify the existence of an organization and provide members with meaning for their activities (Jacobs, 1969). Formal structures represent a means of displaying organizational

Steven J. Taylor and Robert Bogdan. This article originally appeared in *Human Organization*, 39(3): 209–218, 1980.

responsibility and rationality (Meyer and Rowan, 1977:344). Thus organizational goals and structures act as legitimating myths used to gain the support of external publics on which organizations depend for their survival. For instance, the goals and formal structures of universities are designed to legitimate the idea that students have acquired the necessary educational experiences to perform certain roles in society (Kamens, 1977).

Every organization faces the possibility that its legitimizing myths may be shattered. Black shadows fall between what organizations say they do and what they actually engage in: between their espoused goals and everyday practices. Studies of human service organizations reveal a great discrepancy between formal myth and actual reality: mental hospitals do not cure, nursing homes do not comfort, reform schools do not save, drug centers do not rehabilitate, and job training programs do not train.[1]

This paper deals with a type of organization that is engaged in a struggle for survival, institutions—so-called "state schools"—for the "mentally retarded." As used in this paper, "institutions" means "total institution" in Goffman's (1961:xiii) sense.

Of interest in this paper is how organizational standard bearers (institutional professionals and officials holding administrative positions) manage the visible discrepancy between goals and practices. The subjects of our study include persons with the titles of director (superintendent), assistant director, business officer, chief of service (mid-level administrator), and team leader (lower-level administrator). In *Asylums*, Goffman (1961) described the rigid distinction between institutional staff and inmates. What Goffman did not discuss is the ambivalence and even hostility between different levels of staff: ward staff, or attendants, on the one hand, and institutional officials, on the other. Officials share certain elements in common that distinguish them from other levels of staff: their work does not involve direct day-to-day contact with residents, their professional identities and careers are caught up in people work (Goffman, 1961:74), they have been schooled in an ideology of service to humanity, and, as the name "standard bearers" suggests, they represent the organization in relations with the outside world.

To be sure, institutional professionals and administrators may differ from each other according to their responsibilities and positions in the hierarchy. However, we are interested in their common perspectives and reactions to the outside world. Also, although we do not maintain that these common perspectives and reactions are shared by all standard bearers, we do take the position that they characterize the dominant views of those we have studied.

This study is based on qualitative methods and analytical procedures (Bogdan and Taylor, 1975). The sources of data are broad and diverse. A major source of data comes from extensive participant observation at four Northeastern institutions (Central, Cornerstone, Eastern, and Empire State Schools[2]) conducted by the authors and student observers between 1970 and 1977. Three of these institutions are located in one state, and a fourth in another; three are old facilities, established at the turn of the century, whereas the fourth is a new institution, constructed in the 1970s; three are located in small towns, and the fourth in an urban area. These institutions ranged in size from slightly over 250 residents to approximately 3300 at the times they were studied.

We have also used participant observation data collected by student observers at seven additional state schools located in the first-mentioned state. Like Eastern, Empire, Cornerstone, and Central, these state schools vary widely in size, age, and geographical area. Although these data have enabled us to generalize our findings, we have not based any conclusions solely on data collected by others.

In addition, one of us, using a participant observation approach, has visited 11 other institutions in 5 other states: one in a third northeastern state; one in a western state; two in a midwestern state; three in a southern state; four in a midAtlantic state. Three of these institutions were toured in 1979, whereas eight were toured in 1980.

All the participant observations, whether conducted by ourselves or others, focused on ward life at these 15 institutions (see Bogdan et al., 1974; Taylor, 1977). However, semiformal interviews were conducted with at least one and usually several high-ranking officials at each institution. Also, we or the student observers typically received tours of the institutions from officials prior to observing ward life. At several institutions, we reported our findings to institutional officials at the conclusion of our observations. At Empire, for example, we met with the administrative staff to discuss the observations of 15 graduate student observers, each of whom spent 6 full days living at the institution. Of course, on these occasions, we carefully recorded officials' reactions to our findings and observations.

A second source of data is written documents and materials: brochures, policy statements, memoranda, statistical data, and institutional news-letters. On some occasions, we have obtained administrators' written reactions to outside criticism.

Another source is public information, for example, court records and newspaper articles. For institutions for which our sole source of data was public information, we have not attempted to conceal the names of the facilities.

Finally, we have spent time with administrators and professionals at annual professional conventions, social gatherings, and other meetings. Often these contacts provided our best sources of data on administrators' perspectives.

In the following section we describe the events that have challenged the legitimacy of state schools for the retarded. The remainder of the paper is devoted to how institutional standard bearers develop a world view and practical strategies to manage the discrepancy between what their goals and accomplishments are. First, we show how a set of legitimating myths has been developed to justify the existence of institutions. Second, we consider how institutional administrators manage relations with the outside world. Third, we describe the accounts and defense used by standard bearers when faced with outside criticism.

THE ATTACK FROM WITHOUT

State schools for the mentally retarded have been subject to criticism over the past decade and a half. All organizations are subject to criticism at one time or another. What distinguishes state schools is that the criticism has come from a range of respected sources, received widespread publicity, and called into question the legitimacy of the very existence of institutions as a form of service organization.

Exposés

State schools have not been immune to public criticism over the course of their history. A new and constant assault began in the mid-1960s when Senator Robert Kennedy made unannounced tours to a number of state schools in the northeastern United States. Kennedy's outrage at what he observed received nationwide publicity and placed institutional officials in a defensive posture from which they have never recovered. Kennedy toured one of the state schools in this study and was quoted as follows in the *New York Times*: "I was shocked and saddened by what I saw there . . . There are children slipping into blankness and lifelong dependence."

Shortly after Kennedy's exposé, Blatt and Kaplan (1974), the former a well-respected professional in the field of mental retardation and the latter a photographer, published an exposé based on pictures secretly taken on the back wards of state schools in a number of northeastern states. Their book, *Christmas in Purgatory,* depicted degradation, abuse, and squalid conditions, and was later the basis of an article in *Look* magazine, an article that received the largest reader response in the history of that magazine.

The 1970s witnessed a frontal attack on state schools in the form of media exposés. Geraldo Rivera's (1972) exposé of Willowbrook State School in Staten Island, New York, received national publicity. Excerpts of film footage shot at that institution were subsequently shown on the *Dick Cavett Show*. Similar media exposés have occurred in nearly every state in the nation.

The Consumer Movement

The first national organization of parents of retarded persons was founded around 1950. Since that time parent groups throughout the nation have grown increasingly militant in demanding quality services for their children. Whereas at one time parents served a volunteer function at institutions—for example, sponsoring bake sales—today they more often perform a watchdog function. In the majority of institutional lawsuits filed across the country, parent organizations have themselves been plaintiffs. The 1970s also witnessed the development of organizations of retarded persons themselves; the most notable, People First, started in Oregon and now has chapters in a number of states. As implied by its name, People First has demanded that the retarded be given the same rights and privileges enjoyed by other members of society.

The Extension of the Civil Rights Movement

Toward the end of the 1960s, public interest and civil rights attorneys began to direct attention to the plight of the retarded. Their efforts have resulted in a long series of smashing legal victories. In *Wyatt v. Stickney*, a landmark suit in Alabama, a federal district judge in 1972 ruled that institutionalized mentally retarded persons have a constitutional right to treatment under the "least restrictive"—that is, most normal—circumstances. At Willowbrook, another federal judge ruled in *NYSARC v. Rockefeller* that persons at that institution had a constitutional right to protection from harm. Judge Judd, the federal judge in that case, found conditions at Willowbrook "inhumane" and noted "a failure to protect the physical safety of . . . children, and deterioration rather than improvement after they were placed in Willowbrook School." A court ruling in *Halderman v. Pennhurst State School* in Pennsylvania challenged the legality of the very existence of segregated total institutions for the mentally retarded. In this ruling, which has been modified by higher courts and is still under appeal, Federal District Judge Raymond Broderick ordered the State of Pennsylvania to create community alternatives for all the residents of Pennhurst and, in effect, to close Pennhurst State School referred to as a "typical institution" in the case. Similar suits have been won or filed in a large number of states, including Minnesota, Nebraska, Tennessee, Florida, Kentucky, Michigan, West Virginia, Connecticut, Maine, Rhode Island, Massachusetts, North Dakota, New Jersey, and others.

Federal Legislation

Spurred by the widespread negative publicity received by institutions across the country, the U.S. Congress has passed a long series of laws designed to improve existing institutions or to create community alternatives. Foremost among these are Section 504 of the Rehabilitation Act of 1973, which mandated nondiscrimination against persons with disabilities; the Developmentally Disabled Assistance and Bill of Rights Act of 1975, which provided funds to the states to provide services to the mentally retarded; Title XIX Medicaid legislation, which, among other things, provided massive amounts of funds to states to finance institutional and community services for the retarded; and P.L. 94–142 which mandated a "free appropriate public education" for all handicapped children, including the most severely disabled and those in institutions. The legislative testimony surrounding the passage of each of these laws indicates an acute awareness of Congress of the plight of institutionalized persons.

Social Science Perspectives

Traditionally, the field of mental retardation, or as it is better known, "mental deficiency," has been dominated by medical and psychological perspectives. Beginning with the 1960s, however, social science perspectives have played an important role in shaping professional opinion in the field. The studies of Braginsky and Braginsky (1971), Goffman (1961), Tizzard (1970), Vail (1967), and Wolfensberger (1975), all of which, building on sociological or anthropological perspectives, point to the dehumanizing effects of institutionalization, and are widely known and respected among researchers and professionals in the field of mental retardation. Out of social science perspectives has come the principle of normalization, first developed in Scandanavia and publicized in this country by Wolfensberger (1972). The importance of the principle of normalization is that it articulates a clear alternative philosophy and approach to the traditional practice of segregating retarded persons in congregate institutions.

The institutional standard bearers in this study are not only well aware of recent critiques of institutional life, but have themselves been confronted with outside criticism. With one possible exception, all these state schools have received negative public exposure in the 1970s. Some have had special independent investigations of questionable deaths and abusive conditions. At least four have been subjects of lawsuits, whereas others have been attacked by legal or advocacy groups. At Empire State School, 24 attendants were arrested on charges of abuse several years ago as a result of an investigation of an undercover state trooper who posed as an attendant for a year. It is these events that have thrust state schools into a struggle for existence, what one commentator (Wolfensberger, 1975) has called the death throes of the institutional model.[3]

THE SYMBOLIC TRANSFORMATION OF INSTITUTIONS

Traditionally, one or more of three legitimating myths have been used to justify the existence of state schools for the mentally retarded (Davis, 1959; Kanner, 1964; Sarason and Doris, 1959; Wolfensberger, 1975; also see the papers of the founders of the modern institutional model contained in Rosen et al., 1976). First, as the name "state school" suggests, these institutions have been held up as education and training centers for the more mildly and moderately retarded. Education and training has been defined less in terms of academic instruction than moral discipline and hard work, including caring for the severely disabled residents of the institution. Second, institutions have found legitimacy in providing custodial care for the severely and profoundly retarded and multiply handicapped. Some institutions were founded as custodial asylums or infirmaries for the nonambulatory. For instance, Empire was founded in the late 1800s as "Empire State Custodial Asylum for Unteachable Idiots." All institutions, regardless of why they were originally established, eventually developed custodial departments for the care of the severely disabled. Finally, state schools for the retarded have been justified as agencies of social control. Spurred by the eugenics movement around the turn of the century, many institutions were founded to segregate the retarded, especially the "high grade feebleminded," and thereby prevent the distribution of allegedly defective genes associated with crime, feeblemindedness, and degeneracy throughout the population. Thus Central State School was established as "Central State Custodial Asylum for Feebleminded Women of Child-Bearing Age" during the latter part of the nineteenth century.

In the modern—post World War II—period, state schools have had as legitimating myths the education of the more mildly retarded and the custodial care of the more severely disabled. With the waning of the eugenics movement in the 1920s, social control gradually ceased to serve as a legitimating myth for state schools for the retarded. By the end of the World War, professionals and institutional officials were eager to disassociate themselves from the logical extension of eugenics policies as found in Nazi Germany.

Until recently, the modern institution found legitimacy in holding itself up as a place in which the retarded are provided with benign care and treatment. Critics, however, have shattered this image of the institution. As public exposés, scholarly studies, court evidence, and professional critiques have ably demonstrated, state schools have provided neither education nor humane care. Rather than educate, institutions debilitate; rather than provide care, they abuse. Some critics, increasingly, go further than pointing to a discrepancy between goals and conditions by suggesting that the institution, by its nature, is inconsistent with humanitarian, educational, or therapeutic goals.

What is occurring at present is a symbolic transformation of state schools for the mentally retarded in response to attacks from without. The old goals, formal structures, and vocabularies no longer serve to legitimate the existence of state schools to external publics or to institutional officials themselves. The old legitimating myths are being discarded and new ones created. Not surprisingly, the new legitimating myths conform to current ideologies in the field of mental retardation and to the vocabularies used by institutional critics.

The state schools in this study are in a process of changing their goals, structures, and vocabularies along the lines of what has been termed the "developmental model" (Wolfensberger, 1975), the clinician counterpart of the principle of normalization. This trend is epitomized by the renaming of Willowbrook State School, which has become synonymous with snakepit in the public mind, to Staten Island Developmental Center. None of the institutions in the study has accomplished a perfect symbolic transformation. Old structures and vocabularies persist to some extent.

Some institutions have progressed further in creating new legitimating myths than others. An institution's relations with the outside world seem important in influencing the extent to which it has developed new goals, structures, and vocabularies. Thus institutions routinely exposed to outside criticism, whether from courts, reporters, professionals, or parents, seem more likely to subscribe to a developmental model. Those located in remote areas are more likely to cling to the elements of a traditional medical or custodial model. However, our data do not warrant a simple linear explanation. What is important is that all the institutions are moving in the same direction.

Goals

Many of the institutions in this study were originally called "asylums." Some time after the turn of the century they were retitled "state school" or "state hospital." In the 1970s many institutions received yet another name: "developmental center," "regional center," or "education and training center." The state in which Empire, Central, and Cornerstone are located recently renamed all of its institutions "developmental center."

During the early 1970s, institutional goals were phrased in terms of education and custodial care. An official bulletin published by Empire State School around 1972 read as follows:

Empire State School, responsible for the care and treatment of the mentally
retarded, is one of several State Schools in the Department of Mental Hy-
giene of (State) . . . Some of the aims of the School are: (1) To care for
those residents who are unable to help themselves; (2) To help those who
are able to be accepted back into the community as useful citizens; and
(3) To teach each resident to become self-sufficient as possible.

By the mid to late 1970s, many institutions had developed a new set of
goals, emphasizing the residents' potential for growth and development.
A statement prepared by the administration of Central State School
presents the goals of children's service in the following manner:

The objective of the Children's Habilitation Service will be to promote
optimum realization of each individual's potential for successful and satis-
fying adjustment to his environment, adaptation to others in his environment, and contribution to society.

Cornerstone State School, one of the more "progressive" institutions
in the study, adopted the goal of normalization in the mid-1970s. One
official policy statement expresses the goal "to promote programs both
within the facility and in the community which adhere closely as possible
to the principles of normalization." Another publication defines Cornerstone's philosophy as "Normalization—the concept of providing an environment and programs that will enable a handicapped person to function in ways considered to be within acceptable norms for his society." By
the end of the 1970s, the agency responsible for operating institutions in
this state had adopted the goal of normalization for all of its facilities.

Formal Structures

As Meyer and Rowan (1977:346) state, organizations structurally reflect
the social reality constructed by their goals. Traditionally, asylums or
state schools were organized as a rigid medical hierarchy. Governing the
institutions were "medical officers" or "superintendens." Ward service
supervisors, generally nurses, occupied the next level in the institutional
pecking order. Attendants occupied the bottom rungs of the organization. Teachers and other professionals held staff positions and lacked line
authority.

The modern institution is in the process of being reorganized. According to the formal organization of the institution, authority and re-

sponsibility are being decentralized. Elements of the hierarchy remain. There is a director, an assistant director, chiefs of service (e.g., in charge of children's services or adult services), team leaders, unit coordinators, and direct care staff. Typically, administrative positions are staffed by professionals with backgrounds in psychology, education, or management. But, according to the formal structure, day-to-day decision-making follows a "team approach" or "unitization" (Sluyter, 1976). As one optimistic administrator put it, "Our new philosophy is unitization. Service will revolve around the patient and the patient won't live in a way that is simply convenient for the staff." Another standard bearer explained what the team approach would mean at his institution:

> The psychologist could diagnose problems and prescribe services and directions. The social worker could use the community setting to place these men wisely in community activities. The guidance counselors could steer the residents' everyday rocky ship. The physician and nurse could administer medical problems. The school teacher could prepare him basically for his educational needs when he goes into the community. The speech therapist could improve his expressive and acceptance speech and language abilities. Finally, the attendants could follow up the recommendations of any professional consultant rather than babysit.

Another recent trend at institutions is the proliferation of policies governing almost every aspect of residents' care. This reflects an increased emphasis on displaying rationality and responsibility to the outside world as well as the requirements of federal Medicaid standards. Thus at all institutions there are policies concerning the reporting of incidents, abuse, the use of restraints, positioning techniques for nonambulatory residents, housekeeping procedures, the preparation of meals, and so on. In addition, all institutionalized residents have "treatment plans" or "individual habilitation plans" that contain a statement of therapeutic goals, means to accomplish those goals, and measures of progress.

Ironically, our data provides some evidence to suggest that if anything, decision-making has become *more* centralized at institutions over the past decade. In the past attendants made decisions regarding the use of restraints or isolation. Today physicians must certify that such practices are "in the resident's best interests." Further, treatment teams and individual staff avoid making potentially controversial decisions concerning residents' care or ward practices, leaving high-ranking officials with the responsibility of making these decisions.

Vocabularies

Nowhere is the symbolic transformation of state schools more evident than in institutional vocabularies (Meyer and Rowans, 1977:349). As noted, the names of the facilities and titles of staff have been changed to present a new image of institutions. Similarly, inmates are no longer called "patients," but "residents" or "clients." Building and living units have been renamed to reflect current ideological thrusts. At Eastern, custodial buildings have been redesignated "living and learning units." Another institution refers to its wards as "halfway houses." On the wards—"units"—mundane activities and traditional practices carry new names. For example, "motivation training" refers to coloring with crayons and listening to music at one state school. Table 1 contrasts the traditional institutional legitimating myths—goals, formal structures, and vocabulary—with the new developmental legitimating myths created in recent years. Again, not all institutions have incorporated all the elements of the new legitimating myths.

Recent changes in the goals, structures, and vocabulary of institutions communicate a concern with providing individualized and normalized care for residents. These changes are to be seen as symbolic, rather than real. These state schools *are* total institutions. For residents, daily life is routinized and regimented. Our own observations over a period of more than a decade indicate that the conditions and abuses exposed over the last 15 years persist to this day to some extent.

MANAGING RELATIONS WITH THE OUTSIDE WORLD

One of the consequences of institutional exposés, court suits, and public critiques has been to open the operations of a closed organization to the view of all. It is common knowledge these days that institutions are "bad" places. Nearly everyone associated with mental retardation has seen pictures of squalid institutional conditions in the newspapers, in magazines, or on the news. The evils of institutions are so well known that as reported in a recent *Newsweek* article, parents may provide an account for withholding life-sustaining medical treatment for their child on the grounds that he will end up in an institution eventually and should be spared the suffering. In short, the emperor wears no clothes, and must stand naked in plain view for all to see.

Table 1. The Symbolic Transformation of Institutions
Goals, Structures, Vocabularies

	Traditional Model	New "Developmental" Model
Goals	Custodial care Education	Normalization Habilitation
Formal Structure	Rigid, medically dominated hierarchy Policies vaguely formulated Practices governed largely by custom, tradition	Team approach, unitization All aspects of institution and residents' care governed by written policies
Vocabulary		
Facility name	State School, Hospital	Developmental center, regional center, education and training center
Staff titles	Superintendent Supervisor Ward Charge Attendant, Aide	Director Chief of service, team leader Unit coordinator Therapy aide, mental hygiene assistant, advocate
Living quarters	Ward Custodial Ward Punishment Ward	Unit, halfway house, living and learning unit, special treatment unit, behavior shaping unit
Inmate titles	Patients	Residents, clients
Inmate categories	High grade, low grade, moron, idiot, imbecile	Mildly, moderately, severely, profoundly retarded Developmentally disabled
Extensions of the institutions	Colonies	Halfway houses, group homes, community residences
Practices	Straitjackets, camisoles Tripping Isolation	Restraining devices Toileting Time-out
Activities	Activities referred to by descriptive names; e.g., going for walks, coloring	Motivation training, recreation therapy

Institutional standard bearers, like administrators in all organizations, actively manage outsiders' impressions of their facilities by presenting fronts consistent with organizational goals (Goffman, 1959, 1961). This is not new. What is new is that recent events such as exposés, public scrutiny, militant parents, and the like have demanded increasingly sophisticated impression management techniques. No longer can institutions automatically deny access to members of the outside world.

Institutions use many standard public relations techniques in dealing with outside publics. A sign of the times, many employ a public relations specialist for precisely this purpose. Officials write and distribute various literature-brochures, for example, outlining institutional goals and philosophy as well as the wide range of services that are supposed to be available to residents. Institutional literature paints an ironically blissful picture of institutional life. A brochure distributed by Central State School contained these words:

> It has been said that no man is an island. Neither is this Institution nor the people in it. For many it is a bridge—a bridge from an aimless and isolated life in the community to useful and integrated membership in society. For others, it is a haven—offering the kind of care, protection and nurturing which are necessary to foster the blossoming of a delicate plant. For none is it a dungeon of oblivion and neglect, walled up against the rest of the world. Rather it is a place of devotion and dedication which draws upon the good will, resources and services of society and, in turn, contributes to the benefit and welfare of that same society. Yes . . . "This is Central State School."

Similarly, institutions issue press releases announcing special events: field days, picnics, staff recognition awards, the visit of a celebrity. In 1976 one institution sent out a press release to announce the renaming of its buildings along bicentennial lines, for instance, "Independence Hall." Another institution sponsored a widely publicized poster contest at local high schools on the theme, "At (state school), we care."

Officials make regular public appearances to promote the preferred image of the institution. These include speaking engagements before community groups as well as appearances on local radio and television talk shows. One institution's director writes guest editorials for a large urban newspaper. In addition, institutions often operate booths at community gatherings as vehicles to distribute literature.

Institutions receive regular requests from outside groups and individuals to visit or tour the facilities. Officials use a host of strategies to deal with these situations. They may deny access to certain outsiders (university students or unaffiliated individuals) by invoking the *rhetoric of rights;* that is, by using their obligation to respect residents' rights to privacy and confidentiality as a means of keeping conditions hidden from the public view. However, it is difficult to deny access to certain persons (parents, attorneys, advocacy groups, elected officials, and other influential persons) for to do so is to run the risk of the appearance of a cover-up.

Institutions sometimes have special rooms set aside for visits between residents and family members. As Goffman (1961:102) notes, the decor and furnishings of these rooms more closely approximate outside standards than residents' actual living quarters. Staff will usher unexpected visitors to these rooms in order to "protect the privacy of other residents" or "allow you to be alone with your child." Whether or not institutions maintain visiting rooms, staff expect family members to give notice prior to visits. This enables staff to dress residents in normal, as opposed to "state issue," clothes and to make sure they are properly showered or shaved.

Institutions may sponsor an "open house" for members of the community. These tend to be highly staged affairs during which outsiders are taken to model programs, shown the newest equipment and facilities, and introduced to the "institutional characters": a woman 101 years old, a man who paints pictures, a child with an exotic disease. "Open house" is never truly open in the sense of back regions (living units, especially those for more severely disabled residents) being accessible to outsiders. In fact, "open house" may consist of nothing more than staff presentations. At one institution, officials show slides of selected living units during these occasions.

Some institutions do provide tours to interested community groups. All institutions give tours to influential persons. Officials discourage tours on weekends, since institutions are characterized by an utter lack of structured activity at these times, and, if possible, will avoid taking outsiders to typical living units, especially the "back wards" (so-called because custodial units have historically been located the farthest from the administration building).

In preparation for visits by important outsiders, staff will scrub the floors, place new bedspreads on the beds, stock bathrooms with soap and toilet paper, mount decorations on the walls, and make special efforts to keep residents clean and dressed. On one Empire ward, staff maintained a supply of stuffed animals which were placed on residents' beds immediately before a tour and removed and put away immediately afterwards.

Institutional tour guides define (Lyman and Scott, 1970) and predefine (Hewitt and Stokes, 1975) outsiders' experiences and observations at the institutions. The typical tour begins with a brief discussion of the philosophy of the institution, the nature of its clients, its financial and other hardships, and its progress over the years. During the tour, guides tell visitors what to see and how to interpret it. They usually have ready-made interpretations for the absence of programming or any form of meaningful activity: visitors "just miss" or "come too early" to observe the programs offered to residents or they happen to visit on the "school holiday" or "our therapist's day off."

It would be misleading to suggest that the typical official consciously manipulates or lies to outsiders. Administrators and professionals approach their work by highlighting the positive features of their institutions and downplaying the negative features. They organize their work so as to be more familiar with those parts of the institution which more closely approximate the therapeutic ideal than with those in which blatant abuse occurs. As Roth (1971) notes of professionals in public hospitals, state school officials tend to turn their backs on the day-to-day happenings on the wards and spend their time physically isolated in administrative enclaves. They may seldom, if ever, visit the back wards (this is a common complaint among institutional attendants). To a large extent, institutional standard bearers take on a belief in the reality they create for outsiders.

An organization's legitimating myths will structure its standard bearers' accounts for its activities. For example, business executives have ready-made explanations for making excessive profits; prison officials (at least those subscribing to retribution goals) have ready-made explanations for imposing hardships on inmates; military officers have ready-made explanations for taking lives. Institutional officials tend to provide different accounts for abusive or dehumanizing conditions according to whether they subscribe to a traditional custodial model of services or a new developmental model. Of course, since most state schools are in the process of symbolic transformation, different officials at a single state school may offer accounts reflecting either traditional or new legitimating myths. Similarly, a single official may offer a different type of account at different times or in different situations.

What distinguishes officials' accounts is whether they involve a denial or admission of the harmfulness of conditions or practices. If an institution is characterized by traditional legitimating myths, its officials will be inclined to suggest that conditions are not harmful or that they are inevitable. If, on the other hand, the institution is held up as being based on a developmental model, its officials will tend to admit to the harmfulness of conditions, but provide detailed rationales or excuses for why they exist. *Any* official may deny the existence of certain conditions or events. However, critics are usually able to document at least some of their charges, so this defense is of limited usefulness.

Denial of Harm

Officials may account for dehumanizing conditions by attributing them to the nature of their population. As one official commented during a tour, "Conditions are bad here, but what can you expect with severely retarded, acting-out residents." This is similar to what Sykes and Matza (1957) refer to as "denial of the victim" and Ryan (1972) refers to as "blaming the victim."

Historically, state schools never aspired to provide anything more to the severely and profoundly retarded and multiply disabled than pure custodial care—feeding them, supervising them, and cleaning up after them. Officials who cling to traditional perspectives will deny that the lot of more severely disabled residents can be improved. If the wards smell and are unclean, this will be accounted for by the presumed inability of residents to be toilet-trained; if residents rock, bang their heads, remove their clothes, abuse themselves or each other, this will be explained by inherent characteristics of the severely mentally retarded. This line of defense is epitomized by Nelson Rockefeller's account for dehumanizing conditions at Willowbrook offered in response to a question asked during Senate hearings on his confirmation as Vice-President in 1974: "It is very difficult to get people to devote their lives to take care of human beings while really in full fact it is not more than a vegetable."

One way to deny the harmfulness of institutions is to provide examples of abusive and dehumanizing conditions in noninstitutional settings. Some officials claim that even if institutional conditions are not good, they provide better care than the retarded can receive elsewhere. In the words of one administrator, "There will always be a need for institutions . . . as long as we have serious problems like the severely and profoundly retarded. This is the best treatment that some of the kids will ever get." Officials can provide countless examples of abuse and exploitation in group homes, foster families, and even residents' own families. One explained:

> As for this institution, this is the best thing for some of these kids. They are fed, kept warm, and clothed. For some of them this would not have happened because some come from unbelievable home situations.

Officials may also defend their institutions by condemning their critics (Sykes and Matza, 1957). As one standard bearer stated, "People are always criticizing institutions and how they are run and even whether they should exist. Yet they offer no alternatives or solutions." When officials use this defense, they are suggesting critics are naive or misguided in believing that conditions could be otherwise. In short, outsiders "don't know what it's really like." Some officials go further by accusing critics of serving their own self-interests. As they put it, politicians are after votes, reporters are after hot stories, lawyers are after a fast buck, academicians are trying to build their reputations, and parents are attempting to alleviate their own guilt. By condemning their condemners, officials try to get their institutions off the hook.

Any official may use denial as a defense. At any institution, some officials will blame the victim, discredit families and community alternatives, and at least privately question the motives of critics. But this line of defense is inconsistent with current legitimating myths and ideologies. One cannot subscribe to the developmental model and deny residents' potential for development. Nor can abuses in noninstitutional settings or the motives of critics excuse the failure to provide programming or even a safe living environment for the persons under their care. Increasingly, officials account for abusive conditions, not by asserting their inevitability, but by attributing them to circumstances beyond the institution's or their control.

Denial of Responsibility

One pervasive belief among institutional officials is that society—the general public and elected officials—has never provided them with the resources and funds to accomplish their goals. They defend the institution and themselves by pointing a finger of blame elsewhere. One administrator accounted for this institution's problems as follows:

> Money is the problem. We have to work within the budget. But we need more employees and some up-to-date, modern fireproof facilities.

Another official expressed the point more directly: "The public complains, but there is nothing more that can be done if people aren't willing to help and we cannot get more funds."

A corollary of this belief is that institutional conditions have improved over the past and will continue to improve as the public provides greater resources with which to accomplish the institution's noble ends. Officials point to declining populations and increased staffing to demonstrate that things have improved. One Empire administrator stated, "There have been many improvements. In 1965 there were 4300 residents and we have reduced that number greatly and we've hired many more employees." Eastern's director, a relatively new administrator, explained, "You'll find that this institution is probably unlike any other you've ever been to. We've gone through a lot of changes over the past couple years." And a Central standard bearer had this to say: "I've worked here 25 years and I've seen a great many improvements. Of course, everything isn't perfect yet." Institutional officials may also compare their institutions to others to show that conditions are not as bad as they could be. Thus a deputy director at Eastern admitted that his institution was a "hole," but added, "It's the best institution in the state."

Insitutional officials, admitting that their facilities are overcrowded and that more mildly retarded persons should not be institutionalized, increasingly blame the community for their problems. Thus neighborhoods may be blamed for not accepting the retarded: "If the community isn't willing to accept these people, there's not much we can do." Parents and community agencies may be blamed for exerting pressures on the institution to accept more residents than it can accommodate. An official at a Midwestern state school offered this explanation for the failure of his institution to place people in the community:

> . . . the residents ought to be served in training programs in the community. However, these facilities do not exist and thus demands for the use of the institution continues from parents and community agencies . . . We do have an ongoing deinstitutionalization program, but we can only deinstitutionalize to the point that community facilities are available.

By locating responsibility for the institution's problems with the public, legislators, community agencies, parents, and others, officials can maintain their belief in the institution's legitimating myths and avoid organizational and personal responsibility for abuse and dehumanizing conditions. Their institutions are good, even if they are bad.

The Rhetoric of Rights

Earlier we discussed how the rhetoric of rights (specifically, residents' rights to privacy and confidentiality) may be used to keep the institution's operations hidden from public view. Officials may also invoke residents' rights to account for certain practices and conditions.

The rhetoric of rights may be used either to attack mandated changes or to justify benign neglect. An example of the former is found in officials' response to recent laws prohibiting institutional peonage. One administrator commented:

> We used to have them doing all kinds of work, and they liked it. It made them feel important. We can't let them work anymore, so they have to sit around all day doing nothing.

As a justification of current practices, the rhetoric of rights may be used to account for a failure to provide residents with programming or to encourage them to act in socially appropriate ways. At one institution, administrators justified the lack of programming for one profoundly retarded, nonverbal resident on the grounds that he refused to participate in recreation activities. At a Midwestern state school, an official offered this account for residents being naked in ward dayrooms: ". . . if we talk about rights, maybe one should have the right to be naked in one's personal environment." This official justified the dressing of residents in non-normalizing clothing on the same grounds: "We try to provide residents clothing which is 'normal' but some prefer to wear clothing which may appear 'baggy' and inappropriate—which is frequently their choice." The rhetoric of rights is most often used to justify childlike decorations on adult wards and childlike possessions—toys or stuffed animals—for adults. Officials are likely to claim that retarded adults want childlike decorations and possessions, even though no attempt is made to provide them with age-appropriate objects. Of course, the rhetoric of rights goes hand-in-hand with the new legitimating myths of institutions.

The Protection of Policies

One reason for the proliferation of institutional policies is to create the appearance of bureaucratic efficiency and rationality. Another is to avoid organizational and administrative responsibility for the actions of direct care staff.

As noted earlier, institutional officials issue policies covering almost every aspect of residents' care. Policies prohibit physical or psychological abuse; policies define when and how residents may be restrained or placed in isolation; policies specify procedures for reporting accidents and injuries; policies call for the implementation of ward programs. When their institutions are characterized as being abusive or repressive, officials respond by holding up written policies as a way of getting the organization and themselves off the hook. One Midwestern official countered charges that residents were secluded in locked dormitories during the day by stating, "This is not policy." Similarly, the director of a Far Western institution responded to a legal aid organization's charges that physical restraints were used excessively for staff convenience, and as punishment by sending the attorneys the institution's policies on physical restraint and behavior modification.

By using policies as a means of defense, administrators create a definition of abuse as idiosyncratic and uncontrollable. Abuse is presented as a consequence of the failings of attendants. One official explained, "We try to teach our attendants . . . It isn't easy since we're dealing with human beings with all their weaknesses." Another official, speaking at a professional convention, claimed that administrators have no control over attendants' actions:

> I'll tell you what the problem with the institution is. It's those damn civil service regulations and all that civil rights crap. We can't get rid of anyone. We have to give them a hearing . . . If we could start firing people, we wouldn't have abuse.

Officials may account for a lack of ward programming in the same manner. For some, attendants are rather backward folks: "You have to remember that most of them have not graduated high school and have no experience at all. It's one of the bad points about the institution." For others, attendants just don't care:

> Those wards are really bad places. The attendants don't really care about the kids . . . They spend their time on other things rather than on the kids.

To blame attendants for the institutions' problems is to destroy staff morale and create hostility between higher and lower levels of staff. Perhaps for this reason, most officials make frequent public testimonials to the dedication of most attendants and, at least in public statements, blame abuse and policy violations on a "few rotten apples in the barrel." One administrator elaborated on this theme:

> I have some bad seeds in my department as I'm sure you'll find in every organization. I cannot do anything about them because they are smart enough not to get caught. The union has strict rules that protect the bad worker. I will stand up for one of my good workers anytime. If we see something wrong we will write it up and take it to the director's office.

Attendants, for their part, complain that "higher-ups" impose unrealistic expectations on them and scapegoat them for conditions beyond their control (Bogdan, et al., 1974; Taylor, 1977).

CONCLUSION

There are two general conclusions to be drawn from this study. The first has to do with the survival of total institutions for the mentally retarded. As we have argued, institutions have adopted a new image and new legitimating myths in response to external forces for change. And institutional officials have developed increasingly sophisticated strategies and defenses to deal with the outside world.

We cannot predict whether total institutions will be successful in their struggle for organizational survival. But we can say that the battle will hinge on their ability to maintain legitimacy among important external publics. Although direct observation of institutional life reveals a wide discrepancy between goals and practices, the new legitimating myths uphold the image of the institution as a benign, therapeutic setting serving humanitarian ends. Further, as the current furor over institutional abuse and dehumanization dies down, it is possible for total institutions to cloak themselves in the legitimating myths of the past. The institutional model first gained widespread acceptance during the eugenics movement around the turn of the century. Renewed social science interest in the biological bases of behavior and the inheritability of intelligence clearly does not bode well for the mentally retarded. Whatever the case, the institution's struggle for survival will continue to take a symbolic form.

The second conclusion relates to institutional officials and professionals—those we have referred to as organizational standard bearers. These officials are not alone in facing criticism from without. To the contrary, their lot is shared by professionals in a wide range of service organizations accused of harming those they purport to help (Biklen, 1975; Lasch, 1978; Piven and Cloward, 1971; Ryan, 1972; Scott, 1969; Szasz, 1970). What is the effect on human beings who are trained in professional schools to serve the "less fortunate" and then graduate to positions in the labor force in which their activities have a detrimental effect: their activities do not serve clients but rather do society's dirty work? The officials in our study may signal the coming of a crisis for professionals working in human services. Professionals make a large investment in time and training to get to the positions they occupy. With declining job possibilities and career alternatives it is difficult to leave positions in which they are unable to carry out their service orientation—to help people. As their pretenses and excuses become transparent, the trap they find themselves in may be one of the significant problems this generation will have to face. Their crisis may be one of the prices to pay for confronting our human service system directly and liberating its clients.

NOTES

1. Carol Weiss (1972:11) states: "results of evaluation research more often than not, show little positive change." For studies see: Goffman (1961), Wiseman (1970), Gubrium (1975), Bogdan et al. (1974), Scott (1969), Roth (1971), and Kleinmen et al. (1977). Also see recent historical critiques such as Platt (1969) and Roth (1971), as well as Piven and Cloward (1971), and Szasz (1970).

2. All the names used in this paper are pseudonyms.

3. Note that the critics of state schools have not simply called for the liberation of the mentally retarded from institutions, but for the provision of services in small homelike settings, with programming, work, and social activities occurring in different settings in the community. Two, much heralded community service systems are found in eastern Nebraska and the Macomb–Oakland region of Michigan.

13

A Closing Remark

Our purpose in this book has been to introduce qualitative research as an approach to phenomenological understanding. Any book can only take you so far; it is up to you to carry on.

Not everyone can excel in the research approach we have described. Early practitioners suggested that the marginal person, the one caught between two cultures, has the greatest potential to become a good qualitative researcher, since he or she possesses the detachment this kind of research requires. In our experience, people with a diverse range of backgrounds and interests have become successful qualitative researchers. Yet all who do well have had an ability to relate to others on their own terms. They have also shared a passion about what they do. It excites them to be out in the world and to develop an understanding of diverse settings and people. For some, research becomes part of life, part of living.

Research methods can be dull and unexciting, however, if they are learned in a classroom or studied behind a desk. Qualitative research is a craft that can only be learned and appreciated through experience. It requires skills and a devotion that must be developed and nurtured in the real world.

Many, if not most, people who pursue studies in the social sciences are not lured to them by the kind of work that appears in academic journals and publications. Although the culture of the university makes it difficult to admit it, many students come to the social sciences with a desire to understand their world *and* to make it better. These "do-gooders," along with the "journalistic types," are often intimidated by the academic world. This must change if the social sciences are to play important roles in the university and the society.

Throughout this book we have described qualitative methodology as an approach to gaining basic social science knowledge and understanding. This is not the only way in which this methodology can be used.

There is a long tradition of "action research" linked to qualitative studies in the social sciences (Madge, 1953). Indeed, the Chicago School researchers led by Robert Park sought to change conditions in urban slums through their incisive field reports and studies (Hughes, 1971). Based on our research at state institutions for the so-called "mentally retarded," we have prepared in-depth descriptive reports of institutional abuse and neglect for federal courts, the popular media, policy-makers, and organizations composed of people with disabilities and their families.

Howard Becker (1966–1967) argues that researchers cannot avoid taking sides in their studies.[1] Research is never value-free (Gouldner, 1968, 1970; Mills, 1959). When we get close to people, especially those whom society considers "deviant," we develop a deep sympathy for them. We learn that official views of morality present only one side of the picture. Becker takes the position that we should side with society's "underdogs," those who do not have a forum for their views. By presenting their views, we provide a balance to official versions of reality.

Bodemann (1978) takes the activist tradition in qualitative research a step farther than Becker and the Chicago School researchers. According to Bodemann, the field researcher should actively intervene in the lives of people to relieve human suffering. He urges researchers to participate fully in the settings they study by pointing out options to a community that has been deprived of options and returning findings to the community directly.

Bodemann's argument falls squarely in line with C. Wright Mills' call to action expressed two decades earlier in his classic book, *The Sociological Imagination* (1959). For Mills (1959:187), the role of the sociologist, and hence the qualitative researcher, is to help people translate their "personal troubles" into "public issues":

> Whether or not they are aware of them, men in a mass society are gripped by personal troubles which they are not able to turn into social issues . . . It is the political task of the social scientist . . . continually to translate per-

sonal troubles into public issues, and public issues into the terms of their human meaning for a variety of individuals.

For those who feel ill at ease with the strong advocacy stance adopted by Bodemann, Becker, Mills, and others, qualitative evaluation research represents an alternative way of using qualitative methods to address practical issues in the day-to-day world (Patton, 1980).[2] In contrast to most forms of evaluation research, qualitative evaluation focuses on how things actually work as opposed to whether they work. In conducting qualitative evaluation, the researcher sets aside official goals and objectives to explore what is really happening in an organization or program.

Qualitative studies have been conducted since the beginning of what we now call the social sciences. Yet those who have practiced qualitative research have been few. This is an exciting time for those dedicated to qualitative research, for interest in studies produced by this methodology is increasing. We have reached a point where a great many researchers are needed to go to the people. There is much to be learned and many are needed to carry out the work.

NOTES

1. A refusal to take sides is often tantamount to upholding the status quo, whatever that happens to be. Those who believe that researchers can avoid value commitments should take a look at the experience of a group of social researchers who got hoodwinked into collecting intelligence information on Latin America for the U.S. military (see Sjoberg, 1967). Spradley (1980) also reports one case in which the South African government used ethnographic research to attempt to make apartheid more effective.

2. In evaluation and other funded research, the researcher has to be careful not to allow sponsors or funders to exercise undue influence of how the study is conducted and how the results are analyzed and presented (see Warren, 1980).

Appendix

This appendix contains a set of field notes from the state institution study discussed in the text. They are intended to provide an example of what participant observation field notes should look like in terms of form and content.

A brief note of explanation: Since these field notes were recorded during the observer's ninth visit to the setting, they do not describe the setting as thoroughly as they were described in earlier notes. Participant observers must describe their setting in detail only once. As their studies progress, they can omit many of the details already covered.

I drive onto the grounds of the state school and proceed to the rear of the institution. The grounds are almost empty at this time of the evening, with the exception of a few people I see sitting in front of the buildings on the way in. After I park, I see a double line of people (at least 100) walking in the direction of the school building from the women's side of the institution. Although the people are too far away for me to see them clearly, I can hear women's voices.

I walk to Building 27. The small anteroom is empty and dark. To the left of the door are several rows of benches, arranged in such a way that people could look out the windows of the room.

The hallway inside the building is also empty, and relatively dark, a few ceiling lights are on. I walk past the various offices off the hallway: speech and hearing, X-ray, and some others. They are all empty. I proceed to the stairway which is about three quarters of the way down the hall.

OBSERVATIONS AT STATE INSTITUTION

Field Notes#9   Diagram:
Friday, October 20, 1972
6:50 p.m. til 7:55 p.m.

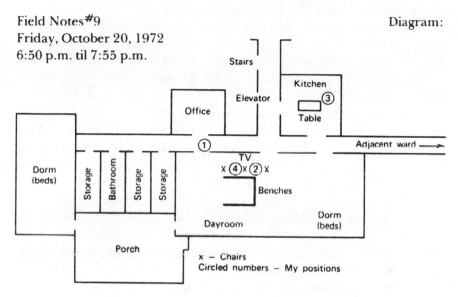

Figure A. A diagram of the state institution ward.

As I reach the stairway, I begin to hear some muffled voices coming from the upper floors. The smell that I first noticed when I entered the building becomes slightly stronger as I reach the stairs. (O.C. It is not as strong as it sometimes is. Perhaps this has to do with the cooler weather.) It is a funny smell—perhaps feces and urine, steamed food, and disinfectant.

I walk up the stairs which are encased in a yellow steel mesh grating. The pastel green walls are worn—paint chipped, stained. My footsteps echo as I walk the stairs. Some of the voices become louder now, especially as I go past the doors which lead to the wards on the various floors. Several windows are open on the stairway; some fresh air blows in as I pass them.

I hear a loud scream as I near the fourth floor. It echoes through the stairway.

I get to the fourth, and top floor. The door is open. A large cartoon wall painting is in the hall as I get to the top floor. It's about five feet long and three high. Blue, orange, and yellow dominate the mural.

I turn right and walk to the central hallway, past the attendants' kitchen and the elevator.

I look down to the left as I reach the hallway. I can see an attendant at the dayroom door of the ward adjacent to Ward 83.

The woman attendant, who is heavy-set, wears a pink nurse's aide type dress and white shoes, has blonde hair and glasses, and is about 50, ignores me as I walk out into the hall. (O.C. The women on this ward neither know me nor want to know me for some reason. They appear content as long as I don't go down to visit their ward. It just occurred to me that many of the women attendants at the institution wear some kind of uniforms—pink, white, or blue—whereas only 2 of the male attendants on "my" ward, out of about the 30 who are assigned to it throughout the day, wear white uniforms. Perhaps this has something to do with how they see their jobs, or maybe it has something to do with sex-role differences. I'll have to try to question some of the attendants about this.)

I can also see a couple of residents in the dayroom of the adjacent ward. Both are boys around 14. One is naked and appears to be just walking around the room. The other is wearing some kind of gray clothes and is sitting in a chair and rocking.

As I turn right down the hall to get to Ward 83, I can hear the loud noise of the TV coming from the dayroom. The hall of 83 is empty now, as well as one of the dorms at the end of the hall. The doors to the dayroom are closed except for one halfway down the hall.

I can see Bill Kelly, a resident in his early twenties, sitting by the dayroom, half in the dayroom and half in the hall. (O.C. According to the attendants, Kelly serves as the "watchdog." From his position, he can see anyone coming down the hall. He warns the attendants when a supervisor is coming.)

Kelly waves to me as I approach. He is smiling. Kelly is wearing gray pants made from some kind of heavy material standard on this ward, a white T-shirt, and black tennis shoes without socks. His hair appears to have been cut recently. The scars on his head stick out. (O.C. Kelly's hair, like the other residents', is never long. The residents' hair seems to be cut every few weeks. Presumably, this is to prevent parasites which would spread rapidly on this ward.)

As I get to the dayroom door, I see that all the residents are in the room. I can only see two attendants: Vince and another younger man. (O.C. It's interesting how I automatically assume that this other man is an attendant as opposed to a resident. Several hints: long hair, moustache, and glasses; cotton shirt and jeans, brown leather boots. He's also smoking a cigarette, and a resident, Bobby Bart, is buffing his shoes with a rag.

Thus this attendant's dress and appearance differ from that of the residents.) Vince, who is 21, is wearing jeans, brown leather boots, and a jersey that has "LOVE" printed on it. He has long hair, sideburns, and a moustache.

I wave to Vince. He half-heartedly waves back. (O.C. I don't think that Vince has quite gotten used to me coming.) The other attendant doesn't pay any attention to me.

Several residents wave or call to me. I wave back.

Kelly is smiling at me. (O.C. He's obviously happy to see me.) I say to Kelly, "Hi, Bill, how are you?" He says, "Hi, Steve. How's school?" "OK." He says, "School's a pain in the ass. I missed you." (O.C. According to the attendants, Kelly attended school at the institution several years ago.) I say, "I missed you too."

I walk over to Vince and the other attendant. I sit down on a hard plastic rocker between Vince and the other atten., but slightly behind them. The other atten. still doesn't pay attention to me. Vince doesn't introduce me to him.

The smell of feces and urine is quite noticeable to me, but not as pungent as usual.

I, along with the attendants and perhaps five or six residents, am sitting in front of the TV, which is attached to the wall about eight feet off the floor and out of the residents' reach.

Many of the 70 or so residents are sitting on the wooden benches which are in a U shape in the middle of the dayroom floor. A few are rocking. A couple of others are holding onto each other. In particular, Deier is holding onto the resident the attendants call "Bunny Rabbit." (O.C. Deier is assigned to "Bunny Rabbit"—to keep a hold of him to stop him from smearing feces over himself.)

A lot of residents are sitting on the floor of the room, some of these are leaning against the wall. A few others, maybe 10, just seem to be wandering around the room.

Maybe three or four residents are completely naked. I make a quick count and see that five are wearing any kind of shoes. Most of the residents are wearing their usual clothes: heavy institutional clothes or remnants of regular clothes.

Apparently, Miller and Poller are "on the bucket." Miller is sitting on one of the beds in the dormitory half of the room. His metal bucket is by his feet. Poller is sitting on the floor with his bucket not far from me.

Tresh comes over to greet me. He grins, waves, and mumbles something that I can't understand. Tresh has a ball of rags which he throws up into the air about five feet and catches. (O.C. There are no other things that the residents can use to throw or play with on this ward. It seems so sad that one must play with rags to have something to do.)

Bobby Bart is still buffing the attendant's shoes. The attendant lights up a cigarette. He says to me and to Vince, "All I need is for the supervisor to come up and catch me smoking in here and letting him shine my shoes. They're not supposed to shine shoes." He says this sort of whimsically. He then goes back to watching TV. The atten. have positioned their chairs so that they can see the whole room but still watch TV.

I ask the atten., "Where are all the other guys tonight? Are a lot of them off?" (O.C. There are usually three or four attendants working on a Friday night, if not more.) Vince answers, "No, they're just out to lunch. They'll be back in a little while." (O.C. It's interesting how men who work the evening shift refer to their evening meal as lunch.)

I ask, "When's Mike coming back?" (O.C. Mike has been working on a ward downstairs for the past month since that ward is short-staffed.) Vince says, "He should be back pretty soon—maybe next week. He was up here for a little while tonight."

Vince says something about the number of residents on this ward. I can't exactly catch what he says. I ask, "Weren't they supposed to transfer some of them?" Vince says, "Yeah, but I don't know how many now. They came up here for some, but Bill wasn't here so they didn't take them."

David Dunn, a resident of about 35–40 years of age, comes over. David is shy, but friendly. He is wearing an orange jersey, jeans, no belt, and tennis shoes. His hair is short and prematurely gray. (O.C. The residents who are better dressed and wear shoes are also those who are considered more intelligent by the atten. Of course, they also tend to be the ward workers. I wonder if the clothes they receive stems from the fact that they work or that they care more about clothing than the others.)

I say to David, "Hi, David, how are you?" He says, "Just fine." Vince interrupts, "David Dunn's not going to Building 48 after all. They're going to keep him here to take care of Igor." (O.C. "Igor" is the attendants' nickname for a tall resident with hard features. They have nicknames for many of the residents. Many of these I consider dehumanizing. Somehow the atten. do not see the residents as true human beings. I noticed here how Vince talked about David in front of him but not to him. This is common. The atten. act as though the residents do not matter at times. Vince's comment reveals something very interesting—placement policies are based not on the welfare of the resident, but on his usefulness on the ward. Atten. hate to lose good workers. David takes care of another resident on a 24-hour basis.)

Bobby Bart finishes shining the attendant's shoes. The atten. says to Bobby, "I don't have any pennies now, Bobby. I'll pay you later."

Bill, the atten. in charge, enters the room with a cup of coffee. Jim and Nick, two other atten., follow him. They all wave to me. I wave back.

Bill comes right over to me and says, "Hi, Steve. Want some coffee? Go get yourself some if you want some." I say, "Not right now, thanks, Bill. Maybe later."

Bill and the other atten. are all wearing dark pants, cotton shirts—various colors, and black tie shoes. All have relatively short haircuts and are older than the two atten. in this room. Bill's about 50 and the other two are about 30. Bill is wearing a "key caddy" from his belt. He also has a name plate on his shirt with his name on it. He is the only one on the ward to have a name plate. (O.C. It seems strange for Bill to have this name plate. The ward gets almost no visitors, and he knows all of the atten. and residents on the ward. A sign of status? It's also interesting that the older atten. seem to stick together.)

As Nick and Jim walk toward me, I see Nick try to whisper something to Jim. Jim doesn't seem to hear him, for he doesn't look at him or acknowledge him. (O.C. I wouldn't be surprised if Nick said something about me being here, like "Oh, no, he's here again.")

Nick comes over to me and gives me a friendly, "Hi, Steve."

Nick and Jim leave the room again.

I notice a resident behind me and to my right who has his pants pulled down and is masturbating. He doesn't seem to be paying attention to anyone else in the room.

Miller gets up and goes over to a puddle of urine to my left. He kneels down, wipes the floor with a wet rag, wrings out the rag, and then throws it back into the bucket. He goes by me as he walks back to his chair. The smell is overpowering. Feces are floating in the water. (O.C. Miller, unlike other residents, automatically cleans up feces or urine on the floor. Many of the others wait for feces or urine to be pointed out to them.)

Miller frequently cleans up feces and urine throughout the time I am on the ward.

Bill, who has been standing near me, pulls a chair over and sits down beside Vince. (O.C. There are five plastic chairs in the room. These are used by the atten. The residents seldom try to sit in any of them. When they do, they are castigated by the atten.)

A resident named Jim is sitting on the floor in front of all of us. Jim is in his late teens, is wearing gray pants and shoes, but nothing else. The new atten. says, "Hello Jim, hello, Jim. O.K. O.K." He says it in a mocking tone. Jim repeats him, "Hello, Gem. O.K. O.K." The atten. says, "O.K., Gem, O.K. O.K." Jim repeats him again. The atten. then says, "Fuck you, Gem, Fuck you." Jim waves his arms around, swatting the air. The atten. all laugh. Bill, laughing, looks over at me, as though to share the laughter. I smile. (O.C. Situations like this are always difficult. I feel guilty smiling, but somehow feel that I don't want to seem like I'm putting the atten. down.)

The new atten. turns around to Bobby Bart. He says, "Fuck you, Bobby," and sticks his middle finger up vigorously. Bobby returns the gesture, laughing. (O.C. Bobby cannot hear, according to the atten., but is quite intelligent.)

This same atten. begins to sing. (O.C. He seems to be joking around.) "It's beginning to look a lot like Christmas. . . ." Bill says, "You're a little early, aren't you?" He says, "Nah, it'll be Christmas any time now."

Romano, about 21, comes running over to me. He has cerebral palsy and is crippled on the left side of his body. Romano says to me, "Hi, Steve." I say, "Hi, Vito, how are you?" he smiles.

Vito walks over behind Bill and starts to rub his back. Bill screams at him, "Get the hell outta here, Vito. I don't want my back rubbed."

Bill points to the new atten. and says, "Go rub his back, Vito." The atten. says, "He won't rub my back 'cause of what I did to him that one night. Remember?" (O.C. The atten. says it in such a way that I don't think I should pursue the matter—too sensitive at this time. I don't want to seem like a snooper.)

The atten. then says to Vito, "What's the matter Vito? Don't you want to rub my back? Don't you like me?" (O.C. He says this mockingly.) Vito is behind me so I can't see his face, but the atten. says, "Why not, Vito? Come on, rub my back." Vito goes over to him and begins to rub his back.

Vince asks me, "Has Vito ever rubbed your back." Then he says to Vito, "Come rub Steve's back." I say, "Yeah, he's rubbed my back." Vince says to Vito, "That's O.K., Vito. Never mind," and then to me, "Oh, then you know what he's like. He really rubs hard."

One of the residents wanders over to the dayroom door. Bill yells at him, "Bates, get away from that door."

The new atten. points to Tresh's ball of rags and says, "Give that to me." Tresh gives it to him. He throws the rags at the resident by the door and hits him in the back. The resident runs away from the door.

Miller is behind me and is wiping up a puddle of urine. A resident near us pulls his pants to his knees and crouches on the floor. Vince yells to Miller, "Miller, get up. Hurry! Take him to the bathroom. Hurry up before he goes on the floor!" Miller grabs the resident's hand and leads him out of the room.

Vito is still rubbing the new attendant's back. This atten. asks Vince, "Should I pay him for the backrub?" Vince says, "I usually give him a nickel if he does a good job. He doesn't deserve it if he rubs too hard."

Bill says something about the trouble he's having trying to keep residents from "pissing and shitting on the floor." He then says something to the effect, "These patients here are low grades."

Bill continues, "I'd love to be able to train them. I really would. But you can't do it. Not here you can't." Bill points to a resident who is a couple of feet away from us and says, "This isn't bad. You can teach him something." He points to Vito and says, "This one isn't bad either. You can teach them something. I mean, you can teach them so much. There's a limit. They have a borderline. You can do so much with 'em, but that's all. They have a borderline and you can't go beyond on them. They can talk so you can tell 'em what to do. If they can talk you can do somethin' with 'em. They can comprehend."

Bill continues, "See, if they can talk, you can do something with 'em. You can tell them to do something, and they'll do it. Most of these here you can't talk to. They only listen to two things." Bill pauses, makes a fist, and says, "This," he makes a slapping motion and says, "Or this."

Bill stands up and asks me, "You want some coffee, Steve? Come on." Bill starts for the door. I stand up and follow him. We walk out of the room and down the hall to the kitchen.

Both of us take a cup and get coffee from a percolator in the room. Bill walks over to a refrigerator in the room and takes out a large carton of milk. He pours some into his coffee and then hands it to me. We sit down at a table in the kitchen. There are five loaves of bread and a box of green bananas on a table by the refrigerator.

Bill lights a cigarette, sits back, and says, "The supervisor just told us that we have to start taking the low grades to a special dance just for low grades. So this Tuesday we have to take them. What we have to do is dress them all up in their own clothes and then one employee has to take them over to the dance and stay with them the whole night. How are we going to do that? We don't have enough employees. We'll get them all dressed up and start taking them over and then one will shit his pants and we'll have to bring them all back."

I ask Bill, "Well, why are they having this special dance?" He says, "I'll tell ya why. It's because they get federal grants for having so many patients in the program. That's why they have so many programs around here. (O.C. From Bill's perspective there are too many programs. Yet very few residents actually receive programming.) See, they get state grants, county grants, and federal grants. They may have the program anyway, but the government gives them more money if they have more patients in it. They had record hops before. They had one employee to run the hi-fi. What they did was add more patients to get the federal grant. Where's the money going? There's still that one employee running the hi-fi. What they did was add more patients to get the federal grant. The money ain't goin' to the patients and it ain't goin' to the employees so where's it goin'? Well, I know where it's goin' and I think you know too—it's goin' to graft. The people runnin' this place are gettin' rich on graft. The people above them know it, but they don't care."

Bill goes on, "I'll tell ya, I know there's graft around here. Every year around January they start cuttin' down on food. See, the year starts in April so January's the end of the year for money. So they start scrimpin'."

I say, "Well, it's not even January and you don't have enough stuff here." Bill says, "That's right. They don't give us enough disinfectant. That's why I have to buy it myself—with my own money. Hell, in 29— the medical building—they have all they need. That's 'cause they get all the visitors there. Nobody comes here, but these are the buildings that need it the most."

I ask Bill, "Where were you before you came up here?" He says, "I was downstairs before. I was second in charge. The charge down there didn't care about nothin'. He never cleaned the place. He said if the place was dirty he wouldn't get any visitors and I guess he was right. I was second charge and every time the charge was off I cleaned the whole place. Then the supervisor told me he wanted me to be charge up here."

Bill goes on, "You see, they knew I was clean. They knew I'd keep this place clean. That's why they wanted me up here. This place was the dirtiest place in the world. The charge up here didn't care. He just put his watchdogs at the door and played cards. I got this place clean too. I just can't stand filth. So now that I'm up here they won't give me the things I need to keep this place clean."

I say, "You must get discouraged." Bill says, "Sure I get discouraged. They won't give us any disinfectant or anything. The state don't care what we take home to our kids. Well, I care. I'm not takin' home hepatitis or somethin' to my kids. I'm gonna keep this place clean. I just can't stand filth."

Bill stands up quickly and says, "If I don't take a leak now, I'm gonna piss my pants. I'll be back in a second. Go ahead, have another cup of coffee." Bill hurries out of the room.

(O.C. Bill has given me important insights into how he defines his supervisors and his job. I'll have to follow up on this graft and this cleanliness thing.)

I pour myself another cup of coffee and sit alone for a couple of minutes.

Bill returns and immediately begins to speak, "Everybody is here for one reason and one reason only—money. That's right. They're all here for money. That's why they took this job. That's why I took this job. I'm 50 years old now and when I came here I was 40. Who's gonna hire you at 40? Nobody wants a guy who's 40 years old."

I ask Bill, "Do you have a problem keeping good men? I mean, is there a lot of turnover?" He answers, "No, I have good employees now. They'll do what I say. They're clean like I am."

Bill continues, "My wife's a supervisor, but she lets people take advantage of her." I ask, "Where does she work—over on the other side?" He answers, "Yeah, over in 18." I ask, "Isn't 18 the children's building?" He says, "Yeah, my wife has them until 12 to 16—whenever they mensurate [sic]. When they mensurate [sic] they put them in another ward. There are only three employees on my wife's ward, and on weekends they only have two. My wife's supervisor was makin' them work eight and a half hours without lunch on weekends. Can you believe that?" (O.C. I am amazed at how many atten. have relatives working at the institution. The institution almost makes this a company town.)

Jim comes into the room with a box and different slips of paper. These are for a lottery on the World Series. Bill fills out a slip and gives Jim one dollar. Jim leaves after some small talk about baseball.

Bill stands up, goes over to the sink, and washes out his coffee cup.

I do the same. We walk back to the dayroom. We had spent about 25 minutes in the kitchen.

Jim and Nick are in the dayroom now and are sitting in front of the TV. Vince and the other atten. are in the dayroom too. Bill walks around the room. I sit down beside Vince.

A resident walks up behind me and stands there. Vince looks at him and screams, "Harris, get out of there. Leave him alone." Vince says to me, "Don't ever let them behind you. You don't know what they might do. They could choke you. One time, Bobby Bart got a kid in a choke hold and wouldn't let go. Nobody could get him off either." (O.C. I've never seen a resident attack or strike an atten. Neither have I ever seen Bobby Bart hurt anyone.)

Bill leaves the room.

Nick and Jim talk about snowmobiles and watch TV.

Vince asks me, "Have you ever seen Frankie tie shoes?" I answer, "No," and he says, "You should see him. He really does it different." Vince looks around the room and calls, "Hey Frankie, come here." Frankie ignores Vince. Instead, he kicks a resident who is sitting on the floor. The resident doesn't do anything. Vince calls to Frankie again. Frankie comes over this time. Frankie is a heavy-set man in his early twenties. He is not wearing shoes but has on institutional clothing.

Vince says to Frankie, "Tie Steve's shoes, Frankie." Frankie unties my shoes and then methodically ties them again without even looking at them.

Vince says to Frankie, "Tie my shoes, Frankie." Vince is wearing boots which do not have shoelaces. Frankie doesn't respond to Vince.

The new atten. says, "Hey Frankie," makes a fist, and points to a young black resident who is sitting against the wall and near the TV. Frankie walks over to the resident and punches him in the head. The resident cringes and runs away toward the dormitory part of the room. Frankie wanders away also. The atten. don't pay attention to what Frankie did. (O.C. There are three black residents on the ward. The atten. all seem to be racist by their behavior toward these residents and by how they refer to them.)

Vince points a puddle of urine out to Miller. Miller goes over to it and wipes it up.

I ask Vince, "What did Miller do to get on the bucket?" He answers, "He didn't do anything. He doesn't mind being on the bucket. He knows that if he's on the bucket, he'll get extra food. We give extra food to whoever is on the bucket. Miller knows that so he doesn't mind. Some of the other ones aren't that smart, but Miller is."

Vince starts to talk to the new atten. about baseball.

I decide to leave. I say to Vince, "Well, I think I'd better get home now. I'll be seeing you." He says, "O.K., I'll see you later." I wave good-bye to the other atten. and to some of the residents. I leave the room. I walk past the office in the hall.

Bill is sitting at the desk in the office. He is filling out some kind of chart. I say, "I'm leaving now, Bill." He says, "O.K., Steve, take it easy. Stop up any time." I leave the ward and the building.

As I walk to my car, a man comes up to me. (O.C. I assume that he is a resident by his clothes—old and baggy, his hair, and the way he speaks.) He says, "I don't have a day off until Sunday. I work all the time." He walks with me. He points to a tree and says, "My brother cut a branch off that tree. He works here. I have another brother who works here too. One at home too."

We get to the parking lot. He asks, "Which one is your car?" I point to it and say, "That one." He says, "I see it. You need someone to wash it? I'll wash it for you some time. It'll only cost you a quarter. I do a good job." I say, "O.K., I'll be seeing you." He walks away. I walk to my car. The man comes back over to me, and says, "I work over in Building 22. Come get me if you want your car washed—inside and out." I say, "O.K.," and leave the institution. (O.C. It was important to this man for me to believe that he was an employee and not a resident here. This probably has something to do with the stigma of being "retarded.")

Bibliography

Academic Freedom and Tenure Committee. "Statements of Principles." *Bulletin of the American Association of University Professors*, 26: 49–54, 1940.

Adams, R. N., and Preiss, J. J. (Eds.). *Human Organization Research*. Homewood, Ill.: Dorsey Press, 1960.

Agar, M. H. *The Professional Stranger: An Informal Introduction to Ethnography*. New York: Academic Press, 1980.

Agar, M. H. "Whatever happened to cognitive anthropology: A partial review." *Human Organization*, 41: 82–86, 1982.

Agar, M. H. "Ethnography and cognition." In R. M. Emerson (Ed.) *Contemporary Field Research*. Boston: Little, Brown, pp. 68–77, 1983.

Allport, G. *The Use of Personal Documents in Psychological Science*. New York: Social Science Research Council, 1942.

Allport, G., Bruner, J. S., and Jandorf, E. M. "Personality under social catastrophe: An analysis of 90 German refugee life histories." *Character and Personality*, 5(10): 1–22, 1941.

Altheide, D. L. "Leaving the newsroom." In W. B. Shaffir, R. A. Stebbins, and A. Turowetz (Eds.) *Fieldwork Experience: Qualitative Approaches to Social Research*. New York: St. Martin's Press, pp. 301–310, 1980.

American Anthropological Association. "Principles of professional responsibility." *Newsletter of the American Anthropological Association*, 11(November): 14–16 (Adopted May 1971), 1970.

American Psychologist. "Ethical standards of psychologists." 18: 56–60, 1963.

American Sociologist Staff. "Toward a code of ethics for sociologists." *American Sociologist*, 3(November): 316–318, 1968.

Anderson, N. *The Hobo*. Chicago: University of Chicago Press, 1923.

Angell, R. *The Family Encounters the Depression*. New York: Scribner, 1936.

Angell, R. "A critical review of the development of the personal document method in sociology 1920–1940." In L. Gottschalk, D. Kluckhohn, and R. Angell, *The Use of Personal Documents in History, Anthropology, and Sociology.* New York: Social Science Research Council, 1945.

Angell, R. D. and Friedman, R. "The use of documents, records, census materials, and indices." In L. Festinger and D. Katz (Eds.) *Research Methods in the Behavioral Sciences.* New York: Holt, pp. 300–326, 1953.

Angell, R. D. and Turner, R. H. "Comment and reply on discussions of the analytic induction method." *American Sociological Review,* 19: 476–478, 1954.

Appell, G. *Ethical Dilemmas in Anthropological Inquiry: A Case Book.* Waltham, Mass.: Crossroads, 1978.

Arbus, D. *Diane Arbus.* New York: An Aperture Monograph, 1972.

Arensberg, C. M. "The community-study method." *American Journal of Sociology,* 60: 109–124, 1954.

Argyris, C. "Diagnosing defenses against the outsider." *Journal of Social Issues,* 8(3): 24–34, 1952.

Arrington, R. "Time sampling in studies of social behavior." *Psychological Bulletin,* 40: 81–124, 1943.

Asad, R. (Ed.) *Anthropology and the Colonial Encounter.* London: Ithaca Press, 1973.

Babchuck, N. "The role of the researcher as participant observer and participant-as observer in the field situation." *Human Organization,* 21(3): 225–228, 1962.

Back, K. W. "The well-informed informant." *Human Organization,* 14(4): 30–33, 1956.

Bader, C. "Standardized field practice." *International Journal of Opinion and Attitude Research,* 2: 243–244, 1948.

Bain, R. "The impersonal confession and social research." *Journal of Applied Sociology,* 9: 356–361, 1925.

Bain, R. K. "The researcher's role: A case study." *Human Organization,* 9(1): 23–28, 1950.

Baldamus, W. "The role of discoveries in social science." In T. Shanin (Ed.) *The Rules of the Game: Cross-Disciplinary Essays on Models in Scholarly Thought.* London: Tavistock, pp. 276–302, 1972.

Ball, D. "An abortion clinic ethnography." *Social Problems,* 5(14): 293–301, 1966–1967.

Banaka, W. H. *Training in Depth Interviewing.* New York: Harper and Row, 1971.

Barber, B. "Research on human subjects: Problems of access to a powerful profession." *Social Problems,* 21(Summer): 103–112, 1973.

Barnes, J. A. "Some ethical problems in modern field work." *British Journal of Sociology,* 14(June): 118–134, 1963.

Bartlett, F. C. "Psychological methods and anthropological problems." *Africa,* 10: 401–420, 1937.

Barton, A. H. and Lazarsfeld, P. F. "Some functions of qualitative analysis in social research." *Frankfurter Beitrage zur Soziologie,* 1: 321–361, 1955.

Bateson, G. "Experiments in thinking about observed ethnological materials." *Philosophy of Science,* 8: 53–68, 1941.

Beals, R. L. "Native terms and anthropological methods." *American Anthropologist,* 59: 716–717, 1957.

Beals, R. L. *Politics of Social Research.* Chicago: Aldine, 1968.

Becker, H. S. "The career of the Chicago public school teacher." *American Journal of Sociology*, 57(March): 470–477, 1952.

Becker, H. S. "The teacher in the authority system of the public school." *Journal of Educational Sociology*, 27(November): 128–141, 1953.

Becker, H. S. "A note on interviewing tactics." *Human Organization*, 12(4): 31–32, 1954.

Becker, H. S. "Interviewing medical students." *American Journal of Sociology*, 62: 199–201, 1956.

Becker, H. S. "Problems of inference and proof in participant observation." *American Sociological Review*, 23: 652–660, 1958.

Becker, H. S. "Notes on the concept of commitment." *American Journal of Sociology*, 66 (July): 32–40, 1960.

Becker, H. S. *Outsiders: Studies in the Sociology of Deviance.* New York: Free Press, 1963.

Becker, H. S. "Problems in the publication of field studies." In A. J. Vidich, J. Bensman, and M. R. Stein (Eds.) *Reflections on Community Studies.* New York: Wiley, pp. 267–284, 1964.

Becker, H. S. "Introduction." In C. Shaw *The Jack-roller.* Chicago, Ill.: University of Chicago Press, 1966.

Becker, H. S. "Whose side are we on?" *Social Problems*, 14(Winter): 239–247, 1966–1967.

Becker, H. S. (Ed.) *The Other Side.* New York: Free Press, 1967.

Becker, H. S. *Sociological Work: Method and Substance.* Chicago: Aldine, 1970.

Becker, H. S. and Carper, J. W. "The development of identification with an occupation." *American Journal of Sociology*, 61(January): 289–298, 1956a.

Becker, H. S. and Carper, J. W. "The elements of identification with an occupation." *American Sociological Review*, 21(June): 341–348, 1956b.

Becker, H. S. and Friedson, E. "Against the code of ethics." *American Sociological Review*, 29: 409–410, 1964.

Becker, H. S. and Geer, B. "Participant observation and interviewing: A comparison." *Human Organization*, 16 (3): 28–32, 1957.

Becker, H. S. and Geer, B. "The fate of idealism in medical school." *American Sociological Review*, 23(February): 50–56, 1958a.

Becker, H. S. and Geer, B. " 'Participant observation and interviewing': A rejoinder." *Human Organization*, 17(2): 39–40, 1958b.

Becker, H. S. and Geer, B. "Latent culture: A note on the theory of latent social roles." *Administrative Science Quarterly*, 5(September): 304–313, 1960a.

Becker, H. S. and Geer, B. "Participant observation: The analysis of qualitative field data." In R. N. Adams and J. J. Preiss (Eds.) *Human Organization Research.* Homewood, Ill.: Dorsey Press, pp. 267–289, 1960b.

Becker, H. S., Geer, B., and Hughes, E. *Making the Grade.* New York: Wiley, 1968.

Becker, H. S., Geer, B., Hughes, E. C., and Strauss, A. L. *Boys in White: Student Culture in Medical School.* Chicago: University of Chicago Press, 1961.

Becker, H. S. and Horowitz, I. L. "Radical politics and sociological research: Observations on methodology and ideology." *American Journal of Sociology*, 78(July): 48–66, 1972.

Becker, H. S. and Strauss, A. L. "Careers, personality and adult socialization." *American Journal of Sociology*, 62(November): 253–263, 1956.

Becker, H. S. et al. (Eds.) *Institutions and the Person: Essays Presented to Everett C. Hughes.* Chicago: Aldine, 1968.

Becker, M. et al. "Predicting mother's compliance with medical regimens." *Journal of Pediatrics,* 81: 843–854, 1972.

Beecher, H. K. *Research and the Individual: Human Studies.* Boston: Little, Brown, 1970.

Beeghley, L. and Butler, E. "The consequences of intelligence testing in public schools before and after desegregation." *Social Problems,* 21(5), 1974.

Beezer, R. H. "Research on methods of interviewing foreign informants." George Washington University Human Resources Research Office Technical Report, No. 30, 1956.

Bendix, R. "Concepts and generalizations in comparative sociological studies." *American Sociological Review,* 28: 532–539, 1963.

Bennett, C. C. "What price privacy?" *American Psychologist,* 22: 371–376, 1967.

Bennett, J. W. "The study of cultures: A survey of technique and methodology in field work." *American Sociological Review,* 13: 672–689, 1948.

Benney, M., and Hughes, E. C. "Of sociology and the interview." In N. K. Denzin (Ed.) *Sociological Methods: A Sourcebook.* Chicago: Aldine, pp. 175–181, 1970.

Bensman, J. and Vidich, A. "Social theory in field research." *American Journal of Sociology,* 65: 577–584, 1960.

Bercovici, S. "Qualitative methods and cultural perspectives in the study of deinstitutionalization." In R. H. Bruininks, C. E. Meyers, B. B. Sigford, and K. C. Lakin (Eds.) *Deinstitutionalization and Community Adjustment of Mentally Retarded People.* Washington, D.C.: American Association on Mental Deficiency, 1981.

Berger, P. "On existential phenomenology and sociology (II)." *American Sociological Review,* 31(April): 259–260, 1966.

Berger, P. L. and Luckmann, T. *The Social Construction of Reality.* Garden City, N.Y.: Doubleday, 1967.

Bergman, A. B. "Psychological aspects of sudden and unexpected death in infants and children. *Review and Commentary, Pediatric Clinics of North America,* 21: 115–123, 1974.

Berk, R. A. and Adams, R. A. "Establishing rapport with deviant groups." *Social Problems,* 18(Summer): 102–117, 1970.

Berk, S. F. and Berheide, C. W. "Going backstage: Gaining access to observe household work." *Sociology of Work and Occupations,* 4: 27–48, 1977.

Bernard, J. "Observation and generalization in cultural anthropology." *American Journal of Sociology,* 50: 284–291, 1945.

Berreman, G. D. "Ethnography: Method and product." In J. A. Clifton (Ed.) *Introduction to Cultural Anthropology: Essays in the Scope and Methods of the Science of Man.* Boston: Houghton Mifflin, pp. 337–373, 1968.

Bevis, J. C. "Interviewing with tape recorders." *Public Opinion Quarterly,* 13: 629–634, 1950.

Bickman, L. and Henchy, T. (Eds.) *Beyond the Laboratory: Field Research in Social Psychology.* New York: McGraw-Hill, 1972.

Bierstedt, R. "A critique of empiricism in sociology." *American Sociological Review,* 24: 584–592, 1949.

Biklen, D. (Ed.) *Human Report 1: Observations in Mental Health, Mental Retardation Facilities.* In collaboration with the Workshop on Human Abuse Protection and Public Policy, Syracuse University, 1970.

Biklen, D. *Patterns of power.* Unpublished dissertation, 1973.

Biklen, D. *Let Our Children Go.* Syracuse: Human Policy Press, 1975.

Bittner, E. "The concept of organization." *Social Research,* 31: 239–255, 1964.

Bittner, E. "Objectivity and realism in sociology." In G. Psathas (Ed.) *Phenomenological Sociology: Issues and Applications.* New York: Wiley, pp. 109–125, 1973.

Bittner, E. "Realism in field research." In R. M. Emerson (Ed.) *Contemporary Field Research.* Boston: Little, Brown, pp. 149–155, 1983.

Black, D. J. and Reiss, A. J. "Police control of juveniles." *American Sociological Review,* 35: 63–77, 1970.

Blalock, H. M., Jr. *Social Statistics.* New York: McGraw-Hill, 1960.

Blatt, B. *Exodus From Pandemonium.* Boston: Allyn & Bacon, 1970.

Blatt, B. *Souls in Extremis.* Boston: Allyn & Bacon, 1973.

Blatt, B., Biklen, D., and Bogdan, R. (Eds.) *An Alternative Textbook in Special Education.* Denver: Love, 1977.

Blatt, B. and Kaplan F. *Christmas in Purgatory.* Syracuse, N.Y.: Human Policy Press, 1974.

Blatt, B., Ozolins, A., and McNally, J. *The Family Papers: A Return to Purgatory.* New York: Longman, 1980.

Blau, P. M. *The Dynamics of Bureaucracy.* Chicago: University of Chicago Press, 1955.

Blau, P. M. *Bureaucracy in Modern Soicety.* New York: Random House, 1956.

Blau, P. M. "Orientation toward clients in a public welfare agency." *Administrative Science Quarterly,* 5(3): 341–361, 1960.

Blau, P. M. *Exchange and Power in Social Life.* New York: Wiley, 1964.

Blau, P. M. and Scott, W. R. *Formal organization.* San Francisco: Chandler, 1962.

Blauner, R. and Wellman, D. "Toward the decolonization of social research." In J. Ladner (Ed.) *The Death of White Sociology.* New York: Vintage Books, 1973.

Bloor, M. J. "On the analysis of observational data: A discussion of the worth and uses of inductive techniques and respondent validation." *Sociology,* 12: 545–552, 1978.

Bloor, M. J. "Notes on member validation." In R. M. Emerson (Ed.) *Contemporary Field Research.* Boston: Little, Brown, pp. 156–172, 1983.

Blum, F. H. "Getting individuals to give information to the outsider." *Journal of Social Issues,* 8(3): 35–42, 1952.

Blumer, H. *An Appraisal of Thomas and Znaniecki's 'The Polish Peasant in Europe and America.'* New York: Social Science Research Council, 1939.

Blumer, H. "Sociological analysis of the 'variable.'" *American Sociological Review,* 21 (December): 683–690, 1956.

Blumer, H. "Sociological implications of the thought of George Herbert Mead." *American Journal of Sociology,* 71(March): 535–544, 1966.

Blumer, H. "Society as symbolic interaction." In J. Manis and B. Mentzer (Eds.) *Symbolic Interaction.* Boston: Allyn & Bacon, 1967.

Blumer, H. *Symbolic Interactionism: Perspective and Method.* Englewood Cliffs, N.J.: Prentice-Hall, 1969.

Boas, F. *Handbook of American Indian Languages*. Washington, D.C.: Bureau of American Ethnology, Bulletin 40, 1911.

Bodemann, Y. M. "A problem of sociological praxis: The case for interventive observation in field work." *Theory and Society*, 5: 387–420, 1978.

Bogdan, R. *A Forgotten Organizational Type*. Unpublished dissertation, 1971.

Bogdan, R. "Learning to sell door to door." *The American Behavioral Scientist*, September/October, 55–64, 1972a.

Bogdan, R. *Participant Observation in Organization Settings*. Syracuse, New York: Syracuse University Division of Special Education and Rehabilitation, 1972b.

Bogdan, R. *Being Different: The Autobiography of Jane Fry*. New York: Wiley, 1974.

Bogdan, R. "Interviewing people labeled retarded." In W. B. Shaffir, R. A. Stebbins, and A. Turowetz (Eds.) *Fieldwork Experience: Qualitative Approaches to Social Research*. New York: St. Martin's Press, pp. 235–243, 1980.

Bogdan, R. and Barnes, E. "A qualitative sociological study of mainstreaming." Mimeographed. 1979.

Bogdan, R. and Biklen, D. "Handicapism." *Social Policy*. April, 14–19, 1977.

Bogdan, R., Brown, M.A., and Foster, S. B. "Be honest but not cruel: Staff/parent communication on a neonatal unit." *Human Organization*, 41(1): 6–16, 1982.

Bogdan, R. and Taylor, S. *Introduction to Qualitative Research Methods: A Phenomenological Approach to the Social Sciences*. New York: Wiley, 1975.

Bogdan, R. and Taylor, S. J. *Inside Out: The Social Meaning of Mental Retardation*. Toronto: U. of Toronto Press, 1982.

Bogdan, R., Taylor, S., de Grandpre, B., and Haynes, S. "Let them eat programs: Attendants' perspectives and programming on wards in state schools." *Journal of Health and Social Behavior*, 15(June): 142–151, 1974.

Bonacich, P. "Deceiving subjects: The pollution of our environment." *American Sociologist*, 5(February): 45, 1970.

Bonaparte, M. A. "A defense of biography." *International Journal of Psycho-Analysis*, 5(20): 231–240, 1939.

Bowers, R. V. "Research methodology in sociology: The first half-century." In R. F. Spencer (Ed.) *Method and Perspective in Anthropology*. Minneapolis: University of Minnesota Press, pp. 251–270, 1954.

Braginsky, D. and Braginsky, B. *Hansels and Gretels*. New York: Holt, Rinehart & Winston, 1971.

Bromley, D. G. and Shupe, A. D., Jr. "Evolving foci in participant observation: Research as an emergent process." In W. B. Shaffir, R. A. Stebbins, and A. Turowetz (Eds.) *Fieldwork Experience: Qualitative Approaches to Social Research*. New York: St. Martin's Press, pp. 191–202, 1980.

Brookover, L. A. and Back, K. W. "Time sampling as a field technique." *Human Organization*, 25: 64–70, 1966.

Brown, C. *Manchild in the Promised Land*. New York: New American Library, 1965.

Bruininks, R. H., Meyers, C. E., Sigford, B. B., and Lakin, K. C. (Eds.) *Deinstitutionalization and Community Adjustment of Mentally Retarded People*. Washington, D.C.: American Association on Mental Deficiency, 1981.

Bruyn, S. T. *The Human Perspective in Sociology: The Methodology of Participant Observation*. Englewood Cliffs, N.J.: Prentice-Hall, 1966.

Brymer, R. A. and Faris, B. "Ethical and political dilemmas in the investigation of deviance: A study of juvenile delinquency." In G. Sjoberg (Ed.) *Ethics, Politics, and Social Research,* Cambridge, Mass.: Schenkman, pp. 297–318, 1967.

Buckner, H. T. "Organization of a large scale field work course." *Urban Life and Culture,* 2(3) (October): 361–379, 1973.

Bulmer, M. "Concepts in the analysis of qualitative data: A symposium." *Sociological Review,* 27: 651–677, 1979.

Burchard, W. W. "Lawyers, political scientists, sociologists—and concealed microphones." *American Sociological Review,* 23: 686–691, 1958.

Burgess, E. W. "What social case records should contain to be useful for sociological interpretation." *Social Forces,* 6: 524–532, 1925.

Burgess, E. W. "Statistics and case studies as methods of sociological research." *Social Forces,* 12: 103–120, 1927.

Burgess, E. W. "Research methods in sociology." In G. Gurvitch and W. Moore (Eds.) *Twentieth Century Sociology.* New York: Philosophical Library, pp. 20–41, 1945a.

Burgess, E. W. "Sociological research methods." *American Journal of Sociology,* 50: 474–482, 1945b.

Burgess, R. G. (Ed.) *Field Research: A Sourcebook and Field Manual.* London: George Allen and Unwin, 1982.

Burr, A. R. *The Autobiography: A Critical and Comparative Study.* New York: Houghton Mifflin, 1909.

Camilleri, S. F. "Theory, probability, and induction in social research." *American Sociological Review,* 27: 170–178, 1962.

Campbell, D. T. "The informant in qualitative research." *American Journal of Sociology,* 60: 339–342, 1955.

Campbell, D. T. "Factors relevant to the validity of experiments in social settings." *Psychological Bulletin,* 54: 297–312, 1957.

Campbell, D. T. "Systematic error on the part of human links in communication systems. *Information and Control,* 1: 334–369, 1959.

Campbell, D. T. and Stanley, J. C. *Experimental and Quasi-Experimental Designs for Research.* Chicago: Rand McNally, 1966.

Cannel, C. F. and Axelrod, M. "The respondent reports on the interview." *American Journal of Sociology,* 62: 177–181, 1956.

Caplow, T. "The dynamics of information interviewing." *American Journal of Sociology,* 62: 165–171, 1956.

Carey, A. "The Hawthorne studies: A radical criticism." *American Sociological Review,* 32(3): 403–416, 1967.

Carroll, J. "Confidentiality of social science research sources and data: The Popkin case." *Political Science,* 6: 11–24, 1973.

Cartwright, A. *Human Relations and Hospital Care.* London: Routledge and Kegan Paul, 1964.

Cartwright, A. *Patients and Their Doctors.* London: Routledge and Kegan Paul, 1967.

Cartwright, D. and French, J. R. P., Jr. "The reliability of life history studies." *Character and Personality,* 8: 110–119, 1939.

Cassell, J. "Risk and benefit to subjects of fieldwork." *American Sociologist,* 13: 134–143, 1978.

Cassell, J. "Ethical principles for conducting fieldwork." *American Anthropologist,* **82**: 28–41, 1980.

Cassell, J. and Wax, M. "Ethical problems of fieldwork." *Social Problems,* **27**: 259–264, 1980.

Castenada, C. *The Teachings of Don Juan: A Yaqui Way of Knowledge.* Los Angeles: U. of California Press, 1968.

Castenada, C. *A Separate Reality: Further Conversations with Don Juan.* New York: Simon and Schuster, 1971.

Castenada, C. *Journal to Ixtlan: The Lessons of Don Juan.* New York: Simon and Schuster, 1972.

Castenada, C. *Sorcery: A Description of Reality.* Ann Arbor: University Microfilms, 1973.

Castenada, C. *Tales of Power.* New York: Simon and Schuster, 1974.

Castenada, C. *The Second Ring of Power.* New York: Simon and Schuster, 1977.

Caudill, W. *The Psychiatric Hospital as a Small Society.* Cambridge, Mass.: Harvard University Press, 1958.

Cavan, R. S. "Interviewing for life-history material." *The American Journal of Sociology,* **35**: 100–115, 1929–1930.

Cavan, S. *Liquor License: An Ethnography of Bar Behavior.* Chicago: Aldine, 1966.

Cavan, S. "Seeing social structure in a rural setting." *Urban Life and Culture,* **3**(October): 329–346, 1974.

Chapin, F. S. *Field Work and Social Research.* New York: Century, 1920.

Charmaz, K. "The grounded theory method: An explication and interpretation." In R. M. Emerson (Ed.) *Contemporary Field Research.* Boston: Little, Brown, pp. 109–126, 1983.

Chesler, M. and Schmuck, R. "Participant observation in a superpatriot discussion group." *Journal of Social Issues,* **19**(2): 18–30, 1963.

Chrisman, N. J. "Secret societies and the ethics of urban fieldwork." In M. A. Rynkiewich and J. P. Spradley (Eds.) *Ethics and Anthropology: Dilemmas in Fieldwork.* New York: Wiley 1976.

Christie, R. M. "Comment on conflict methodology: A protagonist position." *Sociological Quarterly,* **17**: 513–519, 1976.

Church, J. *Three Babies.* New York: Random House, 1966.

Cicourel, A. *Method and Measurement in Sociology.* New York: Free Press, 1964.

Cicourel, A. *The Social Organization of Juvenile Justice.* New York: Wiley, 1968.

Cicourel, A. *Cognitive Sociology: Language and Meaning in Social Interaction.* New York: Free Press, 1974a.

Cicourel, A. "Interviewing and memory." In C. Cherry (Ed.) *Pragmatic Aspects of Human Communications.* Dordrecht, The Netherlands: D. Reidel, 1974b.

Cicourel, A. and Kitsuse, J. *The Educational Decision-makers.* Indianapolis: Bobbs-Merrill, 1963.

Clark, K. *Dark Ghetto.* New York: Harper Torchbooks, 1967.

Clarke, J. "Survival in the field: Implications of personal experience in fieldwork." *Theory and Society,* **2**: 95–123, 1975.

Clyman, R. I. et al. "What pediatricians say to mothers of sick newborns: An indirect evaluation of the counseling process." *Pediatrics,* **63**: 719–723, 1979.

Code of Federal Regulations. "Protection of human subjects." 45 Public Welfare CFR Part 46, Revised October 1. Washington, D.C.: GPO, 1977.

Coles, R. *Children of Crisis*. Boston: Little, Brown, 1964.

Coles, R. *The South goes North*. Boston: Little, Brown, 1971a.

Coles, R. *Migrants Sharecroppers, Mountaineers*. Boston: Little, Brown, 1971b.

Cole, S. *The Sociological Method*. 2nd ed. Chicago: Rand McNally, 1976.

Coleman, J. S. "Relational analysis: The study of social organizations with survey methods." *Human Organization*, 17(4): 28–36, 1958.

Colfax, D. J. "Pressure toward distortion and involvement in studying a civil rights organization." *Human Organization*, XXV (Summer): 140–149, 1966.

Collier, J., Jr. *Visual Anthropology: Photography as a Research Method*. New York: Holt, 1967.

Colvard, R. "Interaction and identification in reporting field research: A critical reconsideration of protective procedures." In G. Sjoberg (Ed.) *Ethics, Politics and Social Research*. Cambridge, Mass.: Schenkman, pp. 319–358, 1967.

Comte, A. *The Positive Philosophy*. Translated by Harriet Martineau. London: George Bell & Sons, 1896.

Conklin, H. C. "Lexicographical treatment of folk taxonomies." In S. A. Tyler (Ed.) *Cognitive Anthropology*. New York: Holt, Rinehart & Winston, pp. 41–59, 1969.

Cook, P. H. "Methods of field research." *Australian Journal of Psychology*, 3(2): 84–98, 1951.

Cooley, C. H. *Human Nature and the Social Order*. New York: Scribner, 1902.

Cooper, K. J. "Rural–urban differences in responses to field techniques." *Human Organization*, 18(3): 135–139, 1959.

Coser, L. A., Roth, J. A., Sullivan, M. A., Jr., and Queen, S. A. "Participant observation and the military: An exchange." *American Sociological Review*, 24: 397–400, 1959.

Coser, R. L. "Comment." *American Sociologist*, 13: 156–157, 1978.

Cottle, T. J. *Time's Children*. Boston: Little, Brown, 1971.

Cottle, T. J. *The Abandoners: Portraits of Loss, Separation, and Neglect*. Boston: Little, Brown, 1972.

Cottle, T. J. *The Voices of School: Educational Images Through Personal Accounts*. Boston: Little, Brown, 1973a.

Cottle, T. J. "The life study: On mutual recognition and the subjective inquiry." *Urban Life and Culture*, 2(3) (October): 344–360, 1973b.

Cottle, T. J. "The ghetto scientists," unpublished paper, 1973c.

Coulter, J. "Decontextualized meanings: Current approaches to verstehende investigations." *Sociological Review*, 19: 301–323, 1971.

Cowley, M. "Sociological habit patterns in linguistic transmogrification." *The Reporter*, September 20, 170–175, 1956.

Craig, K. H. "The comprehension of the everyday physical environment." In H. M. Proshansky, W. H. Ittelson, and L. E. Rivlin. *Environmental Psychology*. New York: Holt, Rinehart & Winston, 1970.

Cressey, D. R. "Criminal violations of financial trust." *American Sociological Review*, 15: 738–743, 1950.

Cressey, D. *Other People's Money: A Study in the Social Psychology of Embezzlement.* Glencoe, Ill.: Free Press, 1953.

Cressey, D. "Limitations on organization of treatment in the modern prison." In R. Quinney (Ed.) *Crime and Justice in Society.* Boston: Little, Brown, 1969.

Cressey, P. G. *The Taxi-Dance Hall.* Chicago: University of Chicago Press, 1932.

Culberg, J. "Mental reactions of women to perinatal death. In N. Morris (Ed.) *Psychosomatic Medicine in Obstetrics and Gynecology.* New York: S. Karger, pp. 326–329, 1972.

Dabbs, J. M., Jr. "Making things visible." In J. Van Maanen, J. M. Dabbs, Jr., and R. R. Faulkner (Eds.) *Varieties of Qualitative Research.* Beverly Hills: Sage, pp. 31–64, 1982.

Dalton, M. *Men Who Manage.* New York: Wiley, 1961.

Dalton, M. "Preconceptions and methods in *Men Who Manage.*" In P. E. Hammond (Ed.) *Sociologists at Work.* New York: Basic Books, pp. 50–95, 1964.

Daniels, A. K. "The low-caste stranger in social research." In G. Sjoberg (Ed.) *Ethics, Politics, and Social Research.* Cambridge, Mass.: Schenkman, pp. 267–296, 1967.

David, C. J. "Grief, mourning and pathological mourning." *Primary Care,* 2: 81–93, 1975.

Davis, A. J. "Sexual assaults in the Philadelphia prison system and sheriff's vans." *Trans-Action,* 6(December): 8–16, 1968.

Davis, F. "The cabdriver and his fare." *American Journal of Sociology,* 63(2): 158–165, 1959.

Davis, F. "Uncertainty in medical prognosis." *American Journal of Sociology,* 66(July): 41–47, 1960.

Davis, F. "Comment on initial interaction of newcomers in Alcoholics Anonymous." *Social Problems,* 8(4): 364–365, 1961.

Davis F. *Passage Through Crisis.* Indianapolis: Bobbs-Merrill, 1963.

Davis, F. "Deviance disavowal: The management of strained interaction by the visibly handicapped." In H. S. Becker (Ed.) *The Other Side,* New York: Free Press, 1964.

Davis, F. "The Martian and the convert: Ontological polarities in social research." *Urban Life and Culture,* 2(3) (October): 333–343, 1973.

Davis, F. "Stories and Sociology." *Urban Life and Culture,* 3(October): 310–316, 1974.

Davis, M. "Physiologic, psychological and demographic factors in patient compliance with doctors' orders." *Medical Care,* 6: 115–122, 1968a.

Davis, M. "Variations in patients' compliance with doctors' advice: An empirical analysis of patterns of communication." *American Journal of Public Health,* 58: 274–288, 1968b.

Davis, M. "Variations in patients' compliance with doctors' orders: Medical practice and doctor patient interaction." *Psychiatry in Medicine,* 2: 31–54, 1971.

Davis, M. S. and Eichhorn, R. L. "Compliance with medical regimens: Panel study." *Journal of Health and Human Behavior,* 4: 240–249, 1963.

Davis, S. P. *The Mentally Retarded in Society.* New York: Columbia University Press, 1959.

Dean, J. P. "Participant observation and interviewing." In J. T. Doby (Ed.) *An Introduction to Social Research.* Harrisburg, Pa.: Stackpole, pp. 225–252, 1954.

Dean, J. P., Eichhorn, R. L., and Dean, L. R. "Observation and interviewing." In J. T. Doby (Ed.) *An Introduction to Social Research,* 2nd ed. New York: Appleton-Century-Crofts, pp. 274–304, 1967.

Dean, J. P. and Whyte, W. F. "How do you know if the informant is telling the truth?" *Human Organization* 17(2): 34–38, 1958.

Dean, L. R. "Interaction, reported and observed: The case of one local union." *Human Organization,* 17(3): 36–44, 1958.

Deegan, M. J. and Burger, J. S. "George Herbert Mead and social reform." *Journal of the History of the Behavioral Sciences,* 14: 362–372, 1978.

Deegan, M. J. and Burger, J. S. "W. I. Thomas and social reform: His work and his writings." *Journal of the History of the Behavioral Sciences,* 17: 114–125, 1981.

de Grandpre, B. The culture of a state school ward. Unpublished dissertation, 1973.

DeLaguna, F. "Some problems of objectivity in ethnology." *Man,* 57: 179–182, 1957.

de Mille, R. *Castenada's Journey: The Power and the Allegory.* Santa Barbara: Capra, 1976.

de Mille, R. *The Don Juan Papers: Further Castenada Controversies.* Santa Barbara: Ross-Erikson, 1980.

Denzin, N. "On the ethics of disguised observation. *Social Problems,* 15: 502–504, 1968.

Denzin, N. (Ed.) *Sociological Methods: A Sourcebook.* Chicago: Aldine, 1970.

Denzin, N. "The logic of naturalistic inquiry." *Social Forces,* 50: 166–182, 1971.

Denzin, N. *The Research Act: A Theoretical Introduction to Sociological Methods.* 2nd ed. New York: McGraw-Hill, 1978.

Department of Health, Education and Welfare. "Protection of human subjects." Washington, D.C.: Federal Register, May 30, 1974 (39 FR18914), 1974.

Department of Health, Education and Welfare. "Protection of human subjects: Institutional review boards." Washington, D.C.: Federal Register, November 30, 1978 (43 FR56174), 1978.

Deutscher, I. "Words and deeds: Social science and social policy." *Social Problems,* 13 (Winter): 233–254, 1966.

Deutscher, I. "Notes on language and human conduct." The Maxwell Graduate School of Social Sciences and the Youth Development Center, Syracuse University, 1967.

Deutscher, I. "The bureaucratic gatekeeper in public housing." In I. Deutscher and E. Thompson (Eds.) *Among the People: Encounters with the Poor.* New York: Basic Books, 1968.

Deutscher, I. "Looking backward: Case studies on the progress of methodology in sociological research." *The American Sociologist,* 4(February): 34–42, 1969.

Deutscher, I. *What We Say/What We Do: Sentiments and Acts.* Glenview, Ill.: Scott, Foresman, 1973.

Deutscher, I. and Thompson, E. *Among the People: Encounters with the Poor.* New York: Basic Books, 1968.

Dewey, J. *Human Nature and Conduct.* New York: Modern Library, 1930.

Dexter, L. A. "Role relationships and conceptions of neutrality in interviewing." *American Journal of Sociology,* 62: 153–157, 1956.

Dexter, L. A. "The good will of important people: More on the jeopardy of the interview." *Public Opinion Quarterly,* 28: 556–563, 1964a.

Dexter, L. A. *The Tyranny of Schooling*. New York: Basic Books, 1964b.

Dexter, L. A. "On the politics and sociology of stupidity in our society." In H. S. Becker (Ed.) *The Other Side*, New York: Free Press, 1967.

Dexter, L. A. *Elite and Specialized Interviewing*. Evanston: Northwestern University Press, 1970.

Diesing, P. *Patterns of Discovery in the Social Sciences*. Chicago: Aldine-Atherton, 1971.

Dingwall, R. "Ethics and ethnography." *Sociological Review*, 28: 871–891, 1980.

Dollard, J. *Criteria for the Life History*. New York: Social Science Research Council, 1935.

Dollard, J. *Caste and Class in a Southern Town*. 2nd ed. New York: Harper, 1949.

Domhoff, G. W. *The Bohemian Grove and Other Retreats*. New York: Random House, 1975.

Dorn, D. S. and Long, G. L. "Brier remarks on the Association's code of ethics." *American Sociologist*, 9(February): 31–35, 1974.

Dornbusch, S. M. "The military as an assimilating institution." *Social Forces*, 33(4): 316–321, 1955.

Doughty, C. M. *Travels in Arabia Deserta*. New York: Random House, 1936.

Douglas, J. D. *The Social Meaning of Suicide*. Princeton, NJ: Princeton University Press, 1967.

Douglas, J. D. (Ed.) *Deviance and Responsibility: The Social Construction of Moral Meanings*. New York: Basic Books, 1970a.

Douglas, J. D. *Observations of Deviance*. New York: Random House, 1970b.

Douglas, J. D. (Ed.) *Understanding Everyday Life: Toward the Reconstruction of Sociological Knowledge*. Chicago: Aldine, 1970c.

Douglas, J. D. *American Social Order: Social Rules in a Pluralistic Society*. New York: Free Press, 1971.

Douglas, J. D. (Ed.) *Research on Deviance*. New York: Random House, 1972.

Douglas, J. D. *Investigative Social Research: Individual and Team Field Research*. Beverly Hills, Calif: Sage Publications, 1976.

Douglas, J. D. and Johnson, J. M. (Eds.) *Existential Sociology*. New York: Cambridge University Press, 1977.

Drass, K. A. "The analysis of qualitative data: A computer program." *Urban Life*, 9(3): 332–353, 1980.

Driscoll, J. *Trans-Action*, 8(5–6): 28–38, 1971.

DuBois, C. "Some psychological objectives and techniques in ethnography." *Journal of Social Psychology*, 285–301, 1937.

Duff, R. S. and Campbell, A. G. M. "Moral and ethical dilemmas in the special-care nursery." *New England Journal of Medicine*, 289: 890–894, 1973.

Duff, R. S. and Hollinghead, A. *Sickness and Society*. New York: Harper and Row, 1968.

Dumont, R. V. "Learning English and how to be silent: Studies in American Indian classrooms." In V. P. Johns, C. B. Cazden, and D. H. Hymes (Eds.) *Functions of Language in the Classroom*. New York: Columbia University, Teachers' College Press, 1971.

Durkheim, E. *The Elementary Forms of Religious Life*. New York: Free Press, 1915.

Durkheim, E. *The Rules of Sociological Method*. New York: Free Press, 1938.

Durkheim E. *Suicide: A Study of Sociology*. Translated and edited by George Simpson. New York: Free Press, 1951.

Duster, T., Matza, D., and Wellman, D. "Field work and the protection of human subjects." *American Sociologist*, 14: 136–142, 1979.

Earle, W. *The Autobiographical Consciousness: A Philosophical Inquiry into Existence*. Chicago: Quadrangle, 1972.

Easterday, L., Papademas, D., Schorr, L., and Valentine, C. "The making of a female researcher: Role problems in fieldwork." *Urban Life*, 6: 333–348, 1977.

Eaton, J. W. and Weil, R. J. "Social processes of professional teamwork." *American Sociological Review*, 16: 707–713, 1951.

Economic Opportunity Amendments. Public Law 92–424, 92nd Congress HR 12350 (Sept.) 1972.

Edgerton, R. B. *The Cloak of Competence*. Berkeley: University of California Press, 1967.

Edgerton, R. and Edgerton, C. "Becoming mentally retarded in a Hawaiian School." In R. Eyman, E. Meyers, and G. Tarjan (Eds.) *Sociobehavioral Studies in Mental Retardation*. Los Angeles: American Association of Mental Deficiency, 1973.

Eggan, R. "Social anthropology and the method of controlled comparison." *American Anthropologist*, 56: 743–763, 1954.

Elementary and Secondary Education Act. Public Law 92–232, Title VI. 1965.

Elling, R. et al. "Patient participation in a pediatric program." *Journal of Health and Human Behavior*, 1: 183–189, 1960.

Elliott, B. A. "Neonatal death: Reflections for parents." *Pediatrics*, 62: 100–102, 1978.

Elsner, H. *Robert E. Park: The Crowd and the Public, and Other Essays*. Chicago: University of Chicago Press, 1972.

Emerson, J. P. "Sustaining definitions of reality in gynecological examinations." In H. P. Dreitzel (Ed.) *Recent Sociology*. No. 2. New York: Macmillan, pp. 74–95, 1970.

Emerson, R. M. "Observational field work." *Annual Review of Sociology*, 7: 351–378, 1981.

Emerson, R. M. (Ed.) *Contemporary Field Research*. Boston: Little, Brown, 1983.

Epstein, A. L. (Ed.) *The Craft of Social Anthropology*. New York: Barnes & Noble, 1967.

Erikson, K. T. "A comment on disguised observation in sociology." *Social Problems*, 14: 366–373, 1967.

Erikson, K. *Everything in Its Path*. New York: Simon and Schuster, 1976.

Etzioni, A. "Two approaches to organizational analysis: A critique and suggestion." *Administrative Science Quarterly*, 5: 257–278, 1960.

Etzioni, A. *A Comparative Analysis of Complex Organizations*. New York: Free Press, 1961.

Etzioni, A. (Ed.) *Complex Organizations*. New York: Holt, Rinehart & Winston, 1962a.

Etzioni, A. *Modern Organizations*. Englewood Cliffs, N.J.: Prentice-Hall, 1962b.

Evans-Pritchard, E. E. *Social Anthropology and Other Essays*. New York: Free Press, 1964.

Evans-Pritchard, E. E. "Some reminiscences and reflections on fieldwork." Appendix IV in *Witchcraft, Oracles and Magic among the Azande*. (Abridged.) Oxford: Clarendon Press, 1976.

Faulkner, R. *Hollywood Studio Musicians*. Chicago: Aldine, 1971.

Faulkner, R. "Improvising on a triad." In J. Van Maanen, J. M. Dabbs, Jr., and R. R. Faulkner (Eds.) *Varieties of Qualitative Research.* Beverly Hills: Sage, pp. 65–102, 1982.

Ferleger, S. and Boyd, P. A. "Anti-institutionalization: The promise of the Pennhurst case." *Stanford Law Review,* 31(4): 717–752, 1979.

Festinger, L. and Katz, D. (Eds.) *Research Methods in the Behavioral Sciences.* New York: Holt, 1953.

Festinger, L., Riecken, H., and Schacter, S. *When Prophecy Fails.* Minneapolis: University of Minnesota Press, 1956.

Feyerabend, P. K. *Against Method: Outline of an Anarchistic Theory of Knowledge.* Atlantic Highlands, N.J.: Humanities Press, 1975.

Fichter, J. H. and Kolb, W. L. "Ethical limitations on sociological reporting." *American Sociological Review,* 18: 544–550, 1953.

Filstead, W. (Ed.) *Qualitative Methodology: Firsthand involvement with the Social World.* Chicago: Markham, 1970.

Fine, G. A. "Cracking diamonds: Observer role in little league baseball settings and the acquisition of social competence." In W. B. Shaffir, R. A. Stebbins, and A. Turowetz (Eds.) *Fieldwork Experience: Qualitative Approaches to Social Research.* New York: St. Martin's Press, pp. 117–131, 1980.

Fischoff, J. and O'Brien, N. "After the child dies." *Journal of Pediatrics,* 88: 140, 1976.

Forcese, D. P. and Richer, S. *Social Research Methods.* Englewood Cliffs, N.J.: Prentice-Hall, 1973.

Form, W. H. "The Sociology of social research." In R. T. O'Toole (Ed.) *The Organization, Management, and Tactics of Social Research.* Cambridge, Mass.: Schenkman, 1971.

Fox, J. and Lundman, R. "Problems and strategies in gaining access in police organizations." *Criminology,* 12: 52–69, 1974.

Fox, R. C. *Experiment Perilous: Physicians and Patients Facing the Unknown.* Glencoe, Ill.: The Free Press, 1959.

Frake, C. O. "The diagnosis of disease among the Subanun of Mindanao." *American Anthropologist,* 63: 113–132, 1961.

Frake, C. O. "The ethnographic study of cognitive systems." In T. Gladwin and W. C. Sturtevant (Eds.) *Anthropology and Human Behavior.* Washington: Anthropological Society of Washington, pp. 72–85, 1962a.

Frake, C. O. "Cultural ecology and ethnography." *American Anthropologist,* 64: 53–59, 1962b.

Frake, C. O. "A structural description of Subanun 'religious behavior'." In W. H. Goodenough (Ed.) *Explorations in Cultural Anthropology.* New York: McGraw-Hill, pp. 111–129, 1964a.

Frake, C. O. "Notes on queries in ethnography." *American Anthropologist,* 66: 132–145, 1964b.

Frake, C. O. "Plying frames can be dangerous: Some reflections on methodology in cognitive anthropology." *The Quarterly Newsletter of the Institute for Comparative Human Development,* 1: 1–7, 1977.

Frake, C. O. "Ethnography." In R. M. Emerson (Ed.) *Contemporary Field Research.* Boston: Little, Brown, pp. 60–67, 1983.

Francis, R. G. *The Rhetoric of Science*. Minneapolis: University of Minnesota Press, 1961.

Frank, A. *The Diary of a Young Girl*. New York: Doubleday, 1952.

Frazier, C. E. "The use of life-histories in testing theories of criminal behavior: Toward reviving a method." *Qualitative Sociology*, 1(1): 122–142, 1978.

Freidson, E. "Dilemmas in the doctor–patient relationship." In A. Rose (Ed.) *Human Behavior and Social Processes: An Interactionist Approach*. Boston: Houghton Mifflin, pp. 207–224, 1962.

Freidson, E. *Profession of Medicine: A Study of the Sociology of Applied Knowledge*. New York: Dodd Mead, 1970.

French, J. R. P., Jr. "Experiments in field settings." In L. Festinger and D. Katz (Eds.) *Research Methods in the Behavioral Sciences*. New York: Holt, pp. 98–135, 1953.

French, K. S. "Research interviewers in a medical setting: Roles and social systems." *Human Organization*, 21(3): 219–224, 1962.

Frenkel-Brunswik, E. "Mechanisms of self-deception." *Journal of Social Psychology*, 5(10): 409–420, 1939.

Friedenberg, E. Z. "The films of Frederick Wiseman." *The New York Review of Books*, 17(October 21): 19–22, 1971.

Friedman, N. *The Social Nature of Psychological Research: The Psychological Experiment as a Social Interaction*. New York: Basic Books, 1967.

Friedman, S. B. "Psychological aspects of sudden unexpected deaths in infants and children." *Pediatric Clinics of North America*, 21: 103–113, 1974.

Friedman, S. B. et al. "Behavioral observations on parents anticipating the death of a child." *Pediatrics*, 32: 610–625, 1963.

Gallaher, A., Jr. "Plainville: The twice studied town." In Arthur J. Vidich, Joseph Bensman, and Maurice R. Stein (Eds.) *Reflections on Community Studies*. New York: Wiley, pp. 285–303, 1964.

Galliher, J. F. "The protection of human subjects: A reexamination of the professional code of ethics." *The American Sociologist*, 8(August): 93–100, 1973.

Galliher, J. F. "Professor Galliher replies." *American Sociologist*, 9: 159–160, 1974.

Galliher, J. F. "The ASA Code of Ethics on the protection of human beings: Are students human too?" *American Sociologist*, 10: 113–117, 1975.

Galliher, J. F. "Social scientists' ethical responsibilities to superordinates: Looking upward meekly." In R. M. Emerson (Ed.) *Contemporary Field Research*. Boston: Little, Brown, pp. 300–312, 1983.

Gans, H. *The Urban Villagers*. New York: Free Press, 1962.

Gans, H. "The participant-observer as a human being: Observations on the personal aspects of field work." In H. S. Becker, B. Greer, D. Riesman, and R. S. Weiss (Eds.) *Institutions and the Person*. Chicago: Aldine, pp. 300–317, 1968.

Gans, H. *The Levittowners*. New York: Random House, 1969.

Gardner, B. B. and Whyte, W. F. "Methods for the study of human relations in industry." *American Sociological Review*, 11: 506–512, 1946.

Garfinkel, H. "Conditions of successful degradation ceremonies." *American Journal of Sociology*. 59(March): 420–424, 1956.

Garfinkel, H. *Studies in Ethnomethodology*, Englewood Cliffs: Prentice-Hall, 1967.

Geer, B. "First days in the field." In P. E. Hammond (Ed.) *Sociologist at Work*. New York: Basic Books, pp. 322–344, 1964.

Geer, B., Haas, J., Vivona, C., Miller, S., Woods, C., and Becker, H. S. "Learning the ropes: Situational learning in four occupational training programs." In I. Deutscher and E. Thompson (Eds.) *Among the People*. New York: Basic Books, 1966.

Geertz, C. "From the native's point of view: On the nature of anthropological understanding." In K. H. Basso and H. A. Selby (Eds.) *Meaning in Anthropology*. Albuquerque: University of New Mexico Press, pp. 221–237, 1976.

Geertz, C. "Thick description: Toward an interpretive theory of culture." In R. M. Emerson (Ed.) *Contemporary Field Research*. Boston: Little, Brown, pp. 37–59, 1983.

Georges, R. A. and Jones, M. O. *People Studying People: The Human Element in Fieldwork*. Berkeley: University of California Press, 1980.

Giallombardo, R. *Society of Women: A Study of a Woman's Prison*. New York: Wiley, 1966.

Gilson, G. J. "Care of the family who has lost a newborn." *Postgraduate Medicine*, 60(6): 67–70, 1976.

Glaser, B. G. "The constant comparative method of qualitative analysis." *Social Problems*, 12: 436–445, 1965.

Glaser, B. G. (Ed.) *Organizational Careers*. Chicago: Aldine, 1968.

Glaser, B. G. *Theoretical Sensitivity*. Mill Valley, Calif.: Sociology Press, 1978.

Glaser, B. G. and Strauss, A. *Awareness of Dying*. Chicago: Aldine, 1965.

Glaser, B. G. and Strauss, A. *The Discovery of Grounded Theory: Strategies for Qualitative Research*. Chicago: Aldine, 1967.

Glaser, B. G. and Strauss, A. L. *Time for Dying*. Chicago: Aldine, 1968.

Glaser, B. G. and Strauss, A. *A Status Passage: A Formal Theory*. Chicago: Aldine, 1971.

Glasser, P. H. and Glasser, L. N. *Families in Crisis*. Evanston: Harper and Row, 1970.

Glasser, P. H. and Navarre, E. L. "The problems of families in the A.F.D.C. program." In P. H. Glasser and L. N. Glasser (Eds.) *Families in Crisis*. New York: Harper & Row, 1970.

Glazer, M. *The Research Adventure: Promise and Problems of Field Work*. New York: Random House, 1972.
1959.

Goffman, E. *The Presentation of Self in Everyday Life*. Garden City, N.Y.: Doubleday,

Goffman, E. *Asylums: Essays on the Social Situation of Mental Patients and Other Inmates*. Garden City, N.Y.: Doubleday, Anchor Books, 1961.

Goffman, E. *Stigma*. Englewood Cliffs, N.J.: Prentice-Hall, 1963.

Goffman, E. *Interaction Ritual*. Garden City, N. Y.: Doubleday, 1967.

Goffman, E. *Relations in Public*. New York: Harper & Row, 1971.

Gold, D. "Comment on 'A critique of tests of significance.'" *American Sociological Review*, 24: 328–338, 1959.

Gold, R. "Janitors versus tenants: A status–income dilemma." *American Journal of Sociology*, 57(March): 486–493, 1952.

Gold, R. L. "Roles in sociological field observations." *Social Forces*, 36: 217–223, 1958.

Golde, P. (Ed.) *Women in the Field*. Chicago: Aldine, 1970.

Goldner, F. H. "Role emergence and the ethics of ambiguity." In Gideon Sjoberg (Ed.) *Ethics, Politics, and Social Research*. Cambridge, Mass.: Schenkman, pp. 245–266, 1967.

Goode, D. A. "The world of the congenitally deaf-blind: Toward the grounds for achieving human understanding." In J. Jacobs (Ed.) *Mental Retardation: A Phenomenological Approach.* Springfield, Ill.: Charles C. Thomas, 1980.

Goode, W. "Community within a community: The professions." *American Sociological Review,* 22(April): 194–200, 1957.

Goode, W. "Encroachment, charlatinism, and the emerging professions: Psychology, Sociology, and Medicine." *American Sociological Review,* 25(December): 903, 1960.

Goode, W. J. and Hatt, P. K. *Methods in Social Research.* New York: McGraw-Hill, 1952.

Goodenough, W. H. "Cultural anthropology and linguistics." *Georgetown University Monograph Series on Language and Linguistics,* 9: 167–173, 1957.

Goodenough, W. H. "Culture, language, and society." Reading, Mass.: Addison-Wesley Modular Publications, 1971.

Gorden, R. L. "Dimensions of the depth interview." *American Journal of Sociology,* 62: 158–164, 1956.

Gordis, L. et al. "Why patients don't follow medical advice: A study of children on long term antistreptococcal prophylaxis." *Journal of Pediatrics,* 75: 957–968, 1969.

Gottschalk, L., Kluckhohn, C., and Angell, R. D., *The Use of Personal Documents in History, Anthropology and Sociology.* New York: Social Science Research Council, 1945.

Gouldner, A. *Patterns of Industrial Bureaucracy.* New York: Free Press, 1954.

Gouldner, A. "The sociologist as partisan: Sociology and the welfare state." *The American Sociologist,* 3(May): 103–116, 1968.

Gouldner, A. *The Coming Crisis of Western Sociology.* New York: Basic Books, 1970.

Green, P. "The obligations of American social scientists." *The Annals of the American Academy of Political and Social Science,* 394: 13–27, 1971.

Griffin, J. H. *Black Like Me.* Boston: Houghton, Mifflin, 1962.

Gross, N. and Mason, W. "Some methodological problems of eight hour interviews." *American Journal of Sociology,* 59(November): 197–204, 1953.

Gubrium, J. *Living and Dying in Murray Manor.* New York: St. Martin's Press, 1975.

Gullahorn, J. and Strauss, G. "The field worker in union research." *Human Organization,* 13(3): 28–32, 1954.

Gurwitsch, A. *Studies in Phenomenology and Psychology.* Evanston, Ill.: Northwestern University Press, 1966.

Gusfield, J. G. "Field work reciprocities in studying a social movement." *Human Organization,* 14(3): 29–34, 1955.

Gussow, Z. "The observer–observed relationship as information about structure in small-group research: A comparative study of urban elementary school classrooms." *Psychiatry,* 27: 230–247, 1964.

Haas, J. *From Punk to Scale: A Study of High Steel Ironworkers.* Unpublished dissertation, University Microfilm, 1970.

Haas, J. and Shaffir, W. "Fieldworkers' mistakes at work: problems in maintaining research and researcher bargains." In W. B. Shaffir, R. A. Stebbins, and A. Turowetz (Eds.) *Fieldwork Experience: Qualitative Approaches to Social Research.* New York: St. Martin's Press, pp. 244–256, 1980.

Habenstein, R. *Pathways to Data: Field Methods for Studying Ongoing Organizations.* Chicago: Aldine, 1970.

Hader, J. J. and Lindeman, E. C. *Dynamic Social Research*. London: Kegan Paul, 1933.

Haley, A. "Epilogue." In Malcolm X *The Autobiography of Malcolm X*. New York: Grove Press, 1966.

Hall, E. T. *The Silent Language*. New York: Doubleday, 1959.

Hammond, P. E. (Ed.) *Sociologist at Work: The Craft of Social Research*. New York: Basic Books, 1964.

Hannerz, U. *Soulside: Inquiries into Ghetto Culture and Community*, 1969.

Hannerz, U. *Exploring the City: Inquiries toward an Urban Anthropology*. New York: Columbia University Press, 1980.

Haring, D. G. "Comment on field techniques in ethnography, illustrated by a survey in the Ryuke Islands." *Southwestern Journal of Anthropology*, 10: 255–267, 1954.

Harrell-Bond, B. "Studying elites: Some special problems." In M. A. Rynkiewich and J. P. Spradley (Eds.) *Ethics and Anthropology: Dilemmas in Fieldwork*. New York: Wiley, 1976.

Harris, R. *The Police Academy: An Inside View*. New York: Wiley, 1973.

Harvey, S. M. "A preliminary investigation of the interview." *British Journal of Psychology*, 28: 263–287, 1938.

Haynes, S. *Change in a State School*. Unpublished dissertation, 1973.

Heap, J. L. and Roth, P. A. "On phenomenological sociology." *American Sociological Review*, 38(June): 354–367, 1973.

Hearnshaw, L. S. *Cyril Burt, Psychologist*. Ithaca: Cornell University Press, 1979.

Heber, R. *A Manual on Terminology and Classification in Mental Retardation*. Washington: The American Association on Mental Deficiency, 1961.

Henry, J. and Spiro, M. "Psychological techniques in projective tests in field work." In Alfred Koreber (Ed.) *Anthropology Today*. Chicago: University of Chicago Press, pp. 417–429, 1953.

Henry, R. and Saberwal, S. (Eds.) *Stress and Response in Field Work*, New York: Holt, Rinehart & Winston, 1969.

Herskovits, M. J. *Man and His Works*. New York: Knopf, 1948.

Herskovits, M. J. "The hypothetical situation: A technique of field research." *Southwestern Journal of Anthropology*, 6: 32–40, 1950.

Herskovits, M. J. "Problems of method in ethnography." In R. F. Skinner (Ed.) *Method and Perspective in Anthropology*. Minneapolis: University of Minnesota Press, 1954.

Hewitt, J. P. and Stokes, R. "Disclaimers." *Sociological Review*, 40: 1–11, 1975.

Heyns, R. W. and Lippitt, R. "Systematic observational techniques." In G. Lindsey (Ed.) *Handbook of Social Psychology*, Vol. 1. Cambridge, Mass.: Addison-Wesley, pp. 370–404, 1954.

Hinkle, R. D., Jr. and Hinkle, G. J. *The Development of Modern Sociology*. New York: Random House, 1954.

Hoffman, N., Horowitz, I. L., and Rainwater, L. "Sociological snoopers and journalistic moralizers: Comment—An exchange." *Trans-Action*, 7(7): 4–10, 1970.

Hoffmann, J. E. "Problems of access in the study of social elites and boards of directors." In W. B. Shaffir, R. A. Stebbins, and A. Turowetz (Eds.) *Fieldwork Experience: Qualitative Approaches to Social Research*. New York: St. Martin's Press, pp. 45–56, 1980.

Homans, G. C. *Social Behavior: Its Elementary Forms*. New York: Harcourt Brace, 1961.

Homans, G. C. "Contemporary theory in sociology." In R. E. L. Foris (Ed.) *Handbook of Modern Sociology.* Chicago: Rand McNally, pp. 951–977, 1964.

Honigmann, J. J. "The personal approach in cultural anthropological research." *Current Anthropology,* 17: 243–251, 1976.

Horowitz, I. L. "The life and death of Project Camelot." *Transaction,* 3(7): 44–47, 1965.

Horowitz, I. L. (Ed.) *The Rise and Fall of Project Camelot.* Cambridge, Mass.: M.I.T. Press, 1967.

Horowitz, I. L. and Rainwater, L. "Journalistic moralizers." *Transaction,* 7(7): 5–8, 1970.

Horton, J. "Time cool people." *Trans-Action,* 4(5): 5–12, 1967.

Huber, J. "Symbolic interaction as a pragmatic perspective: The bias of emergent theory." *American Sociological Review,* 38 (April): 274–284, 1973.

Hughes, E. C. "A study of a secular institution: The Chicago Real Estate Board." Unpublished dissertation, Department of Sociology, University of Chicago, 1928.

Hughes, E. C. "Institutional offices and the person." *American Journal of Sociology,* 43 (November): 404–413, 1934.

Hughes, E. C. "Institutions and the person." In A. L. McClung (Ed.) *Principles of Sociology.* New York: Barnes & Noble, 1951.

Hughes, E. C. *Men and Their Work.* New York: Free Press, 1958.

Hughes, E. C. *The Sociological Eye: Selected Papers.* Chicago: Aldine, 1971.

Humphreys, L. "Tearoom trade: Impersonal sex in public places." *Trans-Action,* 7(3): 10–25, 1970.

Humphreys, L. *Tearoom Trade.* Enlarged ed. Chicago: Aldine, 1975.

Hurley, R. *Poverty and Mental Retardation.* New York: Vintage Books, 1969.

Husserl, E. *Ideas.* London: George Allen and Unwin, 1913.

Hyman, H. H. *Survey Design and Analysis.* New York: Free Press, 1955.

Hyman, H. H., Cobbs, W. J., Feldmen, J. J., Hart, C. W., and Stember, C. H. *Interviewing in Social Research.* Chicago: University of Chicago Press, 1954.

Hyman, J. J. "Do they tell the truth?" *Public Opinion Quarterly,* 8: 557–559, 1944.

Hymes, D. H. "The ethnology of speaking." In T. Gladwin and W. C. Sturtevant (Eds.) *Anthropology and Human Behavior.* Washington, D.C.: Anthropological Society of Washington, 1962.

Hymes, D. H. "Introduction: Toward ethnographies of communication." *American Anthropologist,* 66: 1–34, 1964.

Jackson, B. "Killing time: Life in the Arkansas penitentiary." *Qualitative Sociology,* 1(1): 21–32, 1978.

Jacobs, G. (Ed.) *The Participant Observer.* New York: Braziller, 1970.

Jacobs, J. "A phenomenological study of suicide notes." *Social Problems,* 15(Summer): 60–72, 1967.

Jacobs, J. *The Search for Help: A Study of the Retarded Child in the Community.* New York: Brunner/Mazel, 1969a.

Jacobs, J. "Symbolic bureaucracy: A case study of a social welfare agency." *Social Forces,* 47: 413–422, 1969b.

Jacobs, J. "Perplexity, confusion and suspicion: A study of selected forms of doctor-patient interactions." *Social Science and Medicine,* 5: 151–157, 1971.

Jacobs, J. *Getting By: Illustrations of Marginal Living.* Boston: Little, Brown, 1972.

Jacobs, J. (Ed.) *Deviance: Field Studies and Self Disclosures.* Palo Alto, Calif.: National Press, 1974.

Jacobs, J. (Ed.) *Mental Retardation: A Phenomenological Approach.* Springfield, Ill.: Charles C. Thomas, 1980.

James, W. *The Meaning of Truth: A Sequel to Pragmatism.* Ann Arbor: University of Michigan Press, 1970.

Janes, R. W. "A note on phases of the community role of the participant observer." *American Sociological Review,* 26: 446–450, 1961.

Janowitz, M. "Introduction" to *W. I. Thomas: On Social Organization and Social Personality.* Chicago: University of Chicago Press, 1966.

Johnson, J. M. *Doing Field Research.* New York: Free Press, 1975.

Jonsen, A. R. and Lister, G. "Newborn intensive care: The ethical problems." *Hastings Center Report,* 8(1): 15–18, 1978.

Junker, B. H. *Field Work: An Introduction to the Social Sciences.* Chicago: University of Chicago Press, 1960.

Kahn, R. L. and Cannell, C. F. *The Dynamics of Interviewing.* New York: Wiley, 1957.

Kahn, R. L. and Mann, F. "Developing research partnerships." *Journal of Social Issues,* 8(3): 4–10, 1952.

Kamens, D. H. "Legitimating myths and educational organization." *American Sociological Review,* 42: 208–219, 1977.

Kanner, L. *A History of the Care and Study of the Mentally Retarded.* Springfield, Ill.: Charles C. Thomas, 1964.

Karp, D. A. "Observing behavior in public places: Problems and strategies." In W. B. Shaffir, R. A. Stebbins, and A. Turowetz (Eds.) *Fieldwork Experience: Qualitative Approaches to Social Research.* New York: St. Martin's Press, pp. 82–97, 1980.

Karp, I. and Kendall, M. B. "Reflexivity in field work. In P. F. Secord (Ed.) *Explaining Human Behavior: Consciousness, Human Action and Social Structure.* Beverly Hills: Sage, 1982.

Katz, D. "Psychological barriers to communication." *Annals of the American Academy of Political and Social Science,* Social Science, 250: 17–25, 1947.

Katz, J. "A theory of qualitative methodology: The social science system of analytic fieldwork." In R. M. Emerson (Ed.) *Contemporary Field Research.* Boston: Little, Brown, pp. 127–148, 1983.

Kay, P. "Comment on B. N. Colby, 'Ethnographic Semantics: A Preliminary Survey.' " *Current Anthropology,* 7: 20–23, 1966.

Kay, P. "Some theoretical implications of ethnographic semantics." In *Current Directions in Anthropology.* Bulletins of the American Anthropological Association 3 (no. 3), part 2, 1970.

Kelman, H. C. "Human use of human subjects: The problem of deception in social psychological experiments." *Psychological Bulletin,* 67(January): 1–11, 1967.

Kitsuse, J. I. "Societal reaction to deviant behavior." *Social Problems,* 9(3): 247–256, 1962.

Kitsuse, J. and Cicourel, A. V. "A note on the uses of official statistics." *Social Problems,* II: 131–139, 1963.

Klaber, M. "Institutional programming and research: A vital partnership in action."

In A. A. Baumeister and E. C. Butterfield (Eds.) *Residential Facilities for the Mentally Retarded*. Chicago, Ill.: Aldine, pp. 163–200, 1971.

Klaus, M. H. and Kennell, J. H. *Maternal–Infant Bonding*. St. Louis: Mosby, 1976.

Kleinman, S. "Learning the ropes as fieldwork analysis." In W. B. Shaffir, R. A. Stebbins, and A. Turowetz (Eds.) *Fieldwork Experience: Qualitative Approaches to Social Research*. New York: St. Martin's Press, pp. 171–184, 1980.

Klockars, C. B. *The Professional Fence*. New York: Free Press, 1974.

Klockars, C. B. "Field ethics for the life history." In R. S. Weppner (Ed.) *Street Ethnography*. Beverly Hills: Sage, pp. 201–226, 1977.

Klockars, C. B. and O'Connor, R. W. (Eds.) *Deviance and Decency: The Ethics of Research with Human Subjects*. Beverly Hills: Sage, 1979.

Kluckhohn, C. "Participation in ceremonies in a Navajo community." *American Anthropologist*, 40: 359–369, 1938.

Kluckhohn, C. "Theoretical basis for an empirical method of studying the acquisition of culture by individuals." *Man*, 39: 98–103, 1939.

Kluckhohn, F. "The participant observer technique in small communities." *American Journal of Sociology*, 46: 331–343, 1940.

Kobben, A. J. "New ways of presenting an old idea: The statistical method in social anthropology." *Journal of the Royal Anthropological Institute of Great Britain and Ireland*, 82: 129–146, 1952.

Kolaja, J. "Contribution to the theory of participant observation." *Social Forces*, 35: 159–163, 1956.

Korsch, B. M. "The Armstrong Lecture: Physicians, patients and decisions." *American Journal of the Diseases of Children*, 127: 328–332, 1974.

Korsch, B. M. et al. "Gaps in doctor–patient communication in doctor–patient interaction and patient satisfaction." *Pediatrics*, 42: 855–871, 1968.

Kotarba, J. A. "Discovering amorphous social experience: The case of chronic pain." In W. B. Shaffir, R. A. Stebbins, and A. Turowetz (Eds.) *Fieldwork Experience: Qualitative Approaches to Social Research*. New York, St. Martin's Press, pp. 57–67, 1980.

Kozol, J. *Death at an Early Age*. Boston: Houghton Mifflin, 1967.

Kroeber, A. L. (Ed.) *Anthropology Today*. Chicago: University of Chicago Press, 1953.

Krueger, E. T. "The value of life history documents for social research." *Journal of Applied Sociology*, 9: 196–201, 1925.

Krueger, E. T. and Reckless, W. C. *Social Psychology*. New York: Longmans, 1931.

Kubler-Ross, E. *On Death and Dying*. New York: Macmillan, 1969.

Kuhn, M. "Major trends in symbolic interaction in the past twenty-five years." *Sociological Quarterly* 5(Winter): 61–84, 1964.

Labovitz, S. and Hagedorn, R. *Introduction to Social Research*. New York: McGraw-Hill, 1971.

Lang, K. and Lang, G. E. "The unique perspective of television and its effect: A pilot study." *American Sociological Review*, 18: 3–12, 1953.

Langness, L. L. *Life History in Anthropological Science*, New York: Holt, 1965.

LaPiere, R. T. "Attitudes and actions." *Social Forces*, 13: 230–237, 1934–1935.

Lasch, C. *Haven in a Heartless World*. New York: Basic Books, 1978.

Lasswell, H. D. "The contributions of Freud's insight interview to the social sciences." *American Journal of Sociology*, 45: 375–390, 1939.

LaVor, M. "Economic opportunity amendments of 1972, Public Law 92–424." *Exceptional Children*, November, 1972.

Lazarsfeld, P. F. "The Art of Asking Why." *National Marketing Review*, 1: 26–38, 1935.

Lazarsfeld, P. F. "The controversy over detailed interviews—An offer for negotiation." *Public Opinion Quarterly*, 8: 38–60, 1944.

Lazarsfeld, P. F. "Evidence and interference in social research." In D. Lerner (Ed.) *Evidence and Inference*. New York: Free Press, pp. 107–138, 1959.

Lazarsfeld, P. *Qualitative Analysis: Historical and Critical Essays*. Boston: Allyn & Bacon, 1972.

Lazarsfeld, P. E. and Allen, B. "Some functions of qualitative analysis in sociological research." *Sociologica*, 1: 324–361, 1955.

Lazarsfeld, P. F. and Robinson, W. S. "The quantification of case studies." *Journal of Applied Psychology*, 24: 817–825, 1940.

Lazarsfeld, P. F. and Rosenberg, M. (Eds.) *The Language of Research*. New York: Free Press, 1955.

Leach, E. R. *Culture and Communication*. Cambridge, Mass.: Cambridge University Press, 1976.

Lement, E. *Social Pathology*. New York: McGraw-Hill, 1951.

Lemert, E. M. "Paranoia and the dynamics of exclusion." *Sociometry*, 25: 2–25, 1962.

Lesser, A. "Research procedure and laws of culture." *Philosophy of Science*, 6: 345–355, 1939.

Lesy, M. *Wisconsin Death Trip*. New York: Random House, 1973.

Lesy, M. *Real Life: Louisville in the Twenties*. New York: Pantheon, 1976.

Letkemann, P. "Crime as work: Leaving the field." In W. B. Shaffir, R. A. Stebbins, and A. Turowetz (Eds.) *Fieldwork Experience: Qualitative Approaches to Social Research*. New York: St. Martin's Press, pp. 292–300, 1980.

Levy, C. J. *Voluntary Servitude: Whites in the Negro Movement*. New York: Appleton-Century-Crofts, 1968.

Lewis, O. "Controls and experiments in field work." In A. L. Kroeber (Ed.) *Anthropology Today*. Chicago: University of Chicago Press, pp. 452–475, 1953.

Lewis, O. *Five Families*. Chapter I. New York: Wiley, 1962.

Lewis, O. *The Children of Sanchez*. New York: Vintage, 1963.

Lewis, O. *Pedro Martinez*. New York: Random House, 1964.

Lewis, O. *La Vida*. New York: Vintage, 1965.

Leznoff, M. "Interviewing Homosexuals." *American Journal of Sociology*, 62: 202–204, 1956.

Liazos, A. "The poverty of the sociology of deviance: Nuts, sluts, and perverts." *Social Problems*, 20: 103–120, 1972.

Liebow, E. *Tally's Corner*. Boston: Little, Brown, 1967.

Lindeman, E. C. *Social Discovery*. New York: Republic, 1924.

Lindesmith, A. *Opiate Addiction*. Bloomington, Ind.: Principia Press, 1947.

Lindesmith, A. *Addiction and Opiates*. Chicago: Aldine, 1968.

Lindesmith, A., Weinberg, S. K., and Robinson, W. S. "Two comments and rejoinder to 'The logical structure of analytic induction.'" *American Sociological Review*, 17: 492–494, 1952.

Lipetz, B. "Information, storage and retrieval." *Scientific American*, 215(3): 224–242, 1966.

Littrell, W. B. "Vagueness, social structure, and social research in law." *Social Problems*, 21(Summer): 38–52, 1973.

Lofland, J. "Reply to Davis—Comment on 'Initial interaction.'" *Social Problems*, 8(4): 365–367, 1961.

Lofland, J. *Doomsday Cult: A Study of Conversion, Proselytization, and Maintenance of Faith*. Englewood Cliffs, N.J.: Prentice-Hall, 1966.

Lofland, J. *Deviance and Identity*. Englewood Cliffs, N.J.: Prentice-Hall, 1969.

Lofland, J. *Analyzing Social Settings*. Belmont, Calif.: Wadsworth, 1971.

Lofland, J. "Editorial introduction—analyzing qualitative data: First person accounts." *Urban Life and Culture*, 3(October): 307–309, 1974.

Lofland, J. *Doing Social Life: The Qualitative Study of Human Interaction in Natural Settings*. New York: Wiley, 1976.

Lohman, J. D. "The participant observer in community studies." *American Sociological Review*, 2: 890–897, 1937.

Lombard, G. F. F. "Self-awareness and scientific method." *Science*, 112: 289–293, 1950.

Lopata, H. Z. "Interviewing American widows." In W. B. Shaffir, R. A. Stebbins, and A. Turowetz (Eds.) *Fieldwork Experience: Qualitative Approaches to Social Research*. New York: St. Martin's Press, pp. 68–81, 1980.

Lorber, J. "Deviance as performance: The case of illness." *Social Problems*, 14(3): 302–310, 1967.

Lorber, J. "Good patients and problem patients: Conformity and deviance in a general hospital." *Journal of Health and Social Behavior*, 16: 213–225, 1975.

Lowie, R. H. *The History of Ethnological Theory*. New York: Farrar and Rinehart, 1937.

Lundberg, G. A. "Case work and the statistical method." *Social Forces*, 5(5): 61–65, 1926.

Lundman, R. J. and McFarlane, P. T. "Conflict methodology: An introduction and preliminary assessment." *Sociological Quarterly*, 17: 503–512, 1976.

Lyman, S. M. and Scott, M. B. *A Sociology of the Absurd*. New York: Appleton-Century-Crofts, 1970.

Madge, J. *The Tools of Social Science*. London: Longmans, Green, 1953.

Maines, D. R., Shaffir, W. B., and Turowetz, A. "Leaving the field in ethnographic research: Reflections on the entrance–exit hypothesis." In W. B. Shaffir, R. A. Stebbins, and A. Turowetz (Eds.) *Fieldwork Experience: Qualitative Approaches to Social Research*. New York: St. Martin's Press, pp. 261–280, 1980.

Malcolm X. *The Autobiography of Malcolm X*. New York: Grove Press, 1966.

Malinowski, B. *Argonauts of the Western Pacific*. London: Routledge, 1932.

Malinowski, B. *A Diary in the Strict Sense of the Term*. New York: Harcourt, Brace and World, 1967.

Manis, J. and Meltzer, B. (Eds.) *Symbolic Interaction*. Boston: Allyn & Bacon, 1967.

Mann, F. "Human relations skills in social research." *Human Relations*, 4(4): 341–354, 1951.

Manning, P. K. "Observing the police: Deviants, respectables and the law." In J. Douglas (Ed.) *Research on Deviance.* New York: Random House, 1972.

Manning, P. K. "The researcher: An alien in the police world." In A. Neiderhoffer and A. Blumberg (Eds.) *The Ambivalent Force.* (2nd ed.) Chicago: Dryden Press, 1976.

Mayerson, E. W. *Putting the Ill at Ease.* New York: Harper and Row, 1976.

McCall, G. and Simmons, J. L. (Eds.) *Issues in Participant Observation.* Reading, Pa.: Addison-Wesley, 1969.

McCall, M. "Who and where are the artists?" In W. B. Shaffir, R. A. Stebbins, and A. Turowetz (Eds.) *Fieldwork Experience: Qualitative Approaches to Social Research.* New York: St. Martin's Press, pp. 145–157, 1980.

McCartney, J. L. "On being scientific: Changing styles of presentation of sociological research." *American Sociologist,* 5(February): 30–35, 1970.

McEwen, W. J. "Forms and problems of validation in social anthropology." *Current Anthropology,* 4: 155–169, 1963.

McGinnis, R. "Randomization and inference in sociological research." *American Sociological Review,* 22: 408–414, 1957.

McHugh, P. *Defining the Situation.* Indianapolis: Bobbs-Merrill, 1968.

McIntosh, J. *Communication and Awareness in a Cancer Ward.* London: Cromm Helm, 1979.

McKeganey, N. P. and Bloor, M. J. "On the retrieval of sociological description: Respondent validation and the critical case of ethnomethodology." *International Journal of Sociology and Social Policy,* 1: 332–354, 1981.

McKinney, J. C. *Constructive Typology and Social Theory.* New York: Appleton-Century-Crofts, 1966.

Mead, G. H. *Mind, Self and Society.* Chicago: University of Chicago Press, 1934.

Mead, G. H. *The Philosophy of the Act.* Chicago: University of Chicago Press, 1938.

Mead, M. "More comprehensive field methods." *American Anthropologist,* 35: 1–15, 1933.

Mead, M. and Metruay, R. *The Study of a Culture at a Distance.* Chicago: University of Chicago Press, 1953.

Mehan, H. and Wood, H. *The Reality of Ethnomethodology.* New York: Wiley, 1975.

Melbin, M. "An interaction recording device for participant observers." *Human Organization,* 13(2): 29–33, 1954.

Mensh, I. N. and Henry, J. "Direct observation and psychological tests in anthropological field work." *American Anthropologist,* 55: 461–480, 1953.

Mercer, J. *Labelling the Mentally Retarded.* Berkeley: University of California Press, 1973.

Merton, R. K. *Social Theory and Social Structure.* Revised ed. New York: Free Press, 1957a.

Merton, R. K. (Ed.) *The Student-Physician.* Cambridge, Mass.: Harvard University Press, 1957b.

Merton, R. and Kendall, P. "The focused interview." *American Journal of Sociology,* 51(May): 541–557, 1946.

Metraux, R. and Mead, M. *Themes in French Culture.* Stanford University Press, 1954.

Mey, H. *Field-Theory: Study of its Applications in the Social Sciences.* Translated by Douglas Scott. New York: St. Martin's Press, 1972.

Meyer, J. W. and Rowan, B. "Institutionalized organizations: Formal structure as myth and ceremony." *American Journal of Sociology*, 83(2): 340–363, 1977.

Michels, R. *Political Parties*. New York: Dover, 1957.

Miller, B. and Humphreys, L. "Keeping in touch: Maintaining contact with stigmatized subjects." In W. B. Shaffir, R. A. Stebbins, and A. Turowetz (Eds.) *Fieldwork Experience: Qualitative Approaches to Soical Research*. New York: St. Martin's Press, pp. 212–222, 1980.

Miller, S. M. "The participant observer and 'over-rapport.'" *American Sociological Review*, 17: 97–99, 1952.

Miller, S. M., Roby, P., and Steewijk, A. "Creaming the poor." *Trans-Action*, 8(June): 39–45, 1970.

Miller, S. *Prescription for Leadership: Training for the Medical Elite*. Chicago: Aldine, 1970.

Mills, C. W. "Situated actions and vocabularies of motive." *American Sociological Review*, 5(October): 904–913, 1940.

Mills, C. W. *The Sociological Imagination*. London: Oxford University Press, 1959.

Miner, H. "Body ritual among the Nacirema." *American Anthropologist*, 58: 503–507, 1956.

Mishler, E. G. "Meaning in context: Is there any other kind?" *Harvard Educational Review*, 49: 1–19, 1979.

Moore, J. W. "Social constraints on sociological knowledge: Academics and research concerning minorities." *Social Problems*, 21(Summer): 65–77, 1973.

Morris, P. *Put Away*. New York: Atherton, 1969.

Murdock, G. P. "The processing of anthropological materials." In A. L. Kroeher (Ed.) *Anthropology Today*. Chicago: University of Chicago Press, pp. 476–487, 1953.

Myers, V. "Toward a synthesis of ethnographic and survey methods." *Human Organization*, 36: 244–251, 1977.

Myrdal, G. *An American Dilemma*. (Vol. 2). New York: Harper & Row, 1944.

Nader, L. "Perspectives gained from fieldwork." In Sol Tax (Ed.) *Horizons of Anthropology*. Chicago: Aldine, pp. 148–159, 1964.

Nader, L. "Up the anthropologist—Perspectives gained from studying up." In D. Hymes (Ed.) *Reinventing Anthropology*. New York: Vintage, pp. 284–311, 1969.

Naroll, R. *Data Quality Control*. New York: Free Press, 1962.

Narroll, R. "Native concepts and cross-cultural surveys." *American Anthropologist*, 69: 511–512, 1967.

Naroll, R. and Naroll, F. "On bias of exotic data." *Man*, 25: 24–26, 1963.

Nash, D. "The ethnologist as stranger: An essay in the sociology of knowledge." *Southwestern Journal of Anthropology*, 19: 149–167, 1963.

Nash, D. and Wintrob, R. "The emergence of self-consciousness in ethnography." *Current Anthropology*, 13: 527–542, 1972.

Nathanson, N. L. "Social science, administrative law, and the information act of 1966." *Social Problems*, 21(Summer): 21–37, 1973.

Nejelski, P. and Finster Buch, K. "The prosecutor and the researcher: Present and prospective variations on the Supreme Court's Branzburg decision." *Social Problems*, 21(Summer): 3–21, 1973.

Nejelski, P. and Lerman, L. M. "A researcher–subject testimonial privilege: What to do before the subpoena arrives." *Wisconsin Law Review*: 1085–1148, 1971.

Newcomb, T. M. "An approach to the study of communicative acts." *Psychological Review*, 60: 393–404, 1953.

Nisbet, R. A. *The Sociological Tradition*. New York: Basic Books, 1966.

Oeser, O. A. "Methods and assumptions of field work in social psychology. *British Journal of Psychology*, 27: 343–363, 1937.

Oleson, V. L. and Whittaker, E. "Role-making in participant observation: Process in the researcher–actor relationship." *Human Organization*, 26: 273–281, 1967.

Orlans, H. "Ethical problems in the relations of research sponsors and investigators." In G. Sjoberg (Ed.) *Ethics, Politics and Social Research*. Cambridge, Mass.: Schenkman, pp. 3–24, 1967.

Orne, M. T. "On the social psychology of the psychological experiment." *American Psychologist*, 17: 776–783, 1962.

Osgood, C. "Informants." In C. Osgood (Ed.) *Ingalik Material Culture*. Yale University Publications in Anthropology, 22: 50–55, 1940.

P. S., Newsletter of the American Political Science Association. "Ethical problems of academic political scientists." 1: 3–28, 1968.

Palmer, V. M. *Field Studies in Sociology: A Student's Manual*. Chicago: University of Chicago Press, 1928.

Park, R. *Principles of Human Behavior*. Chicago: The Zalaz Corp., 1915.

Park, R. "Murder and the case study method." *American Journal of Sociology*, 36: 447–454, 1930.

Park, R. "The city: Suggestions for the investigation of human behavior in the urban environment." In *Human Communities: The City and Human Ecology*. Glencoe, Ill.: Free Press, 1915, 1952.

Parsons, T. *The Social System*. Glencoe, Ill.: The Free Press, 1951.

Parsons, T. and Fox. R. "Illness, therapy and the modern urban American family." *Journal of Social Issues*, 8: 31–44, 1952.

Passin, H. "Tarahumara prevarication: A problem in field method." *American Anthropologist*, 44: 235–247, 1942.

Patton, R. *Qualitative Evaluation Methods*. Beverly Hills: Sage, 1980.

Paul, B. "Interview techniques and field relationships." In A. L. Kroeber (Ed.) *Anthropology Today*. Chicago: University of Chicago Press, pp. 430–451, 1953.

Payne, S. L. *The Art of Asking Questions*. Princeton: Princeton University Press, 1951.

Pearsall, M. "Participant observation as role and method in behavioral research." *Nursing Research*, 14: 37–47, 1965.

Pepinsky, H. E. "A sociologist on police patrol." In W. B. Shaffir, R. A. Stebbins, and A. Turowetz (Eds.) *Fieldwork Experience: Qualitative Approaches to Social Research*. New York: St. Martin's Press, pp. 223–234, 1980.

Phillips, D. L. *Knowledge from What? Theories and Methods in Social Research*. Chicago: Rand McNally, 1971.

Pike, K. L. *Language in Relation to a Unified Theory of the Structure of Human Behavior*. Part I. Second edition. The Hague: Mouton, 1954, 1967.

Pitt, D. C. *Using Historical Sources in Anthropology and Sociology*. New York: Holt, Rinehart & Winston, 1972.

Piven, F. F. and Cloward, R. *Regulating the Poor: The Functions of Public Welfare.* New York: Random House, 1971.

Platt, A. M. *The Child Savers.* Chicago: University of Chicago Press, 1969.

Platt, J. "On interviewing one's peers." *British Journal of Sociology,* 32: 75–91, 1981.

Polansky, N., Freeman, W., Horowitz, M., Irwin, L., Papania, N., Rapaport, D., and Whaley, F. "Problems of interpersonal relation in research on groups." *Human Relations,* 2: 281–292, 1949.

Pollner, M. and Emerson, R. M. "The dynamics of inclusion and distance in fieldwork relations." In R. M. Emerson (Ed.) *Contemporary Field Research.* Boston: Little, Brown, pp. 235–252, 1983.

Polsky, N. *Hustlers, Beats and Others.* Garden City, N.Y.: Doubleday, Anchor Books, 1969.

Polya, G. *Patterns of Plausible Inference.* Princeton: Princeton University Press, 1954.

Ponsansky, N. A. *English Diaries.* London: Methuen, 1923.

Posner, J. "Urban anthropology: Fieldwork in semifamiliar settings." In W. B. Shaffir, R. A. Stebbins, and A. Turowetz (Eds.) *Fieldwork Experience: Qualitative Approaches to Social Research.* New York: St. Martin's Press, pp. 203–211, 1980.

Powdermaker, H. *Stranger and Friend: The Way of an Anthropologist.* New York: Norton, 1967.

Prus, R. "Sociologist as hustler: The dynamics of acquiring information." In W. B. Shaffir, R. A. Stebbins, and A. Turowetz (Eds.) *Fieldwork Experience: Qualitative Approaches to Social Research.* New York: St. Martin's Press, pp. 132–144, 1980.

Psathas, G. *Phenomenological Sociology: Issues and Applications.* New York: Wiley, 1973.

Radin, P. *The Method and Theory of Ethnology.* New York: McGraw-Hill, 1933.

Rainwater, L. and Pittman, D. J. "Ethical problems in studying a politically sensitive and deviant community." *Social Problems,* 14: 357–366, 1967.

Reck, A. J. (Ed.). *George Herbert Mead: Selected Writings.* Indianapolis: Bobbs-Merrill, 1964.

Record, J. C. "The research institute and the pressure group." In G. Sjoberg (Ed.) *Ethics, Politics and Social Research.* Cambridge: Schenkman, pp. 25–49, 1967.

Redlich, F. and Brody, E. B. "Emotional problems of interdisciplinary research in psychiatry." *Psychiatry,* 18: 233–240, 1955.

Reinharz, S. *On Becoming a Social Scientist: From Survey Research and Participant Observation to Experimental Analysis.* San Francisco: Jossey-Bass, 1979.

Reiss, A. J., Jr. "Some logical and methodological problems in community research." *Social Forces,* 33: 52–54, 1954.

Reiss, A. J., Jr. "The sociological study of communities." *Rural Sociology,* 24: 118–130, 1959.

Reiss, A. J., Jr. *The Police and the Public.* New Haven: Yale University Press, 1971.

Reissman, L. "A study of role conceptions in bureaucracy." *Social Force,* 27(March): 305–310, 1949.

Reynolds, P. D. "On the protection of human subjects and social science." *International Social Science Journal,* 24: 693–719, 1972.

Rice, S. A. "Contagious bias in the interview: A methodological note." *American Journal of Sociology,* 35: 420–423, 1929.

Richardson, J. T., Stewart, M. W., and Simmonds, R. B. "Researching a fundamentalist commune." In J. Needleman and G. Baker (Eds.) *Understanding the New Religions*. New York: Seabury Press, 1978.

Richardson, S. A. "Training in field relations skills." *Journal of Social Issues,* 8: 43–50, 1952.

Richardson, S. A. "A framework for reporting field relations experiences." In R. N. Adams and J. H. Preiss (Eds.) *Human Organization Research*. Homewood, Ill.: Dorsey Press, pp. 124–139, 1960.

Richardson, S. A., Dohrenwend, B. S., and Klein, D. *Interviewing: Its Forms and Functions*. New York: Basic Books, 1965.

Richardson, W. and Higgins, A. *The Handicapped Children of Acamance County, North Carolina*. Wilmington, Del.: Nemours Foundation, 1965.

Richter, C. P. "Free research versus design research." *Science,* 118: 91–93, 1953.

Riecken, H. W. "The unidentified interviewer." *American Journal of Sociology,* 62: 210–212, 1956.

Riemer, J. W. "Varieties of opportunistic research." *Urban Life,* 5(4): 467–478, 1977.

Riesman, D. and Benney, M. "The sociology of the interview." *Midwest Sociologists,* 18: 3–15, 1956.

Rist, R. "On the relations among education research paradigms: From disdain to detente." *Anthropology and Education,* 8(2): 42–50, 1977.

Rivera, G. *Willowbrook*. New York: Vintage, 1972.

Roadberg, A. "Breaking relationships with research subjects: Some problems and suggestions." In W. B. Shaffir, R. A. Stebbins, and A. Turowetz (Eds.) *Fieldwork Experience: Qualitative Approaches to Social Research*. New York: St. Martin's Press, pp. 281–291, 1980.

Robbins, T., Anthony, D., and Curtis, T. E. "The limits of symbolic realism: Problems of empathetic field observation in a sectarian context." *Journal for the Scientific Study of Religion,* 12: 259–271, 1973.

Robinson, W. S. "The logical structure of analytic induction." *American Sociological Review,* 16: 812–818, 1951.

Rock, P. *The Making of Symbolic Interactionism*. Totawa, N.J.: Roman and Littlefield, 1979.

Roethlisberger, F. J. and Dickson, W. J. *Management and the Worker*. Cambridge, Mass.: Harvard University Press, 1939.

Rogers, C. R. "The non-directive method as a technique for social research." *American Journal of Sociology,* 50: 279–283, 1945.

Rogers, C. R. and Roethlisberger, F. J. "Barriers and gateways to communication." *Harvard Business Review,* 30(4): 46–52, 1952.

Rose, A. "A research note on interviewing." *American Journal of Sociology,* 51: 143–144, 1945.

Rose, A. (Ed.) *Human Behavior and Social Processes*. Boston: Houghton Mifflin, 1962a.

Rose, A. "A systematic summary of symbolic interaction theory." A. Rose (Ed.) *Human Behavior and Social Processes*. Boston: Houghton Mifflin, 1962b.

Rosen, M., Clark, G. R., and Kivits, M. S. (Eds.) *The History of Mental Retardation*. Vols. I and II. Baltimore: University Park Press, 1976.

Rosenhan, D. L. "On being sane in insane places." *Science,* 179(4070) (January): 250–258, 1973.

Rosenthal, R. *Experimenter Effects in Behavioral Research.* New York: Appleton-Century-Crofts, 1966.

Roth, J. "Ritual and magic in the control of contagion." In E. Jaco (Ed.) *Patients, Physicians and Illness.* New York: Free Press, pp. 229–234, 1958.

Roth, J. "Comments on secret observation." *Social Problems,* 9: 283–284, 1962.

Roth, J. *Timetables,* Indianapolis: Bobbs-Merrill, 1963.

Roth, J. "Hired hand research." *The American Sociologist,* 1(August): 190–196, 1966.

Roth, J. "The public hospital: Refugee for damaged humans." In S. Wallace (Ed.) *Total Institutions.* Rutgers: Transaction Books, 1971.

Roth, J. "Turning adversity to account." *Urban Life and Culture,* 3(October): 347–361, 1974.

Roy, D. "Efficiency and 'the fix': Informal intergroup relations in a piecework machine shop." *American Journal of Sociology,* 60(November), 225–260, 1952a.

Roy, D. "Quota restriction and goldbricking in a machine shop." *American Journal of Sociology,* 57(March): 427–442, 1952b.

Roy, D. "Work satisfaction and social reward in quota achievement: An analysis of piecework incentives." *American Sociological Review,* 18: 507–514, 1953.

Roy, D. "Banana time: Job satisfaction and informal interaction." *Human Organization,* 18(Winter): 158–168, 1959–1960.

Roy, D. "The role of the researcher in the study of social conflict: A theory of protective distortion of response." *Human Organization,* 24: 262–271, 1965.

Rubin, L. *Worlds of Pain: Life in the Working-Class Family.* New York: Basic Books, 1976.

Rubin, L. *Women of a Certain Age.* New York: Harper & Row, 1979.

Ruebhausen, O. M. and Brim, O. G. "Privacy and behavioral research." *American Psychologist,* 21: 423–437.

Ryan, W. *Blaming the Victim.* New York: Vintage, 1972.

Ryave, A. L. and Schenkein, J. N. "Notes on the art of walking." In R. Turner (Ed.) *Ethnomethodology,* Baltimore, Md.: Penguin, 1974.

Rynkiewich, M. A. and Spradley, J. P. (Eds.) *Ethics and Anthropology: Dilemmas in Fieldwork.* New York: Wiley, 1976.

Sagarin, E. "The research setting and the right not to be researched." *Social Problems,* 21(Summer): 52–64, 1973.

Sanday, P. R. "The ethnographic paradigm(s)." *Administrative Science Quarterly,* 24: 527–538, 1979.

Sanders, C. R. "Rope burns: Impediments to the achievement of basic comfort early in the field research experience." In W. B. Shaffir, R. A. Stebbins, and A. Turowetz (Eds.) *Fieldwork Experience: Qualitative Approaches to Social Research.* New York: St. Martin's Press, pp. 158–170, 1980.

Sanders, W. B. (Ed.) *The Sociologist as Detective: An Introduction to Research Methods.* New York: Praeger, 1974.

Sarason, S. *The Culture of the School and the Problem of Change.* Boston: Allyn & Bacon, 1971.

Sarason, S. *The Psychological Sense of Community.* San Francisco: Jossey-Bass, 1974.

Sarason, S. B. and Doris, J. *Psychological Problems in Mental Deficiency.* New York: Harper & Row, 1959.

Sawyer, E. "Methodological problems in studying so-called 'deviant' communities." In A. J. Ladner (Ed.) *The Death of White Sociology.* New York: Vintage Books, 1973.

Schatzman, L. and Strauss, A. L. *Field Research: Strategies for a Natural Sociology.* Englewood Cliffs, N. J.: Prentice-Hall, 1973.

Schechner, R. *Public Domain: Essays on the Theater.* New York: Bobbs-Merrill, 1969.

Scheff, T. J. "Control over policy by attendants in a mental hospital." *Journal of Health and Human Behavior,* 2(Summer): 93–105, 1961.

Scheff, T. J. *Being Mentally Ill: A Sociological Theory.* Chicago: Aldine, 1966.

Scheff, T. "The labeling theory of mental illness." *American Sociological Review,* 39(3), 1974.

Schneider, E. V. "Limitations on observation in industrial sociology." *Social Forces,* 28: 279–284, 1950.

Schuler, E. "Toward a code of ethics for sociologists: A historical note." *American Sociologist,* 3(November): 316–318, 1969.

Schur, E. M. *Labeling Deviant Behavior: Its Sociological Implications.* New York: Harper & Row, 1971.

Schutz, A. *Collected Papers, Vol. I: The Problem of Social Reality.* M. Natanson (Ed.), The Hague: Martinus Nijhoff, 1962.

Schutz, A. *Collected Papers, Vol. II: Studies in Social Theory.* M. Natanson (Ed.), The Hague: Martinus Nijhoff, 1966.

Schutz, A. *The Phenomenology of the Social World.* Evanston, Ill.: Northwestern University Press, 1967.

Schwab, W. B. "Looking backward: An appraisal of two field trips." *Human Organization,* 24: 372–380, 1965.

Schwartz, G. and Merten, D. "Participant observation and the discovery of meaning." *Philosophy of the Social Sciences,* 1: 279–298, 1971.

Schwartz, H. and Jacobs, J. *Qualitative Sociology: A Method to the Madness.* New York: Free Press, 1979.

Schwartz, M. S. and Schwartz, C. G. "Problems in participant observation." *American Journal of Sociology,* 60: 343–354, 1955.

Scott, J. "Black science and nation-building." In J. Ladner (Ed.) *The Death of White Sociology.* New York: Vintage Books, 1973.

Scott, M. *The Racing Game.* Chicago: Aldine, 1968.

Scott, M. B. and Lyman, S. M. "Accounts." *American Sociological Review,* 33: 46–62, 1968.

Scott, R. *The Making of Blind Men.* New York: Russell Sage Foundation, 1969.

Scott, R. W. "Field work in a formal organization: Some dilemmas in the role of observer." *Human Organization,* 22(2): 162–168, 1963.

Scott, R. W. "Field methods in the study of organizations." In J. G. March (Ed.) *Handbook of Organizations.* Chicago: Rand McNally, 1965.

Seashore, S. E. "Field experiments with formal organizations." *Human Organization,* 23(2): 164–178, 1964.

Sells, S. B. and Travers, R. M. W. "Observational methods of research." *Review of Educational Research*, 40: 394–407, 1945.

Selltiz, C., Jahoda, M., Deutsch, M., and Cook, S. W. *Research Methods in Social Relations*. Revised ed. New York: Holt, 1959.

Selvin, H. C. "A critique of tests of significance in survey research." *American Sociological Review*, 22: 519–527, 1957.

Shaffir, W. B., Stebbins, R. A., and Turowetz, A. (Eds.) *Fieldwork Experience: Qualitative Approaches to Social Research*. New York: St. Martin's Press, 1980.

Shaw, C. "Case study method." Publications of *The American Sociological Society*, 21: 149–157, 1927.

Shaw, C. *The Natural History of a Delinquent Career*. Chicago: University of Chicago Press, 1931.

Shaw, C. *The Jack Roller*. 2nd ed. Chicago: University of Chicago Press, 1966.

Shaw, C., McKay, N. D., and McDonald, J. F. *Brothers in Crime*. Chicago: University of Chicago Press, 1938.

Shibutani, T. "Reference groups as perspectives." *American Journal of Sociology*, 40 (May): 562–569, 1955.

Shibutani, T. *Human Nature and Collective Behavior: Papers in Honor of Herbert Blumer*. Englewood Cliffs, N.J.: Prentice-Hall, 1970.

Sieber, S. D. "The integration of fieldwork and survey methods." *American Journal of Sociology*, 78: 1335–1359, 1973.

Sjoberg, G. "Project Camelot: Selected reactions and personal reflections." In G. Sjoberg (Ed.) *Ethics, Politics and Social Research*. Cambridge, Mass.: Schenkman, 1967.

Sjoberg, G. (Ed.) *Ethics, Politics and Social Research*. Cambridge, Mass.: Schenkman, 1967.

Sjoberg, G. and Miller, P. J. "Social research on bureaucracy: Limitations and opportunities." *Social Problems*, 21(Summer): 129–143, 1973.

Skipper, J. A. and Leonard, R. D. "Children, stress and hospitalization." *Journal of Health and Social Behavior*, 9: 275–286, 1968.

Sluyter, G. V. "The unit management system." *Mental Retardation*, 14(3): 14–16, 1976.

Smigel, E. "Interviewing a legal elite: The Wall Street lawyer." *American Journal of Sociology*, 64(2): 159–164, 1958.

Smith, H. T. "A comparison of interview and observation methods of studying mother behavior." *Journal of Abnormal and Social Psychology*, 57: 278–282, 1958.

Snow, D. A. "The disengagement process: A neglected problem in participant observation research." *Qualitative Sociology*, 3: 100–122, 1980.

Spector, M. "Learning to study public figures." In W. B. Shaffir, R. A. Stebbins, and A. Turowetz (Eds.) *Fieldwork Experience: Qualitative Approaches to Social Research*. New York: St. Martin's Press, pp. 98–110, 1980.

Spencer, G. "Methodological issues in the study of bureaucratic elites: A case study of West Point." *Social Problems*, 21(Summer): 90–103, 1973.

Spencer, R. F. (Ed.) *Method and Perspective in Anthropology*. Minneapolis: University of Minnesota Press, 1954.

Spindler, G. and Goldschmidt, W. "Experimental design in the study of culture change." *Southwestern Journal of Anthropology*, 8: 68–83, 1952.

Spradley, J. *You Owe Yourself a Drunk*. Boston: Little, Brown, 1970.

Spradley, J. *The Ethnographic Interview*. New York: Holt, Rinehart & Winston, 1979.

Spradley, J. P. *Participant Observation*. New York: Holt, Rinehart & Winston, 1980.

Stanton, A. and Schwartz, M. *The Mental Hospital*. New York: Basic Books, 1954.

Stasz, C. "Text, images and display conventions in sociology." *Qualitative Sociology*, 2(1): 29–44, 1979.

Stavrionos, B. K. "Research methods in cultural anthropology in relation to scientific criteria." *Psychological Review*, 57: 334–344, 1950.

Stimson, G. V. "Obeying doctor's orders: A view from the other side." *Social Science and Medicine*, 8: 97–104, 1974.

Stone, G. P. "Appearance and the self." In A. M. Rose (Ed.) *Human Behavior and Social Processes: An Interactionist Approach*. Boston: Houghton Mifflin, 1962.

Stone, P. J., Bales, R. F., Namenwirth, J. Z., and Ogilivie, D. M. "The general inquirer: A computer system for content analysis and retrieval based on the sentence as a unit of information." *Behavioral Science*, 7: 1–15, 1962.

Stone, P. J., Dunphy, D. C., Smith, M. S., and Ogilvie, D. M. *The General Inquirer: A Computer Approach to Content Analysis*. Cambridge: MIT Press, 1966.

Stouffer, S. A. *Social Research to Test Ideas*. New York: Free Press, 1962.

Strauss, A. *The Social Psychology of George Herbert Mead*. Chicago: University of Chicago Press, 1956.

Strauss, A. and Schatzman, L. "Social Class & Modes of Communication." *American Journal of Sociology*, 60(4): 329–338, 1955.

Strauss, A., Schatzman, L., Bucher, R., Ehrlich, D., and Sabshin, M. *Psychiatric Ideologies and Institutions*. New York: Free Press, 1964.

Strickland, D. A. and Schlesinger, L. E. " 'Lurking' as a research method." *Human Organization*, 28: 248–250, 1969.

Strunk, W., Jr. *The Elements of Style*. Revised by E. B. White. New York: Macmillan, 1972.

Stryker, S. "Symbolic interaction as an approach to family research." *Marriage and Family Living*, 21(May): 111–119, 1959.

Sturtevant, W. C. "Studies in Ethnoscience." *American Anthropologist*, 66: 99–131, 1964.

Sudnow, D. *Passing On: The Social Organization of Dying*. Englewood Cliffs, N.J.: Prentice-Hall, 1967.

Sudnow, D. (Ed.) *Studies in Social Interaction*. New York: Free Press, 1972.

Sullivan, H. S. "A note on implications of psychiatry, the study of interpersonal relations, for investigations in social science." *American Journal of Sociology*, 42: 848–861, 1937.

Sullivan, M. A., Jr., Queen, S. A., and Patrick, R. C., Jr. "Participant observation as employed in the study of a military training program." *American Sociological Review*, 23, 660–667, 1958.

Sutherland, E. *The Professional Thief*. Chicago: University of Chicago Press, 1937.

Suttles, G. D. *The Social Order of the Slum*. Chicago: U. of Chicago Press, 1968.

Svorstad, B. L. "Physician–patient communication and patient conformity with medical advice." In D. Mechanic (Ed.) *The Growth of Bureaucratic Medicine*. New York: Wiley, pp. 220–238, 1976.

Sykes, G. M. *The Society of Captives.* Princeton: Princeton University Press, 1958.

Sykes, G. M. "Feeling our way: A report on a conference on ethical issues in the social sciences." *The Journal of Criminal Law, Criminology and Police Science,* 58(June): 201–213, 1968.

Sykes, G. M. and Matza, D. "Techniques of neutralization: A theory of delinquency." *American Sociological Review,* 22: 664–670, 1957.

Syracuse University, Division of Special Education and Rehabilitation. *Interim report on assessment of the handicapped effort in experimental and selected other Head Start programs serving the handicapped.* Submitted to the U.S. Department of HEW, OCD, by Policy Research, Inc., 1974.

System Research, Inc. *The Status of Handicapped Children in Head Start.* Prepared for the Office of Child Development, Lansing, Mich., 1974.

Szasz, T. *The Myth of Mental Illness.* New York: Hoeber-Harper, 1961.

Szasz, T. *Ideology and Insanity.* Garden City, N.Y.: Doubleday, Anchor Books, 1970.

Szasz, T. S. *Ceremonial chemistry: The ritual persecution of drugs, addicts, and the pushers.* Garden City, N.Y.: Doubleday, 1974.

Taichert, L. C. "Parental denial as a factor in the management of the severely retarded child: Discussion of two patients." *Clinical Pediatrics,* 14(7): 66–68, 1975.

Taylor, S. J. "Attendants' perspectives: A view from the back ward." Unpublished paper presented at the 97th annual meeting of The American Association on Mental Deficiency, 1973.

Taylor, S. J. "The custodians: Attendants and their work at state institutions for the mentally retarded." Ann Arbor: University Microfilms, 1977.

Taylor, S. J. "From segregation to integration: Strategies for integrating severely handicapped students in normal school and community settings." *The Journal of the Association for the Severely Handicapped,* 8: 42–49, 1982.

Taylor, S. J. and Bogdan, R. "Defending illusions: The institutions struggle for survival." *Human Organization,* 39(3): 209–218, 1980.

Taylor, S. J. and Bogdan, R. "A qualitative approach to community adjustment." In R. H. Bruininks, C. E. Meyers, B. B. Sigford, and K. C. Larkin (Eds.) *Deinstitutionalization and Community Adjustment of Mentally Retarded People.* Washington, D.C.: American Association on Mental Deficiency, 1981.

Taylor, S. J., Brown, K., McCord, W., Giambetti, A., Searl, S., Mlinarcik, S., Atkinson, T., and Lichter, S. *Title XIX and Deinstitutionalization: The Issue for the 80's.* Syracuse: Human Policy Press, 1981.

Tax, S. (Ed.) *Horizons of Anthropology.* Chicago: Aldine, 1964.

Thibaut, J. W. and Kelly, H. H. *The Social Psychology of Groups.* New York: Wiley, 1959.

Thomas, P. *Down these Mean Streets.* New York: Knopf, 1967.

Thomas, W. I. *The Unadjusted Girl.* Boston: Little, Brown, 1931.

Thomas, W. I. *Social Behavior and Personality.* New York: Social Science Research Council, 1951.

Thomas, W. I. and Thomas, D. S. *The Child in America.* New York: Alfred A. Knopf, 1928.

Thomas, W. I., and Znaniecki, F. *The Polish Peasant in Europe and America.* New York: Knopf, 1927.

Thompson, J. and McEwen, W. "Organizational goals and environment." *American Sociological Review*, 23(1): 23–31, 1958.

Thorne, B. "Political activist as participant observer: Conflicts of commitment in a study of the draft resistance movement of the 1960's." *Symbolic Interaction*, 2: 73–88, 1979.

Thorne, B. " 'You still takin' notes.' Fieldwork and problems of informed consent." *Social Problems*, 27: 284–297, 1980.

Thorne, B. "Political activist as participant observer: Conflicts of commitment in a study of the draft resistance movement of the 1960s." In R. M. Emerson (Ed.) *Contemporary Field Research*. Boston: Little, Brown, pp. 216–234, 1983.

Thrasher, F. *The Gang*. Chicago: University of Chicago Press, 1927.

Thrasher, F. "How to study the boys' gang in the open." *Journal of Educational Psychology*, 1: 244–254, 1928.

Tibbitts, H. G. "Research in the development of sociology: A pilot study in methodology." *American Sociological Review*, 27(December): 892–901, 1962.

Tiryakian, E. "Existential phenomenology and sociology." *American Sociological Review*, 30(October): 674–688, 1965.

Tizard, J. "The role of social institutions in the causation, prevention, and alleviation of mental retardation." In H. C. Haywood (Ed.) *Social-Cultural Aspects of Mental Retardation*. New York: Appleton-Century-Crofts, pp. 281–340, 1970.

Trice, H. M. "The outsider's role in field study." *Sociology and Social Research*, 41(1): 27–32, 1956.

Trice, H. M. and Roman, P. "Delabeling and alcoholics anonymous." *Social Problems*, 17(4): 538–546, 1969–1970.

Trow, M. "Comment on 'Participant observation and interviewing: a comparison.' " *Human Organization*, 16(3): 33–35, 1957.

Truzzi, M. (Ed.) *Subjective Understanding in the Social Sciences*. Reading, Mass.: Addison-Wesley, 1974.

Turnbull, C. *The Forest People*. New York: Simon and Schuster, 1962.

Turner, R. (Ed.) *Ethnomethodology*. Baltimore: Penguin, 1974.

Turner, R. H. "The quest for universals in Sociological research." *American Sociological Review*, 18: 604–611, 1953.

U.S. Dept. of Health, Education and Welfare, Office of Child Development. *Head Start Services to Handicapped Children*. Second Annual Report to the U.S. Congress, Washington, D.C.: 1974.

Vail, D. *Dehumanization and the Institutional Career*. Springfield, Ill.: Charles C. Thomas, 1967.

Van Maanen, J. "Watching the watchers." In P. K. Manning and J. Van Maanen (Eds.) *Policing*. Pacific Palisades, Calif.: Goodyear, 1978.

Van Maanen, J. "Notes on the production of ethnographic data in an American police agency." In R. Luckham (Ed.) *Law and Social Inquiry*. Uppsala: Scandinavian Institute of African Studies, 1981.

Van Maanen, J. "Fieldwork on the beat." In J. Van Maanen, J. M. Dabbs, Jr., and R. R. Faulkner (Eds.) *Varieties of Qualitative Research*. Beverly Hills: Sage, pp. 103–151, 1982.

Van Maanen, J. "The moral fix: On the ethics of fieldwork." In R. M. Emerson (Ed.) *Contemporary Field Research*. Boston: Little, Brown, pp. 269–287, 1983.

Van Maanen, J., Dabbs, J. M., Jr., and Faulkner, R. R. (Eds.) *Varieties of Qualitative Research*. Beverly Hills: Sage, pp. 103–151, 1982.

Vaughan, T. R. and Sjoberg, G. "Comment." *American Sociologist*, 13: 171–172, 1978.

Vidich, A. J. "Methodological problems in the observation of husband–wife interaction." *Marriage and Family Living*, 28: 234–239, 1955a.

Vidich, A. J. "Participant observation and the collection and interpretation of data." *American Journal of Sociology*, 60: 354–360, 1955b.

Vidich, A. J. and Bensman, J. "The validity of field data." *Human Organization*, 13(1): 20–27, 1954.

Vidich, A. J. and Bensman, J. *Small Town in Mass Society*. Princeton: Princeton University Press, 1958.

Vidich, A. J. and Bensman, J. "The Springdale case: Academic bureaucrats and sensitive townspeople." In A. J. Vidich, J. Bensman, and M. R. Stein (Eds.) *Reflections on Community Studies*. New York: Wiley, 1964.

Vidich, A. J., Bensman, J., and Stein, M. R. *Reflections on Community Studies*. New York: Wiley, 1964.

Vidich, A. J. and Shapiro, G. "A comparison of participant observation and survey data." *American Sociological Review*, 20: 28–33, 1955.

Volkart, E. H. (Ed.) *Social Behavior and Personality: Contributions of W. I. Thomas to Theory and Research*. New York: Social Science Research Council, 1951.

Von Hoffman, N. "Sociological snoopers." *Transaction*, 7(7): 4–6, 1970.

Voysey, M. "Impression management by parents with disabled children: The reconstruction of good parents." *Journal of Health and Social Behavior*, 13: 80–89, 1972a.

Voysey, M. "Official agents and the legitimation of suffering." *Sociological Review*, 15: 533–552, 1972b.

Voysey, M. *A Constant Burden: The Reconstitution of Family Life*. London: Routledge and Kegan Paul, 1975.

Waitzkin, H. and Stoeckle, J. D. "The communication of information about illness." *Advances in Psychosomatic Medicine*, 8: 180–215, 1972.

Wald, A. *Sequential Analysis*. New York: Wiley, 1947.

Walker, A. L. and Lidz, C. W. "Methodological notes on the employment of indigenous observers." In R. S. Weppner (Ed.) *Street Ethnography*. Beverly Hills: Sage, pp. 103–123, 1977.

Wallace, S. *Skid Row as a Way of Life*. New York: Harper Torchbooks, 1968.

Warren, C. A. B. "Data presentation and the audience: Responses, ethics, and effects." *Urban Life*, 9: 282–308, 1980.

Warren, C. A. B. and Rasmussen, P. K. "Sex and gender in field research." *Urban Life*, 6: 349–370, 1977.

Warwick, D. P. "Tearoom trade: Means and ends in social research." *The Hastings Center Studies*, 1: 27–38, 1973.

Warwick, D. P. "Who deserves protection?" *American Sociologist*, 9: 158–159, 1974.

Warwick, D. P. "Social scientists ought to stop lying." *Psychology Today*, 8 (February): 38, 40, 105–106, 1975.

Wax, M. "On misunderstanding *Verstehen*: A reply to Abel." *Sociology and Social Research*, 51: 323–333, 1967.

Wax, M. "Tenting with Malinowski." *American Sociological Review*, 37: 1–13, 1972.

Wax, M. "Paradoxes of 'consent' to the practice of fieldwork." *Social Problems*, 27: 272–283, 1980.

Wax, M. "On fieldworkers and those exposed to fieldwork: Federal regulations and moral issues." In R. M. Emerson (Ed.) *Contemporary Field Research*. Boston: Little, Brown, pp. 288–299, 1983.

Wax, M. and Cassell, J. (Eds.) *Federal Regulations: Ethical Issues and Social Research*. Boulder: Westview, 1979.

Wax, M. and Shapiro, L. J. "Repeated interviewing." *American Journal of Sociology*, 62: 215–217, 1956.

Wax, R. H. "Field methods and techniques: Reciprocity as a field technique." *Human Organization*, 11(3): 34–37, 1952.

Wax, R. H. "Twelve years later: An analysis of field experience." *American Journal of Sociology*, 63: 133–142, 1957.

Wax, R. H. *Doing Fieldwork: Warnings and Advice*. Chicago: University of Chicago Press, 1971.

Wax, R. H. "Gender and age in fieldwork and fieldwork education: No good thing is done by any man alone." *Social Problems*, 26: 509–522, 1979.

Webb, E. J., Campbell, D. T., Schwartz, R. D., and Sechrest, L. *Unobtrusive Measures: Nonreactive Research in Social Sciences*. Chicago: Rand McNally, 1966.

Webb, E. J., Campbell, D. T., Schwartz, R. D., Sechrest, L., and Grove, J. *Nonreactive Measures in the Social Sciences*. Boston: Houghton Mifflin, 1981.

Webb, S. and Webb, B. *Methods of Social Study*. New York: Longmans, Green, 1932.

Weber, M. *The Theory of Social and Economic Organization*. New York: Oxford University Press, 1947.

Weber, M. *The Methodology of the Social Sciences*. Edited by E. A. Shils and H. A. Finch. New York: Free Press, 1949.

Weber, M. *From Max Weber: Essays in Sociology*. Translated and edited by Hans Gerth and C. Wright Mills. New York: Oxford University Press, 1958.

Weber, M. *Economy and Society*. New York: Bedminster Press, 1968.

Weis, R. S. "Alternative approaches in the study of complex situations." *Human Organization*, 25: 108–206, 1966.

Weiss, C. (Ed.) *Evaluating Action Programs*. Boston: Allyn & Bacon, 1972.

West, W. G. "Access to adolescent deviants and deviance." In W. B. Shaffir, R. A. Stebbins, and A. Turowetz (Eds.) *Fieldwork Experience: Qualitative Approaches to Social Research*. New York, St. Martin's Press, pp. 31–44, 1980.

Westley, W. "Secrecy and the police." *Social Forces*, 34(March), 254–257, 1956.

Whyte, W. F. "The social structure of the restaurant." *American Journal of Sociology*, 54(2): 302–310, 1949.

Whyte, W. F. "Observation field methods." In M. Vahoda, M. Deutsch, and S. W. Cook (Eds.) *Research Methods in Social Relations*, Vol. II. 1st ed. New York: Holt, pp. 493–513, 1951.

Whyte, W. F. "Interviewing for organizational research." *Human Organization*, 12(2): 15–22, 1953.

Whyte, W. F. *Street Corner Society*. Chicago: University of Chicago Press, 1955.

Whyte, W. F. "On asking indirect questions." *Human Organization*, 15(4): 21–23, 1957.

Whyte, W. F. "Interviewing in field research." In R. N. Adams and J. J. Preiss (Eds.) *Human Organizational Research*. Homewood, Ill.: Dorsey Press, pp. 352–374, 1960.

Whyte, W. H. *The Social Life of Small Urban Spaces*. Washington, D.C.: The Conservation Foundation, 1980.

Wieder, D. L. *Language and Social Reality: The Case of Telling the Convict Code*. The Hague: Mouton, 1974.

Wiener, J. M. "The attitudes of pediatricians toward the care of fatally ill children." *Journal of Pediatrics,* 76: 700–705, 1970.

Williams, T. R. *Field Methods in the Study of Culture*. New York: Holt, 1967.

Wilson, J. "Interaction analysis: A supplementary field work technique used in the study of leadership in a 'new style' Australian aboriginal community." *Human Organization,* 21(4): 290–294, 1962.

Wilson, T. P. "Conceptions of interaction and forms of sociological explanation." *American Sociological Review,* 35: 697–710, 1970.

Wirth, L. *The Ghetto*. Chicago: University of Chicago Press, 1928.

Wiseman, J. P. *Stations of the Lost: The Treatment of Skid Row Alcoholics*. Englewood Cliffs, N.J.: Prentice-Hall, 1970.

Wiseman, J. P. "The research web." *Unborn Life and Culture,* 3(October): 317–328, 1974.

Wohl, J. "Traditional and contemporary views of psychological testing." *Journal of Projective Techniques,* 27: 359–365, 1963.

Wolf, K. K. "A methodological note on the empirical establishment of cultural patterns." *American Sociological Review,* 10: 176–184, 1945.

Wolfensberger, W. *Normalization*. Toronto: National Institute on Mental Retardation, 1972.

Wolfensberger, W. *The Origin and Nature of our Institutional Models*. Syracuse: Human Policy Press, 1975.

Wolff, K. H. *Trying Sociology*. New York: Wiley, 1974.

Yablonsky, L. "Experiences with the criminal community." In A. Gouldner and S. M. Miller (Eds.) *Applied Sociology*. New York: Free Press, 1965.

Yablonsky, L. "On crime, violence, LSD, and legal immunity of social scientists." *American Sociologist,* 3: 148–149, 1968.

Yancey, W. L. and Rainwater, L. "Problems in the ethnography of the urban underclass." In R. Habenstein (Ed.) *Pathways to Data: Field Methods for Studying Ongoing Social Organizations*. Chicago: Aldine, pp. 245–269, 1970.

Young, F. W. and Young, R. C. "Key informant reliability in rural Mexican villages." *Human Organization,* 20(3): 141–148, 1961.

Zelditch, M., Jr. "Some methodological problems of field studies." *American Journal of Sociology,* 67: 566–675, 1962.

Zetterberg, H. L. *On Theory and Verification in Sociology*. Rev. ed. Totowa, N.J.: Bedminster Press, 1963.

Ziller, R. C. and Lewis, D. "Orientations: Self, social and environmental precepts through auto-photography." *Personality and Social Psychology Bulletin,* 7: 338–343, 1981.

Ziller, R. C. and Smith, D. E. "A phenomenological utilization of photographs." *Journal of Phenomenological Psychology*, 7: 172–185, 1977.

Zimmerman, D. H. and Wieder, D. L. "Ethnomethodology and the problem of order: Comment on Denzin." In J. Douglas (Ed.) *Understanding Everyday Life*. Chicago: Aldine, pp. 285–295, 1970.

Zimmerman, D. H. and Wieder, D. L. "The diary: Diary-interview method." *Urban Life*, 5(4): 479–498, 1977.

Znaniecki, F. *The Method of Sociology*. New York: Farrar & Rinehart, 1934.

Zola, I. K. *Missing Pieces: A Chronicle of Living with a Disability*. Philadelphia: Temple University Press, 1982.

Zorbaugh, H. *The Gold Coast and the Slum*. Chicago: University of Chicago Press, 1929.

Author Index

Subject Index

Access to settings, 20–28, 70
Action research, 73–74, 244
Analytic induction, 81, 125, 127–128, 129, 130, 139, 152
Autobiographies, *see* Life histories

Bargain, 26, 70, 72
Bias, 68, 99, 142
Burt, Pattie, 85, 89, 100, 101, 144, 154

Career, 143
Chicago School, 4, 78, 100, 105, 124, 244
Coding, 59, 130, 136–140, 142, 143
Computer programs, 138, 145
Concepts, 126, 129–130, 132, 133–135, 136–140, 144–145
    concrete, 133
    sensitizing, 133
Confidentiality, 24, 26, 69, 70, 72, 75, 93
Constant comparative method, 126
Cross checks, 98–100, 152
Culture, 5, 84

Diagrams, 56, 59
Discounting data, 130, 140–142, 150

Emic approach, 144–145
Ethics, 23, 25, 28–29, 30, 70–74, 107, 111
Ethnography, 5, 124, 151, 155
Ethnomethodology, 9–11, 12, 57, 75, 108–109, 118–119
Etic approach, 144–145
Evaluation research, 93, 156, 245

Field notes, 25, 27, 34, 52, 56, 58, 59, 66, 68, 104, 137, 138, 143, 151, 246–257
Fry, Jane, 85, 86, 87, 88, 91, 92, 99, 100, 101, 143

Gatekeepers, 20–22, 24–27, 34
Gender, 34–35, 43
Grounded theory, 125–127, 128, 129, 131, 139
Group interviews, 111–112

Hired hand research, 70
Historical research, 69, 114–117, 120–121
Human subjects, protection of, 27, 30
Hypotheses, 41, 49, 67, 126, 127

In-depth interviewing, definition of, 77
Interviewer's journal, 103–104
Interview guide, 92–93

Key informants, 41–42
Key words, 55, 56

Language, 36, 51–52, 55. *See also* Vocabulary.
Life histories, 4, 78, 80, 81, 84–85, 86, 88, 89, 90–91, 92, 100, 113–114, 124–125, 143–144, 154, 155
Log-interview approach, 89, 91

Methodology, definition of, 1
Murphy, Ed, 85, 86, 89–90, 92, 97–98, 100, 104, 144, 154, 155, 157–169

Observer's comments, 49, 60–61, 64, 104, 131, 142
Official documents, 69, 120–121
Over-rapport, 40

Participant observation, definition of, 15
Personal documents, 4, 89, 91–92, 105, 113–114, 118, 122
    definition of, 113
Phased-assertion tactic, 50, 98

301